GREENWAYS FOR AMERICA

Also by Charles E. Little

Challenge of the Land

Space for Survival
(with John G. Mitchell)

A Town Is Saved . . .
(with photographs by Marvin Mort)

Green Fields Forever

Louis Bromfield at Malabar
(editor)

CHARLES E. LITTLE

Greenways for America

THE JOHNS HOPKINS UNIVERSITY PRESS
Baltimore and London

This book has been brought to publication with the generous assistance
of the Conservation Fund, the National Endowment for the Arts, and
the American Conservation Association.

The Johns Hopkins University Press
701 West 40th Street, Baltimore, Maryland 21211
The Johns Hopkins Press Ltd., London

∞ The paper used in this book meets the minimum requirements of
American National Standard for Information Sciences—Permanence of
Paper for Printed Library Materials, ANSI Z39.48-1984.

Maps by Harriet A. Wright. Photographs by Phil Schermeister,
© 1989 Phil Schermeister, or as otherwise noted in the picture credits on page
227, which constitutes a continuation of the copyright page.

Library of Congress Cataloging-in-Publication Data
Little, Charles E.
  Greenways for America / Charles E. Little.
      p.   cm.
  Includes bibliographical references.
  ISBN 0-8018-4066-X (alk. paper)
    1. Greenways—United States.   I. Title.
E160.L58   1990
917.3—dc20   90-34149 CIP

for Richard H. Pough

CONTENTS

Illustrations follow pages xvi, 80, and 160.

FOREWORD

The environment is once again on our national agenda, and in April 1990 we celebrated the twentieth anniversary of Earth Day. The subject of this book, *Greenways for America*, is one of the new environmental solutions now being developed to meet the challenges of the next century. The book tells the story of a grass roots movement that exemplifies the best kind of environmental action. As Charles E. Little notes in his introduction, greenways are "wonderfully rich and diverse—as rich and diverse as human ingenuity and topographical opportunity can make them."

Greenways are a testament to the need to protect our lands and keep them alive, healthy, and green. The community-based, democratic effort to bring greenways about is composed of hard-working, ordinary people who are dedicated to improving the quality of their everyday lives by preserving and connecting remnants of nature near their homes and workplaces.

Although antecedents can be found as early as the 1860s, and the term "greenway" first appeared in the 1950s, the contemporary greenway movement was identified and given national prominence in 1987 by the President's Commission on Americans Outdoors, chaired by then-Governor of Tennessee, Lamar Alexander, with Gilbert M. Grosvenor as vice-chairman. Lamar Alexander, now president of the University of Tennessee system, and Gilbert Grosvenor, chairman and president of the National Geographic Society, were instrumental in giving special emphasis to one of the Commission's recommendations: to "establish a network of greenways across America."

The fifteen-member commission, on which I was privileged to serve, reviewed a vast array of organizations and agencies across America. We discovered that there was a real need for natural areas that are close to home and accessible to citizens of all ages. We learned statistically what was obvious to the eye, that urbanization has fragmented our open countryside, severely jeopardizing the natural corridor systems that protect water supplies, maintain biological diversity, and preserve natural beauty. And new research revealed that recreational activities such as bicycling, jogging, and walking are among the most popular uses of leisure time. These findings clearly suggested a crucial role for greenways in environmental planning and action.

For example, the lands bordering our nation's rivers and streams provide a magnificent 3.2 million miles of potentional greenway corridors. Creating ribbons of green along these streamsides, as well as along other linear resources such as abandoned railroad and utility rights-of-way, need not require massive federal aid. Instead, greenway-making tends to be a state and local endeavor, requiring thoughtful planning and timely action—community by community, state by state. The federal government can help by establishing a program of local matching grants, but making greenways a reality will take more than money. The ultimate success of the greenway movement calls for open dialogue and cooperation between businesses, citizens, private groups such as land trusts, and public agencies. By linking open spaces with natural corridors, greenways can at once provide the many ecological, economic, and recreational benefits that are so essential to healthy, functioning cities and landscapes.

To advance the greenway concept, and to design a comprehensive program for the greenway movement, the Conservation Fund in 1987 created the "American Greenways" program, to follow up on the recommendation of the President's Commission on Americans Outdoors. Keith Hay, a well-known conservationist and professional on natural resources management, was asked to direct the program. *Greenways for America* is one of the program's most significant achievements, and I am very pleased that the Conservation Fund has been able to sponsor the publication of this work, with the generous assistance of the National Endowment for the Arts and the American Conservation Association.

Charles E. Little, whose many books on conservation and community planning have been extremely influential over the years, agreed to take on the research and writing of the work. He has thoughtfully and carefully addressed the many facets of greenways, from their origins in history to the contemporary greenway movement. This book will become an invaluable tool for those who are creating the greenway systems throughout the United States and, I hope, eventually throughout the world. *Greenways for America* captures the indomitable spirit of those Americans—in city neighborhoods, suburban towns, and rural communities everywhere—who are on the front lines of the new environmental agenda, an agenda that will carry us into the 21st century.

PATRICK F. NOONAN, *President*
The Conservation Fund
Arlington, Virginia

GREENWAYS FOR AMERICA

1

Burke-Gilman Trail, Seattle, Washington.

2

3

Oconee River Greenway,
Athens, Georgia (2).

French Broad River, Asheville,
North Carolina (3).

Willamette River Greenway,
Oregon (4).

Frederick Law Olmsted's
Emerald Necklace, Boston,
Massachusetts (5).

4

5

Chesapeake & Ohio Canal National Historical Park, Washington, D.C., and Maryland (6).

31st Street Greenway (now Salt Creek Greenway), suburban Chicago, Illinois (7).

San Juan Islands "Ferryboat Corridor Greenway," Puget Sound, Washington (8).

Stowe Recreation Path, Stowe, Vermont (9).

*Scenes from a network of
greenways in Maryland—
along the C & O towpath (10),
trillium (11), young bikers (12),
night heron (13).*

12

13

W & O D Trail, Northern Virginia.

greenway (*grēn'-wā*) *n.* 1. A linear open space established along either a natural corridor, such as a riverfront, stream valley, or ridgeline, or overland along a railroad right-of-way converted to recreational use, a canal, a scenic road, or other route. 2. Any natural or landscaped course for pedestrian or bicycle passage. 3. An open-space connector linking parks, nature reserves, cultural features, or historic sites with each other and with populated areas. 4. Locally, certain strip or linear parks designated as a parkway or greenbelt. [American neologism: green + way; origin obscure.]

Introduction: Greenways for America

T*his is the story* of a remarkable citizen-led movement to get us out of our cars and into the landscape—on paths and trails through corridors of green that can link city to country and people to nature from one end of America to the other. It is a movement that is not as well known as it should be, for it holds much promise to make the places we live and work a great deal more livable and a great deal more workable. My purpose is to show why and how this is so.

Although modern-style greenways have been around for a generation or so, the citizen movement to create them has until recently been relatively inchoate. And the literature is thin. At the outset of my research for this book, which started in 1987, I conducted a computerized bibliographic data base search for articles on greenways. I came up with exactly one citation, for an article I had written myself. Although I had a suspicion that I might locate more articles (as indeed I did, later on) by making my search more sophisticated, if I wanted to learn anything about this movement, I realized I would have to get virtually all the information at first hand. Accordingly, I placed an author's query in a number of periodicals likely to be read by people interested in greenways: landscape architects and planners, conservationists and environmentalists, and the professionals and officials of various kinds concerned with parks and recreation. The query asked that anyone involved in an "active greenway project," with greenways described broadly as "linear parks, open spaces, and protected natural areas in cities, suburbs, or the countryside," to please get in touch. The result was over a hundred letters in reply (quite a lot for an author's query placed in small-circulation journals) proposing 120 greenways as being ideal examples of the genre.

Some of these greenways were local, others regional or statewide. Some projects consisted of a single linear piece of geography, a converted railroad right-of-way, or a stream valley; others were systems in which a network of linear open space was being assembled. Some greenways were in the country, others in the city, and quite a few in both. Some greenways were for recreation, others were mainly for ecological, aesthetic, or environmental management purposes.

The long and short of it is (and that, too, could describe them!) that the greenway projects I heard from across the United States were wonderfully rich and diverse—as rich and diverse as human ingenuity and topographic opportunity could make them. To be sure, they were not always called *greenways*. For example, in and around certain cities, planners and citizen leaders have adopted the British term *greenbelt*. In the West, where the word does not necessarily connote a highway, greenways are sometimes called *parkways*. In fact, if you take a syllable from each of these terms—*green* from *greenbelt* and *way* from *parkway,* the general idea of *greenway* emerges: a natural, green way based on protected linear corridors which will improve environmental quality and provide for outdoor recreation.

Although greenways resist categorization, it did appear from my correspondence that there are five major project types:

1. Urban riverside greenways, usually created as part of (or instead of) a redevelopment program along neglected, often run-down city waterfronts.
2. Recreational greenways, featuring paths and trails of various kinds, often of relatively long distance, based on natural corridors as well as canals, abandoned railbeds (there are many of these, as we shall see), and other public rights-of-way.

3. Ecologically significant natural corridors, usually along rivers and streams and (less often) ridgelines, to provide for wildlife migration and "species interchange," nature study, and hiking.

4. Scenic and historic routes, usually along a road or highway (or, less often, a waterway), the most representative of them making an effort to provide pedestrian access along the route or at least places to alight from the car.

5. Comprehensive greenway systems or networks, usually based on natural landforms such as valleys and ridges but sometimes simply an opportunistic assemblage of greenways and open spaces of various kinds to create an alternative municipal or regional green infrastructure.

After sorting through the abundance of mail received from my query and making piles along categorical lines such as I have suggested above (although I was to refine the typology continually), I arranged personal visits to some twenty-five representative projects, a journey that took me to twenty states and added 12,708 miles to the odometer of an old Volvo station wagon. For those outstanding greenways that I could not visit, I telephoned my respondents and collected documentary material from them and from others they recommended I speak to. In total, I was able to accumulate substantial information on some eighty active greenways, which provides the reportorial base for this book. (See footnote to the list of Principal Sources for information on how to access this material.)

Because of this research approach, the chapters following come in two different forms. Essay chapters (which are most of them) present the findings of my study organized by topic—the history of the greenway concept; the rise of the modern greenway movement; analyses (in five chapters) of the principal greenway categories outlined above; the nuts and bolts of greenway-making; and an envoi on what I take to be the "greenway imperative." However, two chapters, Chapter 3 and Chapter 9, consist of article-style profiles of individual contemporary projects. This material, entitled "The World of Greenways," is illustrated with maps and galleries of photographs. My criteria for selection, I hasten to add, had to do with creating a representative sample of currently active projects rather than any unseemly personal notions of hierarchy or historic importance. In fact, a good many projects that were not included in the "World of Greenways" are discussed, sometimes at greater length, in the essay chapters.

Although this book may be read straight through, without losing any meaning, from first page to last by any reader choosing to do so, the idea behind the bifurcated organization is to permit (if not encourage) readers to browse around in the project accounts to get a feel for what the present-day greenway movement is all about—in all its range and diversity—before dutifully turning to Chapter 1, wherein the greenway story begins, in time-honored fashion, at the beginning. . . .

1

Origins of an Idea

*Make no little plans; they have no magic to
stir men's blood, and probably themselves will
not be realized. Make big plans: aim high in
hope and work, remembering that a noble,
logical diagram, once recorded, will never die.*

—*DANIEL BURNHAM*

*A*s *it happens,* the tracks of the great park-maker, Frederick Law
Olmsted, are all over the modern greenway movement. Arguably, if any
single person "invented" the idea of greenways, it was he. Born in Hartford, Connecticut, in 1822, Olmsted, like the true prototypical greenway-maker he was, did not begin as a professional designer but ran a rich and
varied vocational gamut as a young man before he came to his calling.
He was, in turn, an apprentice civil engineer, a seaman, a Connecticut
farmer, a Staten Island nurseryman, and a journalist. In this last pursuit,
he was indeed gifted. His book on the pre–Civil War South, *Cotton
Kingdom,* is still in print.

Finally, at the age of thirty-five, the knockabout Olmsted landed an
administrative job as the superintendent of the unimproved site that had
been designated to be a "central park" for New York City. During this
period, Olmsted made the acquaintance of Calvert Vaux, a British architect who had immigrated to America to work with Andrew Jackson
Downing, the successful Newburgh, New York, landscape gardener who

adapted the "picturesque" principles of English garden design to the estates of the newly wealthy in America. Olmsted had long admired Downing (not least because it was Downing who led the effort to establish Central Park) and had gotten to know, and like, Vaux during his Newburgh visits. After Olmsted had taken the superintendent's job for the Central Park site, Calvert Vaux, by then somewhat at loose ends since Downing had died a few years before, persuaded the outgoing Olmsted to join him in submitting a plan for a park design competition. Olmsted, having visited landscape gardens and parks on his European travels, especially in England, had plenty of ideas of his own. He decided to have a go at it. Remarkably, the Vaux-Olmsted plan won the competition, out of thirty-three entries. Although he was not fully aware of it at the time, Olmsted had found his metier, as a landscape architect—not quite garden design and not quite architecture but part of both—although he hated the term. His mind was quick and creative, his energy superhuman. And the Central Park assignment was to bring many commissions in its wake, enabling him to perfect his art and craft.

After a stint during the early part of the Civil War as the secretary of the Washington, D.C.-based Sanitary Commission, devoted to "the sick and wounded of the Army," Olmsted, then forty-one, returned briefly to New York and Central Park. Following a dispute with the Central Park board in the spring of 1863, he and Vaux resigned as landscape architects for the project (although they would be reinstated in 1865). It was during this interlude that Olmsted, with an old Civil War friend, Edwin L. Godkin, conceived of a reform-minded political weekly that would later be called the *Nation*, which is published to this day. But Olmsted, a family man in his forties, needed to earn a living; the publishing prospects were highly speculative, as was, at this point, the landscape architecture business. And so, much to the disappointment of Vaux (although the partnership remained intact), Olmsted shipped out, via the Panama Isthmus (by train across the narrow, jungly neck), bound for California to manage John Charles Frémont's Mariposa estate, the vast northern California landholdings acquired by the famed explorer, territorial governor and later senator, presidential candidate, and Army general. The estate, valued mainly for its gold mines, had been purchased from Frémont for $10 million by a consortium of eastern investors. To attract Olmsted into this far country—for with his Central Park and Sanitary Commission experience, he was a proven administrator—the consortium offered a princely $10,000 a year, with an equal amount annually in gold mine stock options. Fortunately (for the purposes of history), the job did not last long. The mining operation went bust, and Olmsted, although fulfilling his obligations, quit as soon as he could. But he lingered in the West to undertake a number of seemingly attractive design projects—at Yosemite Park (then state owned), a cemetery in Oakland, a commission to create a plan for a major urban park for San Francisco (although this project failed to materialize), and a design for the College of California grounds (now the university) in Berkeley.

With regard to finding an Olmstedian source of the greenway idea, Berkeley may well be where it all started, in the view of Charles E. Beveridge, editor of the Frederick Law Olmsted Papers (a long-term, multi-volume project of American University and the Johns Hopkins University Press). Here, as part of his plan for the college grounds and the immediate neighborhood, Olmsted, says Beveridge, "proposed, for the first time, two 'greenway' elements. One was to take the whole valley of Strawberry Creek above the campus for public parkland, make a pleasure drive and walks along it, ending with a viewpoint at the top of the canyon. He also proposed to link the campus with Oakland by a pleasure drive through the hills that would have been his first road (outside a park) designed primarily for carriages and for scenic experience." Even though only a fragment of the Park and Piedmont Way plan, as Olmsted referred to it, was implemented (a few blocks of roadway), the acceptance of the plan by the trustees of the college might well serve as the point in history at which the time line for greenways should begin. The date was October 3, 1865.

Meanwhile, Olmsted had received an especially urgent letter from his lonely colleague Vaux, for the two had kept up a correspondence, with Vaux always trying to convince his wayward partner to return to full-time design work back East. Now the city of Brooklyn, Vaux wrote, wanted the partnership, formally still intact, to design a large park, and he (Vaux) had sent the city a preliminary plan. Please come home.

Olmsted was perhaps feeling a bit beached in California, with the Mariposa riches having evaporated and the intermittent design jobs not enough to sustain him. Clearly, the time had come to return. Olmsted wrote back, "My heart really bounds (if you don't mind poetry), if we work together about it . . ."

Back in the East at last, the park assignment secured, Olmsted let his famous imagination run as he looked over the maps of Brooklyn and its neighboring city across the bay, New York.[1] Who knows what synapses obtain in the creative mind to bring fresh ideas from a jumble of impressions, facts, and experience? For Olmsted, there was the strong influence of British landscape gardening, which found expression in Central Park, and in the opinion of many was to be perfected in the design of the Brooklyn project, Prospect Park. This park was, to be sure, Olmsted's own favorite. But there was another element in the Brooklyn plan which Olmsted wanted to try, suggested in part no doubt by his Berkeley linear park and scenic drive concept and, in the view of Charles Beveridge, by his admiration for the broad boulevards of Paris and Brussels, where he had visited in 1856 and 1859. Perhaps Olmsted was even influenced by the train trips across the lush Panama Isthmus. As he wrote to his wife, Mary, about the effect of the view along the linear rail corridor, "Simply in vegetation it is superb and glorious and . . . produces a very strong moral impression through an enlarged sense of the bounteousness of nature."

The idea that came to him in Brooklyn was, of course, the linear Park Way, which biographer Elizabeth Stevenson believes may be Olmsted's own coinage. Just as the lush, green corridor in Panama which linked the Atlantic and Pacific Oceans had worked a strong moral impression on Olmsted, the great designer wished to offer a parallel moral impression to the visitors to Prospect Park—by means of a parkway as the principal access corridor. A parkway, he believed, could prepare the minds and hearts of visitors as they approached the park, creating an affection that

1. The consolidation of five boroughs to make up New York City was completed in 1898. Before that, the counties, and the cities within them (such as the city of Brooklyn, in Kings County), were separate.

would lead to the fullest measure of peace and aesthetic appreciation once arrived within. Prospect Park, even more than Central Park, was to be a replicated rural landscape utterly removed (through the artful use of berms) from the toilsome city surrounding it.

According to historian David Schuyler (in his impressive study of nineteenth-century urban design, *The New Urban Landscape*), it was the Prospect Park assignment that led Vaux and Olmsted to a full realization that no single park, no matter how large and how well designed, would provide the citizens with the beneficial influences of nature. Parks needed to be linked to one another and to surrounding residential neighborhoods, they decided. In their 1866 proposal to Brooklyn, therefore, they urged the creation of a "shaded pleasure drive" from the park's southern end which, winding through the countryside, would terminate at the oceanfront of Coney Island. Another drive, they suggested, should lead from the park to the East River, then, after a bridge or ferry crossing, continue up the island of Manhattan to create a linkage with Central Park. Although the Brooklyn city fathers were not interested in the Central Park linkage, they did eventually permit Olmsted to build Ocean Parkway, which connects Prospect Park to Coney Island through Flatbush, and Eastern Parkway, which angles off from the park to the northwest border of what is now the borough of Queens. The two parkways are wide, six-lane carriageways with wooded margins thirty-two feet wide on each side. The total width is 260 feet. They were among America's first greenways and are now part of the new Brooklyn-Queens Greenway, profiled in Chapter 9.

The parkway idea was employed in other famous Olmsted and Vaux designs at the time. According to David Schuyler, an 1868 parkway for Buffalo created the first linked park system. And in that same year, the firm designed a parkway linking suburban Riverside, Illinois, with Chicago. The best known of the Olmstedian park-and-parkway plans is probably the "Emerald Necklace" in Boston (proposed in 1887). Once known as the Olmsted Parkway, the units create what some call a *strip park,* linking Boston Common with Franklin Park via the Back Bay Fens and the Muddy River in a 4.5-mile arc around the city. According to Charles Birnbaum, a landscape architect involved in the restoration of the parks, the Emerald Necklace "is considered to be the greatest greenway achievement" of the Olmsted firm.

The park-and-parkway idea was carried forward in many American cities, not only by Olmsted and his firm but by others, notably H. W. S. Cleveland, a contemporary of Olmsted who designed what many believe to be the first and finest urban open-space network, the Minneapolis-St. Paul metropolitan park system, completed in 1895.

It is important to understand that the early parkways and strip parks were for pedestrians, carriages, and horseback riders. Not even bicycles were in use when Olmsted conceived Piedmont Way in Berkeley and Ocean Parkway in Brooklyn, much less automobiles. The "ordinary" bicycle (high-wheel) was virtually unknown in America until the 1870s, and the pneumatic-tired "safety" bicycle (chain-driven) did not appear in any numbers until the 1890s. As for motorcars, the first U.S. make, the Duryea, was offered for sale in 1893. Mass production didn't start until 1902, with the Oldsmobile. The Ford Model T appeared in 1908. Accordingly, our modern experience, which suggests that a parkway is just a landscaped highway for automobile commuting, can lead us into a false impression about the relation the early "park ways" and the strip parks bear to the modern greenway movement. Many of these parkways were as sylvan and as natural as any present-day greenwayite might wish.

The mass-produced automobile was, of course, to change these early characteristics of the parkway, although not immediately. In 1910, there were fewer than a half-million motorcars in the United States, a ratio of one for every two hundred people. They were still considered recreational vehicles, not transportation necessities. In metropolitan America, streetcars, trains, and ferryboats (if not shank's mares) were for getting to work. Motors were for fun, and as their numbers increased, they multiplied the recreational potential of parkways.[2] The first parkway designed for recreational motor use was the Bronx River Parkway, perhaps the most beautiful suburban road ever built. The twenty-three mile route was to connect New York City with rural Westchester, particularly the

2. Nonmetropolitan parkways were also planned, notably the Blue Ridge Parkway, conceived in 1909, although construction did not start until 1935.

Kensico Dam and associated water supply reservoirs with their extensive watershed lands in the northern part of the county. Legislation providing authority for the road was enacted in 1906, but work was not begun until 1913. Although used today for ordinary traffic, the *park* part of the parkway was so generously proportioned that the corridor is still popular for walking, picnicking, and nature study, with a walker's guide available from the county for a footpath from Kensico Dam in Valhalla to Soundview Park in the Bronx. The parkway still provides, as its planners promised nearly a century ago, "for the refreshment of the mind and body plus the well-being and happiness of the people."

After the success of the Bronx River Parkway, the automotive parkways in Westchester County and Long Island began to proliferate, a good many of them under the astonishing reign of New York's master builder, Robert Moses. In fact, Moses (1888–1981) may have created more parks and parkways than any other single person in the history of the world—along with bridges, housing projects, dams, and nearly everything else, including the world's fairgrounds in Queens and the site of the United Nations in Manhattan. According to biographer Robert Caro, Robert Moses "built public works costing, in 1968 dollars, twenty-seven billion dollars."

Although the works of Moses were varied, what has affected and will affect the life of every single New Yorker from 1920 to the end of time were, and are, his parkways. In Westchester County and the Bronx, he built or expanded the Hutcheson River Parkway, the Taconic Parkway, the Saw Mill River Parkway, and the Cross County Parkway; in Manhattan, the Henry Hudson Parkway, and revisions to Olmsted and Vaux's Riverside Drive and Riverside Park; and in Brooklyn, the Belt Parkway. But that was just for starters. It was in Queens and Long Island that Moses took the parkway idea and drove it right into the ground: Grand Central Parkway, Northern State Parkway, Southern State Parkway, Interborough Parkway, Laurelton Parkway, Cross Island Parkway, Meadowbrook State Parkway, Bethpage State Parkway, and Ocean Parkway (not Olmsted's). And this list does not count the expressways, including the clogged L.I.E. (Long Island Expressway), today familiarly known as the world's longest parking lot.

Actually, Moses's initial impulse was to create a recreational network for the citizens of teeming New York, not commuting routes. As the demand for auto access to recreational areas increased dramatically during the 1920s, Moses saw that both Westchester and New Jersey—until then the destinations of choice—could provide only limited opportunities for weekend outings. In Westchester, many parks and golf courses were off-limits to all but Westchester residents; in New Jersey, in those pre-bridge, pre-tunnel days, getting to the magnificent Palisades Park, established in 1900, took such a tediously long time that many were discouraged from embarking on the trip. Where to turn? To Long Island, Moses decided. Just a skip across the narrow, eminently bridgeable East River, and the whole of this great rural region of farms, seashores, ponds, streams, woods, and great estates could be made available as a playground for the city.

Moses planned his Long Island parkways to link existing parks, although he often created new parks to have a parkway *to*. This approach produced, aside from famous single parks like Jones Beach, many of his own strip parks, especially in Queens, which in turn have formed the basis—together with Olmsted's earlier parks and parkways—for the new Brooklyn-Queens Greenway, a hiking and biking trail linking the North Shore of Long Island with Coney Island and the Atlantic Ocean on the south. But in the end, the great parkway builder became, in effect, a highway builder. As highway design requirements changed to accommodate the increased speed and numbers of automobiles, landscape values became subsidiary to the formulations of the highway engineers, and the parkways began to overpower, if not obliterate, the natural scenes they meant to celebrate and make available. To cite one infamous example, Moses wanted to extend his Ocean Parkway along Jones Beach on to Fire Island, the barrier dunes of the South Shore, to the horror of nearly everyone who treasured this ecologically fragile natural resource and the beach communities along it. Not to worry, Moses said. The parkway would stabilize the dune. The plan was preempted finally by making Fire Island a part of the Gateway National Recreation Area in 1972.

Another Robert Moses Waterloo (and there were many at the end of his career) was the Richmond Parkway, which he had long wanted to build along the beautiful wooded ridge of the escarpment on Staten Island. In 1963, citizen leaders mobilized to fight the plan, proposing a Staten Island greenbelt in its stead, with a trailway running through it—the Olmsted Trailway, in fact, named after the erstwhile nurseryman who had lived on the island as a young man and who had himself proposed a linear park along the ridge. Moses was unmoved, figuring the greenbelt/trailway idea was just a public relations dodge cooked up by a bunch of elitist tree-huggers and daisy-sniffers wanting to keep the island to themselves. They were, in the epithet of one pro-Moses parkway advocate, "Those suede-o conservationists." But in the end, the suede-os won, and Moses and the road builders, those gratified drivers of bulldozers, lost. The Staten Island Greenbelt remains one of the first and most inspirational greenway projects in the country. We shall return to it later.

In 1981, Moses died in Connecticut, a bitter old man. The hated Richmond Parkway alignment was officially demapped in 1989. The Olmsted Trail replaced the non-Olmstedian super highway and is now part of the Staten Island Greenbelt, a three thousand-acre aggregation of public and quasi-public open spaces along the proposed parkway route.

Indeed, the greenbelt concept is itself an important historic source for the greenway idea—fully as important as Olmsted's parkways. As mentioned in the introduction, the two terms create the portmanteau word *greenway*, which borrows a syllable from each. Although in the United States the term *greenbelt* conveys any relatively wide swath of open land (and in some areas is used interchangeably with *greenway*), in Britain, where the concept originated around the turn of the century, the greenbelt has the quite particular function of separating communities to preclude "conurbation," as Lewis Mumford points out in *The City in History*. Mumford cites British economist Alfred Marshall, who made the point this way in an 1899 paper: "We need to prevent one town from growing into another," Marshall wrote, "or into a neighboring village; we need to keep intermediate stretches of country in dairy farms, etc., as well as public pleasure grounds."

Marshall's idea of intermediate stretches expressed more or less exactly the "garden city" concept of Ebenezer Howard, the great British social reformer and author of *To-Morrow: The Peaceful Path to Social Reform,* published in 1898, a book that is better known as *Garden Cities of To-Morrow,* the title of a popular 1902 reissue. Howard proposed an agricultural "country belt" around the garden city to maintain its urban integrity by maintaining the rural integrity. Architect and planner Raymond Unwin later called these protective, surrounding lands *green belts,* which is the term still used in Britain and more loosely in the United States.

According to British town-planning authority Frederick J. Osborn, Howard was unaware of the several American communities called Garden City (although, according to David Schuyler, he resided in Chicago for a time and might well have been aware of Olmsted's use of open spaces woven through his 1868 plan for Riverside, Illinois). The first of the American garden cities was built on Long Island by A. T. Stewart in 1869, and by 1900 there were a number of others in the United States with the same name. Howard's idea, in any case, unlike these American versions, was not concerned with creating a city *of* gardens but rather a city *in* a garden—a city contained within a permanent agricultural landscape. He was, Lewis Mumford writes, primarily concerned with a "stable marriage between city and country, not a weekend liaison. . . . To achieve and express this reunion of city and country, Howard surrounded his new city with a rural greenbelt. The two-dimensional horizontal 'wall' would serve not merely to keep the rural environment near, but to keep other urban settlements from coalescing with it; not least, it would, like the ancient vertical wall [of medieval cities], heighten the sense of internal unity. Apart from the [garden cities] concept as a whole, the principle of establishing permanent greenbelts around urban communities was a major contribution."

In Britain, Howard's contribution took two forms. The first was his own plan for Letchworth, in 1903, which gave rise later to the many "new towns" of England, Scotland, and Wales which were a direct outgrowth of the garden city idea, beginning with Welwyn, designed by Unwin and built in 1920 some twenty miles north of London. Each of these small cities (30,000–50,000 population) not only had an inner network of open spaces for amenity and recreation but a surrounding greenbelt as well. The second adaptation of Howard's idea was to create a country belt around London itself. In 1938, the London Green Belt Act was passed, giving recognition to publicly owned open spaces surrounding the city. A more elaborate plan was created in 1944 by Sir Patrick Abercrombie, proposing a belt five or more miles deep, consisting of both public open spaces as well as private holdings which would be regulated to preclude suburban development. At length, in 1955, the expanded plan was adopted and has been added to since. Private landowners were offered compensation for any loss of development value which they could effectively demonstrate. Today, the London Greenbelt appears to be a permanent fixture despite Thatcherite disaffection for such "socialist" ideas.

In the United States, there has been nothing approximating the London Greenbelt, except possibly in the San Francisco Bay area, where planners have long maintained that the rural area around the bay should be considered a greenbelt de facto, even though it is a long way from de jure (see the discussion in Chapter 9). On a somewhat smaller scale, the city of Boulder, Colorado, has been piecing a greenbelt around itself over the last twenty years.

The new town version of the greenbelt idea was adopted pretty much intact, however, in the New Deal greenbelt towns of the 1930s, built under the leadership of Rexford Tugwell, a Roosevelt brain truster charged with resettling rural people driven off the land by drought and economic depression. The three model towns in Maryland, Ohio, and Wisconsin still survive—Greenbelt, Maryland, now a suburb of Washington, D.C., being the best-known example. Here, a partial greenbelt does in fact separate the community from the undifferentiated housing developments that surround it. The greenbelt concept, as a means of separating communities, was also proposed in the plan for Radburn, New Jersey, the pioneering suburban new town designed by Clarence Stein and Henry Wright during the 1920s.

Although these town planners' contributions are of interest, perhaps the most germane adaptation of the British greenbelt theory of importance to modern greenway-making may well be found in the work of Benton MacKaye. He was the son of the famous artist, actor, and playwright Steele MacKaye, who designed Madison Square Theater and invented overhead lighting and folding theater seats, and younger brother of the well-known playwright Percy MacKaye (*The Canterbury Pilgrims, The Scarecrow*). Benton, however, chose not to enter the family business. Instead, he trained as a forester and later became an important figure in the regional-planning movement of the 1920s. He is best known as the originator of the Appalachian Trail, which he proposed in a 1921 magazine article. He championed wilderness preservation as well as metropolitan regional planning all his life. He was a cofounder, with Aldo Leopold, Robert Marshall, and others, of the Wilderness Society in 1936, and he was also an active member of the Regional Planning Association of America.

Deeply concerned that post–World War I "metropolitanism" was capable of overrunning the rural countryside, MacKaye suggested that dams and levees of open space be established, primarily along ridgelines, to contain and direct the outward metropolitan flow. "If left alone," MacKaye wrote in his book *The New Exploration* (1928), "the metropolitan deluges will flow out along the main highways (and side highways) . . . distributing the population in a series of continuous strings which together would make a metropolitan cobweb."

MacKaye's prescription to stem what we now call urban sprawl was "a common public ground" that could serve as a limiting "embankment" that would hold back the tide of urban development. In a hypothetical urban region (not unlike Boston, near his long-time home in Shirley Center, Massachusetts), he describes the effect this way: "The outstanding topographic feature consists of the range of hills and mountains encircling the locality, together with the four ridges reaching toward the central city. . . . It would form a linear area, or belt around and through the locality, well adapted for camping and primitive travel (by foot or horseback).

"These open ways along the crestlines," MacKaye continues, "mark the lines for developing the primitive environment, while the motor ways mark the lines for extending the metropolitan environment. The motor ways form the channels of the metropolitan flood, while the open ways (crossing and flanking the motor ways) form 'dams' and 'levees' for controlling the flood." Significantly, MacKaye saw the open ways not only as devices to guide development and encourage decentralized economic growth but also as natural corridors that would provide necessary recreational opportunities to large metropolitan populations.

By combining recreation with the use of corridors following natural landforms to control urban growth, MacKaye adds a significant detail to the country belt idea of Ebenezer Howard and perfectly prefigures the modern trail-based greenway system. He calls for "numberless walking-circuits" to be provided by "these open ways around and about the various cities and towns." The concept, although developed over sixty years ago, is a fairly exact description of two current greenway projects—the Ridge Trail/Bay Trail effort in the San Francisco Bay area and the Bay Circuit project around Boston (see Chapter 9 for details of both). Both these plans involve a circumferential "belt," and their planners also hope to establish radial open ways penetrating to the urban core.

The open-way greenbelt concept was, of course, an elaboration of the Appalachian Trail idea. What is important to understand was that MacKaye did not see the *AT,* as it is now familiarly known, as simply a walking route. He envisioned it as the starting point for a giant dam and levee system for the entire Eastern Seaboard. The trail would follow a wide belt of protected open land that would have laterals descending eastward through the Piedmont all the way to coastal cities. "This open way," MacKaye wrote, "when it really opens, would form the base throughout eastern populous America for controlling the metropolitan invasion."

Although the trail was eventually completed—two thousand miles from Maine to Georgia—the primary open-way concept was never implemented. In 1972, however, Stanley A. Murray, then president of the Appalachian Trail Conference (ATC), proposed an Appalachian greenway. According to board minutes, the ATC would "seek the establishment of an Appalachian Greenway encompassing the Appalachian Trail and [additional land] of sufficient width to provide a nationally significant zone for dispersed types of recreation, wildlife habitat, scientific study, and timber and watershed management." To this end, the ATC commissioned planner Ann Satterthwaite to conduct a feasibility study, which was to succeed in reviving interest in MacKaye's larger, regional planning-oriented conception, as opposed simply to the preservation of a relatively narrow trailway corridor. Unfortunately, the timing was bad. Murray and Satterthwaite were too far ahead of the curve. Despite impressive symposia with national and international experts, articles in the popular and professional magazines, and the publication of a well-written, handsome brochure,[3] the revisitation of Benton MacKaye's open-way plan as the new Appalachian Greenway did not take off. Now, with greater national interest in large-scale greenway projects, Murray hopes that "the Appalachian Greenway may again be of interest."

Equally germane to modern greenway theory was MacKaye's approach to the protection of the scenery in undeveloped areas not located in an open way. He called these spaces *intertowns,* which would, typically, consist of relatively low-intensity land uses—truck farms, dairies, and managed woodlands; for example. He did not believe that the intertowns were especially vulnerable to overdevelopment except along the stretches of highway which would traverse them. To deal with the adverse effects of strip development (to use the modern term), MacKaye proposed establishing along each side of the road a five hundred-foot-deep zone in which no buildings (or the billboards he hated) could be erected. This concept, too, prefigures another kind of contemporary greenway—those that are along scenic or historic auto routes, such as Canopy Roads in Florida or California Route 1 in the Big Sur country (profiled in Chapters 9 and 3, respectively). "The alternative to the intertown," MacKaye wrote, "is the 'roadtown'—a continuous tunnel of structures from one end . . . to another." Little did he know how ghastly the tunnels would become when he wrote that sentence. But he was to learn. Benton Mac-Kaye died in 1975, having lived to the age of ninety-six.

So far, on the historic time line for greenways, we have dots for the Olmstedian park way concept of 1865–66, and the strip park as exemplified by his Emerald Necklace of 1887, and then a dot at 1895 repre-

3. Written by John G. Mitchell and designed by Robert Hagenhofer, who had collaborated on a similar publication for the Staten Island Greenbelt. Mitchell later worked on the Redding, Connecticut, Greenbelts and Hagenhofer on the Sourland Mountain trail system in central New Jersey.

senting H. W. S. Cleveland's Minneapolis-St. Paul park system. Charles
Eliot, John Charles Olmsted (nephew and adopted stepson), Frederick
Law Olmsted, Jr. (son), and a crowd of others working briefly or for long
periods at the Olmsted firm should have their own sprinkle of dots along
the line, too. Robert Moses must have his dot, I guess, somewhere in the
1920s—although with a footnote on hubris. No asterisk is needed for the
brilliant planners of the Bronx River Parkway of 1906–13, led by Gilmore
D. Clarke.

Then there is Ebenezer Howard in 1898, plus Raymond Unwin,
Patrick Abercrombie, Clarence Stein, the great New Deal reformer Rexford Tugwell, plus a good many more in the early part of the twentieth
century working on new town and regional planning—all originators of
the greenway idea in one way or another. In the 1920s, a big dot—almost
as big as Olmsted's—goes to Benton MacKaye for the open ways.

In quite recent times, those espousing an ecological approach to
planning have also powerfully informed the contemporary greenway
movement. The best-known practitioner of modern ecological planning
is doubtless Ian McHarg, whose notion of "physiographic determinism"
is now *de rigueur* for virtually all regional planners. McHarg's method is
to establish priorities for development (or nondevelopment) based on
natural processes. Wetlands, for example, provide society with certain
values—acting as a sponge for flooded rivers, providing a habitat for important plants and animals, serving as a buffer between developed areas,
and possessing significant recreational and aesthetic attributes. These
values, McHarg argues, which represent the economy of nature, are no
less important (perhaps more so) than the value that represents the economy of money in determining where the highway should be routed, the
mall built, the parkland preserved. In fact, a superficial reading of potential land value in dollars (high-priced land for development, low-priced
land for conservation) can lead planners into economic disasters. A great
many waterfront greenways, for example, can be justified on McHargian
analysis of natural processes (water runs downhill and can hurt you) and
the economic effects those processes imply.

McHarg's basic method is to create overlay maps of areas impacting
on or impacted by natural processes in a given area. Each physiographic

feature—steep slopes, for example, or the location of wetlands, rock out-crops, ridgelines, and streamways—is individually plotted with a trans-parent color on a clear Mylar sheet. When all the sheets are done, they are placed upon a white-paper base map of the region in question. Where no critical physical feature is present, the whiteness of the base map shows through the clear overlays. But where these features *are* present, the base map is darkened—a little bit, where only one or two of the determinants obscure the whiteness beneath, to almost black where a larger number of determinants "pile up." Accordingly, those areas where the map is light-est are the best places for development; the areas that are the darkest are the worst and should be protected from development. McHarg's book *Design with Nature* (1969), which describes this procedure, is well thumbed and often quoted by a good many conservationists and greenwayites, for his technique can produce persuasive evidence of the ecological value of greenways. Since 1969, refinements to McHarg's basic premise have em-phasized the importance of cultural and historical determinants as well as of natural ones.

A somewhat more eclectic approach to determining the public values of a potential greenway corridor may be found in the work of a landscape architecture professor named Philip Lewis. Now director of the Univer-sity of Wisconsin's Environmental Awareness Center in Madison, Lewis has, over the past thirty years, consistently been the most inventive (and occasionally controversial) figure in regional landscape-planning theory in the country. His most recent idea, a method to predict urban form, is based on analysis of nighttime satellite imagery.

What has occupied most of Lewis's waking hours, however, has been the concept of the *environmental corridor*. The corridors are, typically, along stream valleys. As Lewis has described it, "The flat, rolling farm-lands and the expansive forest have their share of beauty. But it is the steam valleys, the bluffs and ridges, the roaring and quiet waters, mellow wetlands, and sandy soils that combine in elongated designs, tying the land together in regional and statewide corridors of outstanding land-scape qualities."

To determine the exact location and relative landscape value of an environmental corridor, Lewis has created a method of landscape analysis involving some 220 environmental values, with a symbol for each which can be placed on a base map of the region to be studied. For the upper Midwest, the symbols represent natural and man-made water resource values such as waterfalls and reservoirs; various types of wetlands; topographic values such as exceptional glacial remains or nature trails; significant vegetation such as virgin woodlands; historic and cultural resources such as old mines, art museums, even restaurants; archeological features such as Indian burial grounds or shell middens; wildlife and game; and a final category called *the visual quality of space,* which provides a way to record outstanding aesthetic attributes.

Lewis has found that when the symbols representing his 220 values are applied to a regional map, they tend to array themselves in a linear fashion along natural corridors. "Most of the features," writes Lewis, "are found within the combined patterns of water, wetlands, and steep topography of 12.5 percent or greater." These findings comport with McHarg's, although they are arrived at by a slightly different method.

Therefore, we shall give Lewis a dot on the time line, and McHarg, too. It is hard to think of any modern greenway project that does not reflect the important contribution of these two men, whether directly or indirectly through their many students who are now on the front lines of greenway-making.

The penultimate dot goes to whoever it was who invented that most useful term, *greenway*. The first mention of the word that I have been able to find is by William H. Whyte in his 1959 monograph *Securing Open Space for Urban America,* published by the Urban Land Institute. The term comes up in a discussion of the work of Edmund Bacon, who prepared a greenway network plan for an undeveloped, semirural area of northwest Philadelphia. As Whyte describes the plan, it would "lay down the basic [open space] pattern *before* the developers got there. The conventional device of asking developers to dedicate a portion of the land to public use wouldn't be enough; all too frequently, the 3, 4, or 5 percent turns out to be the useless patches the developer couldn't do anything with. The planners [i.e., Bacon] assumed the initiative: they laid out the whole street pattern and in doing so they provided for a series of cohesive neighborhood units, with a series of 'greenways' and parks in between." And so, a provisional dot for Bacon, assuming he was indeed the coiner.

Actually, Whyte discusses greenways in most of his books and papers on open space. In *Cluster Development* (1964), a monograph published by the American Conservation Association, he describes a greenway plan proposed by Karl Belser for Santa Clara County, California, in 1961. The plan would create a creek-based greenway system as well as another greenway using utility rights-of-way. Later in the 1960s, greenways were proposed in Oregon, Colorado, and North Carolina. Also during this period of intense urban development (1955–65), there were a good many projects called *parkways* and *greenbelts,* although virtually all of them are actually greenways. These terms continue to be used, confusing matters somewhat since not all the parkways include a roadway as one might expect, and few of the greenbelts are the classic girdle of regulated agricultural land intended (as in Britain) to contain urban sprawl but rather are simply linear open spaces. Since the early 1970s, however, there has been a marked preference for the word *greenway* as the categorical term of choice. For this we should probably thank William H. Whyte who not only introduced the word to a large audience, but also did much to advance the basic concept. Readers should get hold of Whyte's *The Last Landscape* (Doubleday, 1968) and study the chapter entitled "Linkage." It is a still-useful and quite inspirational essay-length explanation of the greenway idea. As he writes, "There are all sorts of opportunities to link separated [open] spaces together, and while plenty of money is needed to do it, ingenuity can accomplish a great deal. Our metropolitian areas are crisscrossed with connective strips. Many are no longer used, . . . but they are there if only we will look." A great big dot on the greenway time line—and our last—for William H. Whyte.

Such are the manifold origins of the greenway idea—concepts that span a century and a quarter. In the chapters to follow, we shall see how a *movement* was created based on these concepts and how it has been expressed in various contexts—ranging from urban riverside redevelopment projects to rural trails to vast greenway networks. In these accounts, I believe the reader will be able to identify the contributions of Olmsted,

Howard, MacKaye, Lewis, and Whyte, among many others. It is good to know about these people and their works, for without knowing where the greenway movement has come from, it would be well-nigh impossible to figure out where it is going.

2

The Greenway Movement

> *When a piece of work gets done in the world,*
> *who actually does it? Whose eyes and ears do*
> *the perceiving, whose cortex does the thinking,*
> *who has the feeling that motivates, the will*
> *that overcomes obstacles? Certainly not the*
> *social environment; for a group is not an*
> *organism, but only a blind unconscious*
> *organization. Everything that is done within*
> *a society is done by individuals.*
>
> —ALDOUS HUXLEY

A movement is about people, individuals. And so, before getting into any technicalities, it might be useful first to meet a few of the individuals who are behind the hundreds of greenway projects being started every year in cities and towns across the country and to inquire into their purposes. They are unusual, talented, generous, and committed people in the main. As I have mentioned elsewhere in this book, there is something about greenways which attracts a refreshingly different kind of civic leader.

Take Leslie Luchonok, for example, a planner for the Bay Circuit, a one hundred-mile greenway that is to encircle the Boston metropolitan area. A slightly built, balding man in his mid-thirties, Luchonok lives with his wife and daughter in a Boston suburb. A straight-A student at Georgetown University during the early 1970s, Luchonok in his senior year suddenly decided to drop out in order to join the Findhorn Community in Scotland, a counterculture mecca of biodynamic gardening, closed-loop living, and "getting in touch." Among other skills acquired at Findhorn Luchonok learned the art of massage—learned it so well, in fact, that he decided to take his "gifted hands" to Europe to teach the healing art to others. Moving from spa to spa, he came to appreciate the cultural landscape of old Europe, which is underrepresented in most regions of the United States except perhaps in New England. Three years later, Luchonok returned home with a mission. He enrolled in the planning program at Rutgers, graduated with honors, went to Boston, and wound up landing a job on the Bay Circuit project. There this articulate, thoughtful, and highly motivated young man is helping—against terrific odds—to create a one hundred-mile-long healing band of cultural landscape around this great city. The project is profiled in Chapter 9.

Down in Florida, there is a home builder named Chuck Mitchell, whom a code inspector once called the *mad dog builder of Tallahassee* because Mitchell engaged in such unconventional practices as energy conservation, interesting design, and not tearing up a site to get every last possible house built on it. As recounted in another project profiled in Chapter 9, the building firm came to be known as the Mad Dog Construction Company, and it is now one of the biggest in north Florida. An old friend, a psychiatric nurse who worked in a private mental hospital, once sent Mitchell a drawing by one of her patients to whom she had described the Mad Dog Construction Company. The patient then drew a twenty-legged dog pulling a wheeled Valentine's day heart which so entranced Mitchell that he sometimes uses the drawing to promote his business. One day Mitchell and the Appalachee Land Conservancy, of which he is a board member, decided to save Tallahassee's beautiful and historic Canopy Roads—dirt roads so old that Hernando de Soto probably used them in his bloody foray northward in the mid-1500s. The resultant project is now well on its way to success. Mitchell, meanwhile, won a citation from the National Park Service for halting construction at a site that turned out to harbor the remains of some of Hernando's buildings. Arch-eologists now believe this to be the first permanent community built by Europeans in the United States.

In Poughkeepsie, New York, it was a refugee from a village near war-torn Hanover, Germany, who created much of the intellectual foun-dation and civic support for the most ambitious greenway project in America—the Hudson River Valley Greenway. Klara Sauer had spent countless nights of her childhood huddled in a bunker lest the British bombadiers might make a bad guess and blow up her village rather than the nearby munitions factory that was their target. After the war there was no work, so her father took his children to Canada. Klara finally came to the United States at the age of twenty-one, with an eighth-grade education, for schooling had been nearly impossible in postwar Ger-many, and she had to take a job in Canada to help support the family. After marriage and children, Klara decided to make up her lost years of education. She passed a high school equivalency examination and en-rolled in a local community college where she did so well that she was emboldened to apply to Vassar, which was interested in mature women wishing to complete their college training. For months she haunted the mailbox for a reply but heard nothing. Finally, in resignation and despair she called the college, only to learn that her application had never been received. With only days to go before the admissions deadline, Klara hur-riedly completed the forms again and in a few weeks was accepted into the junior class, with a sizable scholarship. She was thirty-four years old. Now Klara Sauer, B.A. and M.A. in urban studies, is the executive direc-tor of Scenic Hudson, Inc., and is determined to make the Hudson Valley a greenway. "America has given so much to me," she says with only the barest hint of an accent and with no pridefulness at all about how much she is giving back.

Such are the greenway people. And there are thousands more be-sides: historians, economists, ecologists, and anthropologists, even a fashion model; there are publicity men and advertising women, journal-ists, lawyers, minor and major government officials, musicians, writers, artists, and a good many people with no visible means of support.

How did the greenway idea attract such a diverse and dedicated cast of characters? Part of the answer, I think, is because our metropolitan areas—where most greenway projects are located—are a mess.

In the cities, homelessness, crime, and physical decay have been increasing at an alarming rate. The anomie of drugs and despair persists. The summertime park-sleepers and wintertime grate-dwellers, scarcely in evidence in downtown shopping and office districts ten or fifteen years ago, are now common everywhere, even in small cities. On the industrial edges, an economic exodus has condemned waterfronts and riverfronts to abandonment and ruin. The shells of once prospering industrial buildings, now with every window broken, line the abandoned railroad tracks. The riverways themselves reek of the unspeakable urban fluids they are asked to absorb and drain away.

Some of the older suburbs are not much better off, although enclaves of privilege remain. Yet even these leafy places are beset, surrounded by gridlocked highways swollen with commuters, one to a car, driving in from even more remote suburban places or from one suburban place to another. The pleasant little towns along the railroads or at the end of the trolley lines are now indistinguishable in a wallow of undifferentiated development, their denizens choking on the fumes of passing traffic. The milieu is fiercely automotive and deadly, and yet a vacant lot now sells for three or four or five times the money that house and lot together sold for fifteen years before.

Meanwhile, in the metropolitan countryside there is no countryside. Formerly rural regions have become an "outer" city, with sprawling automobile dealerships (autos costing more than some houses), gratuitous row house condominium developments, great plazas of stores and office buildings (some even high-rise), each with its own industrial suburb of body shops, plate glass emporia, and chain store warehouses. Across America, some three million acres a year are consumed this way. And between and beyond the outer cities, the corn fields and pastures are bounded by the roads of ruin—the incredibly ugly commercial strips that run from the perimeters of one metropolitan area to the perimeters of the next.

It is within this context that the impulse among certain citizens to create greenways has arisen. Greenways, as defined in the introduction to this book, do not themselves solve the problems of downtown blight, suburban gridlock, the inappropriate development of outer cities, the rural roads of ruin. But these social and environmental issues have clearly informed, if not inspired, a growing movement in creative land conservation which is really quite novel. It is to develop an entirely new infrastructure category, no less, a system of green ways—down rivers and streams, across ridgelines, over abandoned railbeds, along scenic and historic routes—which, in terms of any quality of life measure worth considering, may be one of the most significant people-oriented efforts in civic improvement to be mounted in the postwar era.

Although greenway-making may be seen as an antidote to our general civic malaise, the makers would not wish for us to view their work in the abstract. Their message is in their action, for there are concrete and quite immediate social, environmental, and economic benefits that their greenways confer upon the cities, suburbs, and countryside areas in which they are located. For example:

—Greenways really can improve urban recreational opportunities and quite dramatically so for those (and who is not?) interested in walking, jogging, biking, and hiking. The Platte River Greenway in Denver passes through rich and poor neighborhoods alike and is the most popular recreation facility in the city.

—Greenways also provide vital ecological functions in that natural processes (along waterways, especially) can be left in a natural state rather than obliterated by culverts and concrete. Moreover, greenways offer corridors for wildlife—in fact, they can bring wildlife to the very heart of a city. The elusive, nocturnal kit fox prowls silently through the mesquite bosques in the protected floodways of Tucson, for example.

—Greenways can even, praise be, reduce public costs or produce public money for a locality, and sometimes they do both. They reduce costs by helping to eliminate bad development that can be a liability to a muncipality. And greenways can produce money by helping to attract new development that creates jobs and tax-ratables. In fact, a greenway called Riverpark in Chattanooga, Tennessee, is based entirely on that principle. A public/private investment of three quarters of a billion dollars in redevelopment projects along the greenway is envisioned.

What is especially fascinating about the greenway movement—the thing that makes it so different from past land conservation efforts—is that it has arisen not because there are economic resources available to produce the kind of good results outlined above, but because there are not. Let me explain.

Twenty years ago, the name of the game in land conservation was *the race for open space,* a race between developers and conservationists for the remaining tracts of open land on the metropolitan fringe. As undeveloped parcels became increasingly scarce owing to a protracted post–World War II development boom, a good many landowners—farmers, ranchers, and the proprietors of great estates alike—simply sold out rather than pass their holdings along to the next generation. And so the specter of uncontrolled growth loomed over the hills and valleys of the metropolitan countryside. A single development of a couple of hundred tract houses, or even fifty, could utterly eliminate the rural ambience for miles around and, to add injury to insult, could be expected to drive up local taxes as well in order to provide for municipal services. Rarely could a development of single-family houses pay its own way. Public school costs alone would be higher for such a development—each house containing 3.2 school-age children in those baby-boom times—than the development would return to the community in property taxes. Add to that the costs of fire, police, refuse removal, sewage treatment, highway maintenance, and other services required by the new residents.

"Conservation is not contraception," complained the exasperated planning director of suburban Westchester County, outside New York City, so besieged was he by demands during the 1960s that this or that farm or estate be purchased as a county park or reserve to preclude development. But of course that was the whole idea. So open spacers (including this writer) got the grants and raised the funds to buy hunks of land (or talked their owners into donating them as nature sanctuaries) wherever they could as a kind of rearguard defense against the oncoming bulldozers. Today the pattern of what we did can be seen on road maps of any urban region: blobs of green, some large, some small, floating in a sea of suburban streets.

Finally, some began to wonder about the efficacy of this approach. The blobs, acquired almost entirely on an opportunistic basis, were unrelated either to natural processes or to social need. Indeed, most of the public funds and semipublic philanthropic efforts devoted to open-space preservation in those days benefitted the well-off who lived in estate country. Very little of the newly acquired open-space land appeared in the inner city or older suburbs, despite a light sprinkling of vest-pocket parks here and there. The charge of elitism was leveled at the land-savers, and, in hindsight, perhaps accurately so. Conservationists had an argument for their strategy, of course: that while having "parks where the people are" is desirable, the only land available for parks was where the people are not. Still, the elitism charge was politically damaging. Land conservation was painted by its enemies as no longer a public necessity but merely the frivolous preoccupation of the privileged. "Open space," said one black Illinois legislator who represented a ghetto district in southside Chicago, "does not draw a great deal of attention in the poolroom."

And so, by the mid-1970s, the old open-space action days were drawing to a close. The money was drying up as the nation struggled with its debts from Vietnam. The Department of the Interior claimed it was over $4 billion in arrears in terms of promised land purchases and recreational development. In an inflation-fighting effort, President Carter cut the Interior Department's grant-making Land and Water Conservation Fund severely. The open-space grant program of the Department of Housing and Urban Development, inaugurated in 1960, had long since disappeared, swallowed up by the municipal block-grant program, an invention of the Nixon administration. After the creation of three urban national recreation areas (in New York, San Francisco, and Cleveland-Akron, Ohio), the National Park Service was largely out of business in terms of acquiring metropolitan open space. Then the Reagan administration assumed power, slashing further, including especially housing programs that had to take a higher priority than land conservation at the state and local levels. Some governments simply could not handle it. In

California, the reactionary Proposition 13 had already reduced the ability of local governments to increase taxes to make up for the federal government's abrogations. Parks were closed, as were libraries and schools and much else that had provided amenity and quality of life.

Then the worst economic downturn since the 1930s struck—the recession of 1982–83. If the land-savers had held out any lingering hope of a return to the days when they could acquire large chunks of open space with public money to protect their environment, it was now utterly dashed. A few years later, even private money would be cut into, as tax reform provisions limited the deductibility of donated land or the money to buy it. Meanwhile, the cost of land soared. Although a few states have passed open-space acquisition bond issues in recent years (California and New Jersey, for example), in general, public funds are but a small fraction of what they were twenty years ago in terms of open-space purchasing power. And the strictures of the Gramm-Rudman-Hollings Act to limit the national deficit have suggested to most conservationists that the palmy days of open-space grants from the federal level will not be revived any time soon, if ever.

It is from these ashes that the modern greenway movement has arisen.

The home truth that it is an ill wind that blows nobody good applies especially well in the case of greenways. In fact, the greenway movement was created because of, rather than in spite of, the lack of money for open-space preservation. It was the very lack of it, indeed, that forced conservationists to focus on land resources with inherent, broadly based environmental values rather than on lands whose conservation importance was often quite local. One salubrious result has been that civic leaders of all kinds representing many interests have become attracted to the greenway movement, in contrast to the open spacers of the 1960s who tended to be white, middle class, and suburban. Accordingly, this new leadership has seen to it that instead of dealing mainly with land that is extremely expensive to acquire and is of benefit to only a slender minority of the population, conservationists should now utilize what might be called the *linear commons* of a community, which often costs a great deal less (or nothing at all) to acquire and which benefits the great mass of people.

Historically, a *commons* described a public green at the epicenter of a New England town, where the livestock were grazed. Or in earlier times, it was the waste beyond the furlongs of an Anglo-Saxon open field village. But in modern metropolitan America, there are other kinds of common lands in which there is a demonstrated overriding public interest. The land along a stream or river, for example, has historically been subject to a limited right of public access to the waterway for transportation and other resource needs. More recently, communities have exercised control more broadly over the use of riparian lands for self-protection in the event of flood. If the waters are public, then the banks that contain them also have an implicit public importance.

Linear commons such as these can also be found in the lands along a ridgeline of hills that, because they demark watersheds and possess visual dominance of the valley settlements they separate, are often already in public or quasi-public ownership. Yet another common-land resource is the right-of-way of an abandoned railroad or, less frequently, a canal. Condemned many years past for use by a public carrier, such land can remain intact as a public route, for walkers or cyclists, replacing trains and barges. The land along a road that is agreed to be historic or scenic also has common value, as part of the public landscape, in maintaining a community's sense of itself. Although the title to ownership of such lands may be lodged in private hands, the public's interest in their use and conservation is generally understood.

These linear commons share some interesting characteristics. Almost invariably they follow the topographic logic of a place: streamways, ridgelines, transportation corridors. They are often unsuitable (although not always, of course) for many land uses that would give them great private economic value; being long and thin, they do not offer the dimensional chunks of land favored by those who wish to build shopping malls, residential subdivisions, distribution center warehouses, or office and industrial complexes. Moreover, in many cases, linear common-interest lands are strictly regulated by the community to preclude certain kinds of uses: floodplain zoning along the riversides, or, less often, aesthetically inspired restraints along ridges and sometimes along the scenic roads. On the urban waterfronts or close to the railroad tracks, development is often limited to heavy industry, meaning that the land may lie idle or remain only lightly used, as a materials storage yard, for example. These days, new industry tends to locate near interstate cloverleafs or the airports and less often along the old transportation routes of riversides and rail lines.

Another characteristic shared by linear commons is that in many places they are still largely intact, unsegmented. Despite the intense urban growth since the 1950s, new development has often jumped over these linear land resources because they were physiographically unsuitable for building, were regulated against development, or were in an economically unattractive location.

Thus, green and good, new kinds of land resources presented themselves to conservationists as opportunities they had previously overlooked—the metropolitan linear commons that could affordably be converted to greenways.

Now no one should conclude that greenway-making, because it is affordable, is somehow less valid a land conservation strategy than the earlier emphasis on preserving large discontinuous open-space parcels in the metropolitan countryside. In fact, *cheaper* might even be *better* in certain respects since a greenway program can confer two quite remarkable attributes not realizable when open-space preservation is confined to single chunks of land. One of these attributes is *edge,* and the other is *linkage.*

The edge effect is almost magical. For most people, the great utility of preserved open space of almost any kind is not measured by its area but by its edge: that is, what you see when walking or riding down a street alongside it or taking a pathway through it. From the edge, a wooded park that might be a mile across looks the same as one that is two hundred feet in width. Clearly, therefore, a long, thin greenway can provide a great deal more *apparent* open space per acre than a consolidated parcel of land. Now bear with me a moment for some kitchen-table math to demonstrate the economic implications of the edge effect.

Let us take a round blob of a park that is one hundred acres in area.

The radius of the blob is 1,177.8 feet. Remembering that the circumference of a circle is two times Pi times the radius, you come up with an edge of 7,396.7 feet.

Now, let us unpeel this park into a long strip of green which is one square acre wide (209 feet)—in effect, laying one acre next to another in a line. To find the length of the edge of one hundred acres in this configuration, you multiply the number of acres (one hundred) times the width, *times two,* since there are two sides to this strip. The result is 41,800 linear feet, 5.65 times as much apparent open space in a long thin greenway as compared with a large, more or less circular park with the same number of acres. That is the edge effect. To put the ratio in crass economic terms, for every dollar of tax money spent on a traditional blob park, you can get the same edge effect (assuming an equal price per acre) with an expenditure of eighteen cents for a greenway.

No one should take this little exercise so literally that a movement starts to sell off all the massive parks to buy land for greenways or to forego an opportunity to acquire large natural or historic properties whenever possible. Most of those big-acreage assets are priceless, and localities that possess them are fortunate. But the idea of converting our common-interest linear land resources to greenways is susceptible to powerful economic justification, based on the edge effect.

The second great advantage of a greenway is linkage. Many of the individual parks and nature sanctuaries acquired during the 1960s and early 1970s are intersected by linear commons of some sort—usually a stream valley, less often an open-space ridgeline, or an abandoned transportation route. What greenways can do is to multiply the utility of existing parks—ecologically, recreationally, and aesthetically—by linking them together like beads on a string. This, too, is an old idea. Park planners of the past often recommended such corridors; but in the postwar fervor to beat the bulldozer to those choice hunks of open space, linkage was often forgotten. Now rediscovered, the possibilities of linkage have excited more conservationists than almost any other attribute of greenways. One benefit is that linked parks and reserves provide for what ecologists call *species interchange,* the sine qua non of biological diversity and therefore ecological stability. The wide movement of wildlife, even plants, along a natural corridor is essential for the survival of some species, especially those fairly high up on the food chain. If confined to a single nature reserve, even a quite large one, species such as fox or owl can become an island population and possibly perish.

Moreover, the linking of parks along natural or even man-made corridors produces a remarkable recreational advantage. In Portland, Oregon, for example, a 140-mile greenway around the city will connect some thirty parks and reserves, substantially increasing their aggregate benefit to the community. Almost everyone is also entranced by the possibility of interregional long-distance linkages. Wrote the enthusiastic authors of *Americans Outdoors,* the 1987 report of the President's Commission on Americans Outdoors, "Imagine walking out your front door, getting on a bicycle, a horse, or trail bike, or simply donning your backpack and, within minutes of your home, setting off along a continuous network of recreation corridors which could lead across the country."

The report-writers may have engaged in a flight of prose fancy, but their image of a green network across America—one of the commission's key recommendations—nevertheless caught the imagination of a number of journalists and authors (including me) who were struck by the boldness and the sheer *timeliness* of the idea. Although modern greenways had been in evidence since the mid-1960s (and their predecessors a century before), the idea of linking them from coast to coast seemed compelling for a nation that was, in many ways, splitting apart. The report's emphasis on a nationwide system of greenways and the attendant publicity the recommendation engendered have doubtless had a significant coalescing effect on the greenway movement.

Indeed, *linkage* carries a powerful symbolic message and is, clearly, the philosophic core of the greenways movement, regardless of the prospects of a national system, which perhaps works better as a metaphor rather than a literal policy initiative in any case. The point is that this movement is not merely an aggregation of conservationists undertaking similar projects but a cadre of civic leaders, however disparate, who devoutly believe in the emblematic, as well as actual, importance of linkage: of recreational and cultural resources, of wildlife populations, and most of all, of neighborhoods and towns and cities and people of all colors and stations not only in the use of the greenways but also in the making of them.

To make a greenway, as you will find as you read further in this book, is to make a community. And that, above all else, is what the movement is all about.

3

The World of Greenways: Part I

FATHER OF THE GREENWAYS

The Capital Area Greenway, Raleigh, North Carolina

The plan for the Capital Area Greenway, which is thought to be the earliest comprehensive local greenway *system* in the country, was created not by a famous consultant with offices in major cities, not by a much-published authority in comprehensive planning, not even by a team of planning professionals. It was the work of a twenty-five-year-old North Carolina State University graduate student whose major qualifications were that he needed a thesis project, that he had a passion for keeping his native city of Raleigh as green and good as he knew it while growing up, and that he was convinced, as he now puts it, that "natural environmental functions do not need to be displaced as cities expand."

The year was 1970, and the student, Bill Flournoy, now acknowledged to be "father of the Raleigh Greenways," saw how he could use his master's thesis requirement to plan not a single streamside park but a network of greenways running into and out of all the city's neighborhoods. The basic idea of greenways in Raleigh was not original with Flournoy. Linear parks had been proposed during the 1950s and mentioned again in

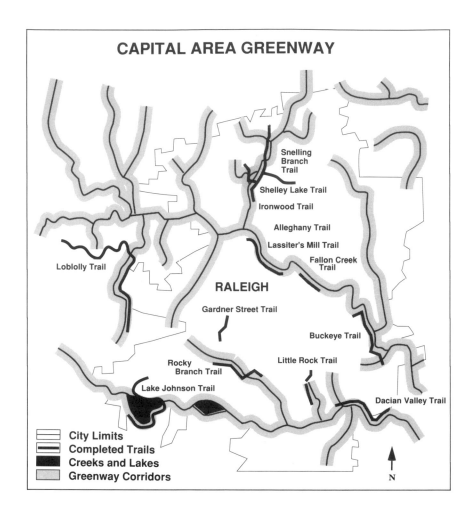

a recreational plan in 1969 which, for the first time in North Carolina, actually used the term *greenway*. What Flournoy did was to show how to make the greenways happen—by writing a report that he says was "one hundred pages of consciousness building." In fact, the report is a master-piece of specificity and has become something of an underground classic among greenway-makers. It described how floodplain zoning could be employed, how easements could be acquired, how paths should be built, and where. And most significantly, it provided politicians and the public alike with persuasive rationales for taking action—the social, economic, environmental, and aesthetic benefits of greenways.

The basic concept involved, Flournoy states, "is the fact that linear open space has significantly more perimeter or edge than traditional consolidated parks. This edge may be used to buffer competing land uses, and soften the urban image." The benefits of an edge system like Raleigh's, Flournoy says, are manifold. "Linear open spaces can connect traditional parks and other activity centers such as schools and shopping centers. They can also accommodate popular recreational activities such as jogging, walking, bicycling, and canoeing which may be incompatible with traditional urban parks. When associated with streams, which are also linear systems, the open space allows flooding to occur without damage to buildings, or disruption of the local economy or individual lives. Environmentally, linear open space acts as a vegetated buffer along streams to protect water quality and fragile natural ecosystems such as wetlands. Further, the urban environment is enhanced through air quality, temperature, and noise moderation resulting from the conservation of vegetation. Finally, these areas function as wildlife corridors, allowing a greater diversity of animals to travel through and survive within urban areas." Such benefits as these are fully realized in Raleigh, where the greenways wind through the thick woodlands characteristic of the Piedmont, along the rivers, creeks, brooks, runs, branches, and forks that make up a skein of waterways which patterns the city.

Flournoy's comprehensive multicreek greenway program was inaugurated in 1974 in association with a rigorous floodplain protection ordinance, after devastating flooding had persuaded the city's political leadership that housing or commercial development on floodplains should be restrained. Floods were causing, on the average, over a million dollars in damages per year, a cost that would doubtless increase exponentially as housing and commercial development reached out into the countryside surrounding the city.

Thanks to support by civic groups and environmental organizations, most particularly the Sierra Club, some twenty-seven miles of pathways were developed along the floodplains over the next fifteen years. During this period, the reorganization of city government helped to encourage greenway action in that council members stood for election on a district basis rather than at large, which gave individual neighborhoods a stronger voice in municipal affairs. And the neighborhoods wanted greenways. Accordingly, greenway corridors were acquired via easement dedication by residential builders, sometimes by landowner donation, sometimes by purchase, and sometimes even by piggybacking a greenway on a sewerline right-of-way. The trails were mostly asphalted and used by joggers, cyclists, picnickers, and people who liked to get from one place to another through the quiet woods rather than over the toilsome roads by car.

In time, as Flournoy's bouquet of benefits became evident to more and more of Raleigh's citizens, the pace of greenway-making picked up in the late 1980s after a bit of a lull. By the year 2000, Raleigh's current greenway-planners hope to reach their goal of two hundred developed miles. Old-hand Flournoy is not quite as optimistic but believes the mileage could well exceed one hundred before the next decade is out.

As an idea, the Capital Area Greenway has become the model for over thirty-five local greenways systems in North Carolina cities plus an untold number of other places throughout the Southeast as well as the United States as a whole. Flournoy, now a state official in the Department of Environment, Health, and Natural Resources, keeps his hand in the greenway movement as a director (and founder) of both the Triangle Land Conservancy and the Triangle Greenway Council, which seek to connect the greenways in the Research Triangle cities of Raleigh, Durham, and Chapel Hill into a regional system. All this was from a thesis/greenway plan that cost the city of Raleigh the astonishingly modest sum of $1,500. The plan has turned out to be a priceless contribution not only for this capital city but also for the scores of other municipalities that have sent their planners to Raleigh to learn how to make greenways happen in their own cities.

So how does greenway-father Flournoy feel about his baby now? Very good indeed, although he is so averse to self-praise that few students of the modern greenway movement realize how influential his work has been. But that is Bill Flournoy's way. As he puts it, "Someone once said you get to do as much as you want, if you don't want the credit." Maybe so, but American conservationists ought to pin a medal on this landscape architect's chest. It is doubtful that without him the modern greenway movement could have developed as rapidly as it has.

NOT JUST AN ORDINARY STRIP OF LAND

The Heritage Trail, Dubuque County, Iowa

For good or ill, it was the railroads, beginning in the early 1800s, that changed the great American prairie—all of the tall-grass prairie and most of the short. The trunk lines and spurs relocated existing towns, created new towns, connected every county seat with every other, redirected trade (and therefore politics) from north–south along the corridors of the Mississippi and its tributaries to east–west, the new transcontinental axis of economic growth provided by rail rather than water. Within a handful of decades, the buffalo were nearly exterminated, the Indians driven out, and the prairie grasses turned under by oxen and moldboard plow to create the American heartland, the richest agricultural region in the world.

It still is the richest agricultural region in the world, but the infrastructure of iron rails and rights-of-way which brought it into being no longer dominates. Semis plying the interstate highways carry the freight, and autos and airplanes carry the passengers that once relied on the elaborate skein of railroads throughout the Middle West. Beginning in the early 1960s, as the railroad companies increasingly abandoned their lines, civic leaders throughout the country and especially in heartland states such as Iowa sought to convert the unneeded rights-of-way to new public uses such as wildlife habitats or recreational trails. Their pleas to save these corridors of land were scarcely heeded at first, during a time when fencerows were being removed to create more land to farm. From the windows of a speeding passenger train—an experience then within recent memory of most—the landscape that these rights-of-way traversed seemed dull or at best ordinary. But the trailmakers knew that up close, afoot or from the saddle of a bike, there were prairie wonders to

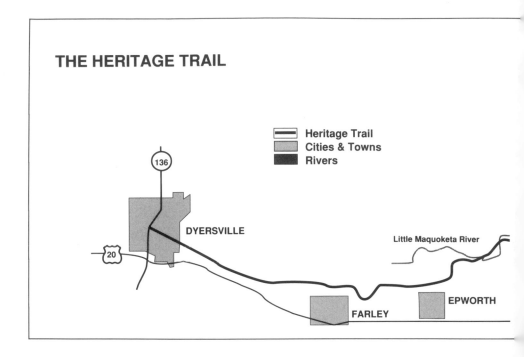

behold—old towns and farms, streamsides and woods, even some of the primordial tall grass itself. They knew, too, that a recreational trail on a refurbished railbed could bring new economic life to rural areas and re-connect communities that had grown apart after the rail lines had been abandoned.

A good many *railroad conversions,* as they are called—over two hundred projects have been undertaken since the beginning of the rails-to-trails movement a quarter-century ago—provide a kind of natural and cultural cross-section of the land through which they travel. In this regard, a conversion called the Heritage Trail, running from the unglaciated Driftless Area of eastern Iowa, with its gorges and sheer escarpments, westward into the rolling bluestem plains may be an outstanding example. As writer Pat Nunnally of the University of Iowa describes the Heritage Trail, "This is not just an ordinary strip of land across Iowa's prairies."

Indeed not. Beginning northeast of Dubuque and traveling west, the

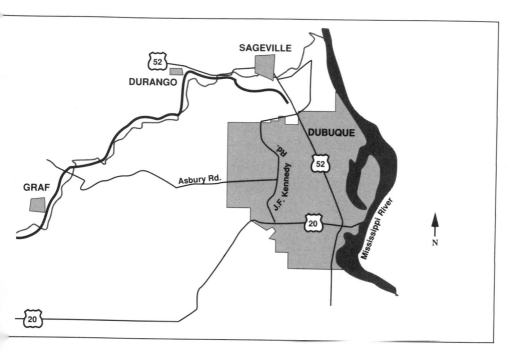

walker or bicyclist encounters, in turn, wetlands; Indian burial mounds; an 1868 cast-iron truss bridge; wood duck nesting sites; a deep valley with sheer limestone cliffs; the lead mine boom-and-bust-town of Durango; an iron ore mine; the remnants of old stagecoach roads; a fabulous fishing spot where channel cat and lunker bass lurk in the pools; a split rock just wide enough for a 4-8-4 steam engine to negotiate; dolomite fossil beds; remnants of dry prairie with side oats grama grass and prairie roses; a number of nineteenth-century grist mills; Paleozoic outcroppings; the birthplace of famed natural scientist W. J. McGee; remnant tall-grass prairie with big bluestem; oak savannas; and artifacts such as the old railroad coaling stations, bridges, and abandoned equipment which bespeak the plains commerce of yesteryear.

The Heritage Trail is built on the right-of-way of the Chicago Great Western Railroad's main line from Chicago to St. Paul, on which passenger service ceased in 1956. In 1968, the CGWR sold out to the Chicago and North Western; and by 1979, when the last freight train rumbled over these rails, the CNW was willing to sell off the right-of-way after it removed the track for reuse in new coalfields in Wyoming and Montana.

As soon as the offer was made, the trailmakers formed a nonprofit sponsoring group, Heritage Trail, Inc., and campaigned to focus interest on a conversion project under the auspices of the Dubuque County Conservation Board. The board was interested, but the county supervisors, as the elected officials to whom the conservation board answered, were concerned about the political fallout from the opponents of the trail idea who quickly showed themselves to be vociferous, if not obstreperous, in their reaction. A stand-off lasted for two years until formal railroad abandonment proceedings took place in 1981, bringing the issue to a showdown. A year later, in 1982, the county supervisors held a hearing to take up the question of converting the right-of-way to a hiking and biking trail as requested by the county conservation board and Heritage Trail, Inc.

The trailway group was at first hopeful that favorable action was at hand. But when they arrived at the meeting, ready to make their presentation, they were shocked to find the auditorium packed with right-of-way neighbors emotionally claiming that a recreational trail would bring "criminal elements" from Dubuque into their rural communities. Many had assumed they owned a reversionary interest in the right-of-way, although their deeds showed otherwise. Moreover, since there had been a history of trespassers and vandals abusing railroad property, the abutting owners and their allies assumed that a trail would compound the problem. Many of the trail neighbors simply wanted some measure of control over the use of the railbed land. Others, more fearful, vowed they would burn the bridges before they would allow the Heritage Trail to be built. They were referring to the wooden trestles that crossed and recrossed the Little Makoqueta River, which the rail-trail followed along part of the proposed twenty-six-mile route. All that was needed to scotch the plan, the extremists figured, was a few crucial missing links, since it would be beyond the means of the project to build new bridges. And then the land would be theirs.

Such opposition did, in fact, intimidate the supervisors, who voted for a study and then finally denied the funding request. But the controversy also stimulated broad public interest in the plan. The ugly hearing got banner headlines in all the county newspapers, which in turn brought the Heritage Trail idea to the attention of the general population. "Despite the early negative publicity," one of the trail organizers later observed, "many new people heard about the trail and offered to help."

The most practical problem faced by the trail proponents was money. The railroad at first asked for $400,000, although after negotiations they agreed to $235,000. But the supervisors, reacting to the nastiness of the preliminary hearing, provided no apparent source of funding. When the railroad, impatient with the delays, pressed for a nonrefundable $24,000 down payment and a payment schedule for the rest, the Dubuque County Conservation Board, reaching into its own very limited budget, found it could piece together $160,000 from other recreation projects. But that was the outside limit, and it was far short of the negotiated price. Fearing the whole project could go under, the Heritage Trail board of directors, led by Doug Cheever, an agricultural equipment engineer, each put up a thousand dollars of their own money. In addition, with some creative financing, Heritage Trail, Inc. managed to swing a loan for $50,000 more—to assure that the complete trail corridor could be purchased. And so, the work of piecing the trail together was begun. The funding for trail development, never enough, was put together by combining private and government funds over a period of years.

Despite the progress made by Cheever and his colleagues, some of the trailway's opponents remained adamant. They had raised the specter of vandalism, yet it was to vandalism they themselves turned in order to stop the project. According to Nunnally, "Many times . . . the trail project seemed doomed to failure. Another bridge would be fired (there were nine burnings by 1986, with three bridges total losses), a source of money would fall through, or another lawsuit would be filed." Nevertheless, the development of the trail continued on, mile by mile, segment by segment, until finally in June of 1986, five years after the project had started, the Heritage Trail was formally dedicated.

According to Doug Cheever, the project was a success because "it was an idea whose time had come," because the trail proponents were backed up by the official county conservation board, and because the nonprofit sponsoring group, Heritage Trail, Inc., which did all the planning, fund raising, and development, had the flexibility "to move fast (or slow) as required for best results."

Just an ordinary strip of land? Hardly. Today, thousands of hikers and bicyclists use the trail every year. When they pass over the charred timbers of a fired bridge, they can thank a handful of visionary leaders who could not be intimidated in their effort to preserve this short stretch of prairie land and history in Iowa. And that is a part of the trail's heritage, too. Says Cheever, "Most of our Heritage Trail board members grew up on a farm, and though they might now live in town, they knew what being close to the land meant to them. They wanted a chance to share that 'sense of the land' with others and saw the trail as a way to do it."

FROM FLOODWAYS TO GREENWAYS

The Pima County River Parks, Tucson, Arizona

It was the flood of 1983 that finally brought everything into focus, that made the connection between flood control and greenways vivid for the people of Tucson, and that gave Charles F. Huckelberry, civil engineer, a way to get a whole system of linear parks under way in his city. Although the beginnings were small, they are encouraging.

Easterners may think that the largest problem for cities such as Tucson in the arid Southwest is too little water. The fact is just the opposite. The largest problem is too much water coming too fast. When the pelting rains of autumn descend on the impervious surfaces of the desert mountains, baked to hardness all summer long, most of the water simply runs off, unabsorbed by the soil and unimpeded by vegetation that is sparse and separated. If it keeps raining, the myriad rills lacing the mountain steeps become quickly engorged, and then they join with one another in a constantly accelerating series of larger and larger confluences that multiply geometrically.

In a matter of minutes, massive walls of water can form to roar down the canyons and into the floodways of the desert floor—the wide, wide

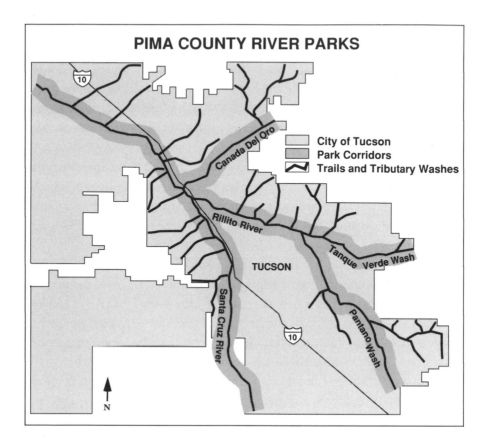

washes where cottonwoods, mesquite bosques, palo verde trees, and desert shrubs and flowers provide a natural garden rich in wildlife. Such
places can flourish undisturbed by destructive flooding for a number
of years, perhaps even decades. But in those rare "one hundred-year"
events, the rainwater tears through the floodway gardens like a runaway
freight train with a cargo of slurried soil, boulders, uprooted trees and
bushes, houses once perched along the banks, horses, parts of bridges,
and automobiles, sometimes with people in them.

The city of Tucson, with mountains rising all around it, has always
been susceptible to serious flash flooding, but the water could be managed with the standard repertoire of flood-control engineering—pretty
much a matter of excavating a permanent channel, making it wide and

deep, and lining it with concrete. This will work well as long as a city stays small. But Tucson did not. As it spread outward along previously undeveloped canyons and washes during the growth-oriented affluent 1960s, the economic distress and human tragedy caused by flooding increased. Finally in 1972, the city passed a stiff floodplain ordinance limiting any further new building in flood-prone areas. All well and good, for five years or so.

Then an era of floods hit the city—not just one flood, but a whole series beginning in 1977 and continuing through 1983, the likes of which most folks in Tucson had never seen. In six years, four Pima County floods were declared federal disasters by the president of the United States.

The last of these, the flood of 1983, was the worst. The rain began pummeling southern Arizona beginning September 29, and it did not let up until October 2. The waters surged down the Santa Cruz River and its tributaries, tearing through the heart of Tucson at twice the volume of any previous one hundred-year flood event. The Federal Emergency Management Agency (FEMA) estimated that in the Santa Cruz basin 154 houses were destroyed and nearly 400 more were damaged. Four bridges were washed out, fifteen required extensive repairs, and forty-two had to be closed for safety reasons during the flooding. Thirteen people were killed and 221 injured. Some four hundred people had to be evacuated by rescue squads. In all, nearly six thousand people were given emergency shelter.

In the aftermath, the tragedy caused the civic leaders of Tucson to reexamine their whole approach to flood control, giving special recognition to land-use remedies such as establishing floodplain parks that would preclude development, and therefore flood damage, rather than undertaking after-the-fact structural remedies. Tucson had already shown an interest in linear parks along its rivers and washes, having established a 1.5-mile downtown park along the Santa Cruz floodway in the early 1970s. But the flood of 1983 brought the U.S. Army Corps of Engineers into the picture. The corps required the city to protect the banks as a preventive measure, and this in turn provided conservationists with good arguments to create an expanded park system along floodways throughout the city. In fact, Huckelberry, then director of the Pima County Department of Transportation and Flood Control District (DOT & FCD) argued that the acquisition of flood-prone land along floodway banks should be the method of first resort rather than the last in flood-control planning. He urged that a substantial fraction of a flood-remediation bond issue, passed in 1984, be devoted to land acquisition.

The idea met with favor but not much money. Of the $64 million in revenues for flood repair approved by Pima County voters in 1984, only $8.3 million was earmarked for riverbank land purchase. Huckelberry nevertheless turned the money he did get to good account, acquiring key parcels along the Rillito River and other tributaries and washes. The following year he made another pitch to the Pima County Board of Supervisors, asking for a second bond issue that would "allow more land beset by critical flood hazards to be acquired in the immediate future, at the lowest overall costs."

Huckelberry asked for $40 million, and he got half that amount, which was not bad since traditionally flood control had been largely a matter of moving earth and pouring concrete, not of buying land. Most persuasive to the supervisors and the voters was an economic analysis that Huckelberry directed be done of the structural approach versus the nonstructural (land acquisition) approach. In one area studied, in which a mobile-home subdivision had occupied flood-prone land on the west branch of the Santa Cruz, the DOT & FCD estimated that the cost of structural flood-control facilities would be $3.5 million. The actual cost of buying the land and relocating the mobile homes turned out to be less than half a million, including the cost of land, the purchase and improvement of a parcel for relocation, and the moving of the mobile homes to the new site. In another example, the Cañada del Oro (Brook of Gold) Wash, the cost of a flood-control structure was estimated to be $12.4 million, whereas the cost of land acquisition and relocation of affected residents was only $4.5 million. This was obviously the kind of arithmetic which Pima County officials liked to hear.

With the passage of the $20 million bond, the DOT & FCD developed a general policy to obtain an additional fifty-foot right-of-way adjacent to all major watercourses—by means of purchase, voluntary easement, or through mandatory open-space dedication required of new residential subdivisions or commercial developments. This would provide the basis for a linear park system with trails and recreational nodes spotted here and there along the way. Natural vegetation would be restored where it had been washed out, and the landscaping of recreational areas would use native plant materials. By 1988, the department had developed parks along the banks of about 3.5 linear miles of floodway on the Rillito River as part of an overall program that could eventually total as much as 105 miles when completed. Certainly, public demand for such parks had been growing. The stretch along the Rillito River, according to Keith Oliver, a landscape architect and planner for the DOT & FCD, had become one of the most popular parks in Pima County. Fifteen more miles along the Rillito are currently in the design stage.

In the planning for these greenways, the DOT & FCD works closely with the U.S. Army Corps of Engineers, which, under the provisions of Section 404 of the Clean Water Act, must issue a permit for all flood-mitigation projects on navigable watercourses. (The definition of *navigable* is obviously a broad one, covering even the intermittent flows of Tucson's "rivers," which are dry most of the year.) In addition, the Environmental Protection Agency and the U.S. Fish and Wildlife Service (which has a special interest in the protected floodways as wildlife corridors) are involved, also under the provisions of Section 404.

Civic support has been impressive. A citizen-led open-space committee gave top priority to the preservation of desert washes in its 1988 report to the Pima County Board of Supervisors. They pointed out that the washes provided simultaneously a wildlife habitat; natural beauty; archeological sites (where prehistoric tribes settled on the natural terraces); and recreational opportunity for horseback riding or hiking in the washes themselves in dry seasons, or walking, jogging, or biking along the banks. Taken together, the system of river floodways and washes could give Tucson what the committee calls the "primary linkages in a communitywide open-space system that will tie the urbanized areas and the surrounding mountains together." Without a remediation approach like Huckelberry's, many of these natural areas would simply be channelized and thus partially destroyed. His river park plan—although still in an embryonic stage in Tucson—can provide for the acquisition of many linear miles of flood-prone land adjacent to the washes and the removal and relocation of any structures that could sustain flood damage. Progress in implementing the plan has seemed to be painfully slow to young planners like Keith Oliver who envision a vast network of natural corridors and recreational parks along the washes. On the Rillito River, Oliver complains, "only a few miles, out of about sixty, are being spared. The flood-prone land acquisition program only works where development is sparse enough to make this an affordable proposition. What is spared is beautiful, but bank protection [i.e., hardening with concrete] is still the primary flood-control strategy."

Still, Oliver has hopes that the program will gather some momentum. Certainly, it is easy to wax lyrical about nature's glories in a system of bankside parks along the desert wash greenways. Here is the route by which the coyotes come down from the mountains on nighttime forays in search of cottontails, javelina, or lesser meals. Here, the roadrunners dodge through the mesquite bosques, the hummingbirds busy themselves with the myriad desert blossoms, and the redtail and Harris hawks circle above, riding the thermals. Closer to the ground are the frogs and toads, including the miraculous spadefoot toad that grows from egg to tadpole to mature adult, breeds, and lays eggs of its own in the handful of days between the first drop of rain and the time that the evanescent puddles permitting the astonishing cycle to begin dry up and disappear. There are geckos hiding in the yucca, and whiptails among the cholla, a dozen different species of lizard in all; and nineteen species of snake, including four kinds of rattlers. And through all the seasons, the wildflowers light the scene—the penstemon, flax, and desert marigolds, the verbena and primrose, the asters and salvia. It is a naturalist's paradise indeed.

And yet, the motive for its protection is ever so practical. Charles Huckelberry, like many of his Tucson neighbors, is a lover of the desert's natural beauty. But it may well be his engineer's dry prose that will turn out to be the most convincing: "Flood-damage reduction through flood-prone land acquisition," he wrote in his recommendation for the park plan, "is a viable and effective flood-control tool which assists government in its role of assuring public safety, while contributing to other community goals such as recreation and open space." It ain't poetry, but it may well serve to turn a floodway into a greenway for the generations to come.

A CASE OF ACUTE FORESIGHT

The Redding Greenbelts, Redding, Connecticut

Redding, Connecticut, a woodsy municipality on the commuting fringe of the New York metropolitan area, has traditionally been favored by artists and photographers (Edward Steichen), writers (Stuart Chase), musicians (Charles Ives), wealthy estate owners (who are everywhere on the perimeters of Gotham), and large numbers of nature lovers. Perhaps this creative heritage has made Redding, more than most exurban places, a standout in the game of demographic prediction. In the late 1950s and early 1960s, Chase and a number of younger writers such as Mary Anne Guitar, who was later to become first selectman (mayor), saw the need to mount some sort of defense against encroaching suburbanization that, having tackified the potato farms of Long Island, was now hell-bent to tear into the Connecticut woods.

Although many neighboring Connecticut towns scorned applying to the federal government for grants to snatch open space from under the bulldozer's blade (being unwilling to permit nonresidents to use the land so acquired for recreation—a stipulation), Redding's creative conservationists decided it was better to be a small-*d* democrat than paved over. So they set about to learn the art of open-space grantsmanship. And they learned it well. Under the leadership of Conservation Commission Chairman Sam Hill, an owner of considerable acreage himself, the town set a goal of preserving 25 percent of its land area as open space. To help achieve this, they made twelve applications to the Department of the Interior for grants from the Land and Water Conservation Fund (LWCF) program and to the Department of Housing and Urban Development for grants under the Open Space Program. The result was unbelievable: they batted exactly 1,000. Before the effort, the town of Redding owned

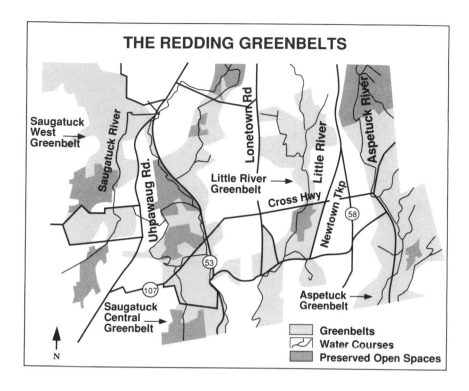

THE REDDING GREENBELTS

but 1.2 acres of protected open space. By 1975, it had acquired 1,256 acres. In total, Hill and company raised well over a million dollars from state and federal sources and persuaded the town voters to come up with $1.3 million on their own. In the midst of those great days of open-space action, Stuart Chase wrote admiringly, "Town officials and residents in general have shown acute foresight in supporting this vital form of insurance against Malthusian disaster."

But soon, the federal money played out. During the 1970s, the LWCF's annual budget was shrinking while land prices were soaring. President Ford offered no solution and let the appropriations dwindle. Then President Carter cut the LWCF severely as an inflation-fighting measure. President Reagan restored it for a few years and then the fund more or less withered away, in a perverse imitation of Marxian theory. During these years, the open spacers in towns like Redding were all asking themselves the same question, "What do we do now?" For many towns, the answer was "nothing." The impetus to save open space slowed or stopped altogether. And the wooded parcels simply sat there, environmentally valuable but unused and unadded to.

This was not the case in Redding, which had succeeded so spectacularly in the game of grantsmanship. The federal grants required that the lands purchased with public money be open to the public that helped to buy them. This was logical but, in the sylvan enclaves around the edges of the expanding metropolis, not entirely popular. Images of hoodlum gang members with boom boxes, of lurking silverware thieves, and even of marauding *liberals* came easily to the minds of some. Redding, nevertheless, was able to suppress any uncharitable feelings and turned what some thought might be a problem into an opportunity. Under the direction of musician Clois Ensor and a crew of volunteer trailmakers, the town constructed footpaths not only through the land purchased with federal help but through all the other open spaces as well.

The trails are probably too modest to be attractive to the alien life-forms that some citizens feared. There is no asphalt here—merely cleared foot- and bridle paths through the woods, marked with blazes. But this is ideal recreational development for nature lovers, which describes nearly every grown person in Redding, Connecticut. There are now fifty-five miles of woodland paths, all charmingly described in a handsome ninety-five-page guide with maps and directions covering some thirty different walks. *The Book of Trails* (1985) is a publication of the Redding Conservation Commission and two nonprofit conservation organizations, Redding Open Lands, Inc., and the Redding Land Trust. It was written by Joan Ensor, the journalist-wife of musician-trailman Clois; and John G. Mitchell, a field editor for *Audubon* magazine.

The trails and the trail guide that encourages their use have also had a far-reaching effect on open-space planning, well beyond the acquisition of parcels of open space. The familiarity that the townspeople of Redding gained by tramping through their woods led to a larger vision. In the second edition of the Ensor-Mitchell trail guide, the so-called *long trails* are shown—the result of connecting open-space acquisitions along the major stream valleys and ridgetops into four greenbelts running through the town. As the Redding open-space plan (written by Mitchell for the

Conservation Commission) describes these corridors, "What nature has provided is a series of parallel ridges and stream valleys. . . . What happenstance provides is a mosaic of large tracts of open land lying within the corridors of these ridges and valleys and creating, in aggregate, unencumbered swaths that run like fingers through the town."

To keep the fingers from being chopped off, the Conservation Commission recommended that future acquisition efforts be concentrated in the environmentally critical greenbelts and that municipal zoning and subdivision regulations be adapted to their special requirements as waterways. Accordingly, the protection of Redding's charming landscape does not rest entirely on isolated, individual parcels of land opportunistically acquired, as it did in the earlier open-space days. It now envisions protecting sizable tracts of land based on ecological considerations. And the four greenbelts constitute not a quarter of the town's area but rather nearly half of it.

This is the way Stuart Chase's acute foresight has worked in Redding and has built upon itself. As First Selectman Mary Anne Guitar puts it, "Here we have living proof that true conservation is for people, that nature is best enjoyed close at hand, that one small town could—and did—control its own destiny."

THE REBIRTH OF AN OLD-TIME RIVER

The Meramec Greenway, St. Louis to Sullivan, Missouri

This is the story of the Meramec River—from its Pleistocene beginnings, through some good times, then some bad, and now good again, for this river is making a comeback, as a greenway.

The Meramec rises in the Missouri Ozarks. It has done so for 600 million years, since the formation of the Ozark Dome. From the dome, the river heads northeast toward the city of St. Louis in a looping, undulating meander through a lush oak-hickory forest alternating with pasture and row-crop farmland. Here and there as it approaches the city, it slides in long curves beneath towering rock-faced bluffs. The Meramec's meander is *entrenched,* as the geologists say, which means the channel is

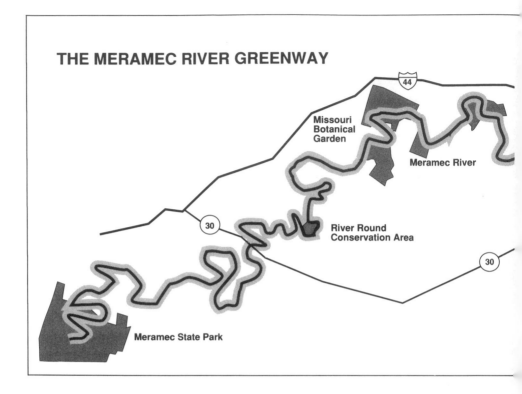

now relatively permanent, having worn down through uplifted sedimentary rock. But entrenchment seems less permanent in times of flood, when the otherwise shallow river retakes its ancient floodplain with a vengeance.

Because of the floods and the varied topography and because the river provides insufficient depth for barges to carry the products of rural fields and forests to market at St. Louis, the Meramec was never fully developed as a river of commerce, unlike the wide Missouri and the even wider Mississippi. Nevertheless, a Meramec Valley railroad line opened in 1853 and encouraged some industry at various places along the lower reaches. Valley Park, for example, thirty miles upstream, once had a glassworks, a stove factory, and a granary. The town boomed, and by the turn of the century it boasted two thousand enterprising souls. Then in 1915, the Meramec flooded thirty-five feet above its banks. End of boom, al-

58

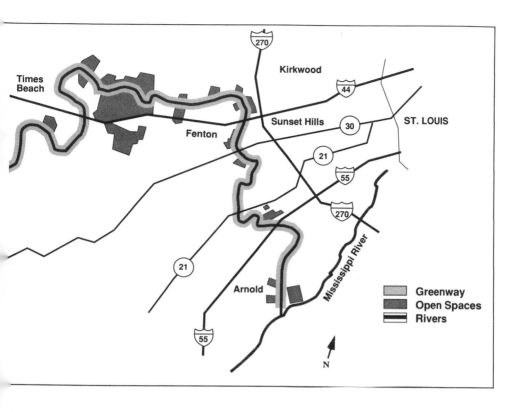

though not of Valley Park, now a St. Louis suburb just beyond Webster Groves and Kirkwood.

What the railroad encouraged even more than industry in those early days was the use of the river as a summertime retreat from the discomforts of the noisome city. Resort communities began to be built on the Meramec as early as 1872, but the greatest amount of development took place between the turn of the century and the late 1920s, when boating clubs, summer cottages, and resort hotels dotted the river bluffs and floodplains (with structures on stilts) for a hundred miles upstream. It was fun, it was grand, it was the bees' knees to take the train from St. Louis up the lazy river, just an hour or two away, and dance the Charleston on balmy nights in the great open-air river pavilions and bathe and paddle and fish the cool waters during the heat of the day.

Some of the resorts have remained, of course, but the Depression of the 1930s and the war of the 1940s began a period of great decline along the Meramec. The clubs were not rebuilt after the floods; the cottage communities became seedy and unkempt. After the war, as prosperity slowly replaced the long years of hard times that had come with the crash of 1929, an affluence even greater than that of the mid-1920s had arrived. But the Meramec was not to benefit from it. Instead of taking a train up the river, you went to see the U.S.A. in your Chevrolet. For the Meramec, this was an era of effluence, not affluence. Pollution, trash and litter, and the destruction of areas of natural and historic interest characterized it in the postwar era. The river community of Times Beach, with its deadly deposits of cancerous dioxin, bespoke the Meramec, not the palmy days of pavilions and play. The old river was forgotton by all but a few—those who kept the faith and who could see beyond the gravel pits, the river-edge dumps of old tires and refrigerators, and the cans and bottles of a throwaway America.

By 1967 the river's champions feared that the river itself, or at least the stretch within metropolitan St. Louis, was going to be thrown away in the great urban expansion of those years. They proposed to save the Meramec by turning the lower river into a national recreation area, to be owned and operated by the National Park Service along the lines of the Cuyahoga Valley NRA between Cleveland and Akron in Ohio. A study was made which was, in fact, the first comprehensive inventory of the Meramec's natural and cultural resources ever undertaken. The governor of Missouri commended the NRA idea to the Department of the Interior. The Missouri congressional delegation was united in its support. But when an official assessment was made by the National Park Service, the Meramec was judged to be below standard. Not to put too fine a point on it, the river seemed "too far gone" for inclusion in the pantheon of national parks. But if this news was a blow to the faithful and their supporters, it was a yawn for everyone else in the St. Louis metropolitan area. They had forgotten or were too young to know about the treasure they had in their own backyard as they sped out of town on the interstate, bound for Yellowstone or Vegas.

One of the early river-preservation advocates during the 1960s was a St. Louis public relations man and writer named Al Foster, who specialized in outdoor recreation. Foster, then in his thirties, spent as much time as he could on the river, fishing, canoeing, and studying its natural and cultural history. He still does. He loved the river, of course, but he had a valued skill as well: as a publicist, he knew how to "get some ink" for the plight of the Meramec. It was natural that other river lovers would turn to Foster for advice. If the media could be enlisted in the battle, they figured, then maybe some other way could be found—after the NRA debacle—to return the Meramec to its former glory.

So Al Foster thought the problem through. The river was not really destroyed—at least not yet. It just looked like hell. The answer, obviously, was not to induce the federal government to take over the Meramec but for St. Louisans to save it themselves and thereby acquire a personal—and permanent—stake in its protection. Thus did Operation Cleanstream spring from Foster's publicity man's brow. Under the aegis of the St. Louis Open Space Council, Operation Cleanstream recruited volunteers to "get their hands dirty," as Foster now puts it, to rid the river of the old stoves and refrigerators and tires and cans and bottles that had accumulated over the years of neglect. Politicians and business leaders lent their support and gave their weekend hours to the project. So successful was it (and still is, in fact: between four hundred and six hundred people turn up every year for their assignments) that the Izaak Walton League adapted the idea for a national program now called Save Our Streams.

The pride was back. It came slowly at first but picked up momentum as the citizens picked up the trash. At length, in 1975, something called the *Meramec Concept* was developed which called for an intergovernmental, public-private cooperative effort to save the landscape along the river's bluffs and bends and floodplain flats. This concept led the governor to declare as the Meramec River Recreation Area the lower 108 miles of the river, running through three counties and eight towns. A government-sanctioned coordinating committee was formed which later became the Meramec River Recreation Association (MRRA), now a private, non-profit body consisting of representatives of local governments as well as conservation organizations. The current part-time executive director, Susan Sedgwick, doubles as a planning official for St. Louis County.

The result? Over the past twenty years, there has been a steady accumulation of greenspace along the lower riverway, protecting on one side or the other, and sometimes both, nearly one-quarter of the 108 river miles in the project area. This achievement has come about through a multiplicity of efforts on the part of governments, developers, and nonprofit groups along the river. The citizens of St. Louis County passed two bond issues, one in 1977 and another in 1988, providing a total of $3 million for land acquisition (with emphasis recently on land that would link preexisting parks and open spaces) and recreational development. Municipalities have purchased land on their own as well, creating riverfront parks locally and with remarkable success have encouraged residential builders to dedicate strips of land at least three hundred feet back from the water's edge in the course of developing their sites. Additionally, private donations of land and money to purchase land are encouraged by the St. Louis Open Space Foundation. Recently, MRRA's Sedgwick has been working with, ironically, the National Park Service to prepare a booklet, slide show, and videotape presentation directed to individual landowners in the Meramec Valley to encourage private stewardship of river resources.

Perhaps the most effective technique developed by the MRRA is to use the provisions of the federal flood insurance program, administered by FEMA (Federal Emergency Management Administration) to convert flood-damaged properties into permanent open space. FEMA has a small budget to help municipalities acquire flood-damaged properties, paying the difference between the pre-flood appraised value and the insurance adjustment on severely damaged properties. Under the law, the federal government will not provide flood insurance to communities that permit structures damaged to the extent of 50 percent or more to be rebuilt, except by elevating them above the one hundred-year floodplain—for the obvious reason that otherwise the government would be paying damages over and over again. On the Meramec, a serious flood can be expected every six years.

After a disastrous flood in 1982, which had a devastating effect on the lower part of the river as it passes through St. Louis County, Sedgwick and her colleagues on the MRRA had an idea. Instead of the typical town-by-town competition for FEMA buyout funding, the MRRA persuaded the eight municipalities and three counties involved to work together in an appeal to the FEMA authorities in Washington to provide the wherewithal for a comprehensive floodplain acquisition program. The figure was $2 million, and they got it. Since then, more than 150 structures have been removed from the riverside, with the land transferred to local authorities and dedicated as permanent open space.

The river is getting beautiful again, thanks to Operation Cleanstream and the MRRA land-saving work. Since 1975 they have presided over the preservation of seven thousand acres of riverbank and encouraged private owners and governments to create greenway linkages that will connect large regional open-space resources such as state and county parks and lands owned by Washington University and the Missouri Botanical Gardens. Now it is called the Meramec Greenway. Every year, to raise money, the big event is the Great Meramec River Raft Float, with the most fanciful barge winning first prize.

And so the happy days along the river are coming back to the Meramec. Why, if you squint your eyes just so, you can almost make out a fellow in a bright straw boater over there by the far bank, paddling a canoe with his girl, a pink parasol hiding her face as she trails her fingers in the water. And then, in the soft evenings, if you listen hard, you might just hear a ukelele strumming, as if from an old pavilion. "Ja-da, ja-da, ja-da ja-da jing jing jing." By golly, it's the bees' knees all over again.

A TOUGH ASSIGNMENT FOR THE AMERICAN RHINE

The Hudson River Valley Greenway, New York City to Albany–Troy, New York

The majestic Hudson. It is that and more: chock-a-block with history, from Henry Hudson's voyage in the *Half Moon* onward through the commercial development of a waterway that would link the Great Lakes with the greatest port on the Eastern Seaboard, New York Harbor. The riches from trade built mansions—even Rhineish castles—on the river's bluffs.

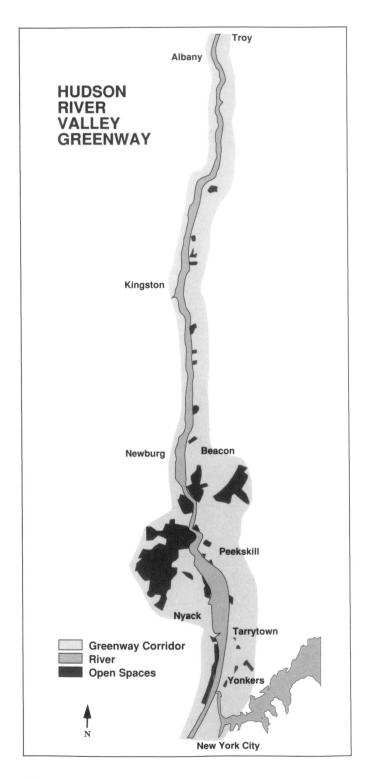

HUDSON
RIVER
VALLEY
GREENWAY

Troy

Albany

Kingston

Newburg   Beacon

Peekskill

Nyack

Tarrytown

Yonkers

Greenway Corridor
River
Open Spaces

N

New York City

The cloves and glens and streams and sweeps of landscape inspired a generation of painters—the Hudson River School. Its brackish waters created major commercial fisheries: striped bass, sturgeon, shad.

In modern times, the Hudson has been the focus of some of the most remarkable conservation achievements in our history: the preservation of the riverside from 72nd Street in Manhattan upriver to the northern tip of the island. Across the river, conservationists preserved the dramatic Palisades, and further along they established the magnificent state parks of the Hudson Highlands. Another success, astonishing even to those who worked to bring it about, is the de-pollution of the Hudson's waters. Fish populations are up sharply (although there are lingering PCB problems affecting some of the game and commercial fisheries), and the water is more swimmable and drinkable than at any time in the postwar period. Most fittingly of all, it was the Hudson River Valley that provided the venue for what is surely the most instructive and ennobling environmental battle ever waged to save a bit of scenery—the fight, ultimately victorious, for Storm King Mountain.

Although the recent greenway concept for the Hudson River owes something to all these past efforts, it is perhaps Storm King, forty miles north of New York City, that provided the necessary political and organizational context for the greenway idea to take hold and flourish. For those who may have only a dim memory of this event, in 1962 the Consolidated Edison Company announced (quietly, in a small-circulation rural newspaper, to meet the barest minimum the law allowed in the matter of informing the public of its plans) that they intended to build a cement lake near the top of the mountain as reservoir for a "pumped storage" electric generating plant to produce wattage for periods of peak demand. First, three units of electricity would be used during off-peak hours to pump the water uphill from the river, incidentally sucking in, and killing, untold numbers of striped bass fingerlings in a river judged one of the most productive nurseries for this commercially fished species on the East Coast. Then, at peak periods of electricity demand, the water would be released through penstocks to generate two units of electricity during hot afternoons when office air conditioners might cause a brownout on Wall Street or Madison Avenue. For lovers of the history and scenery of the Hudson River, the project was anathema. For the fishermen, it was an outrage. A protest was mounted and then a protracted lawsuit that, many years and many millions of dollars later, the environmentalists finally won. Storm King was one of the first great struggles among many that would ensue from coast to coast in the years of the environmental awakening, and it provided the legal inspiration for the National Environmental Policy Act, the epochal 1969 federal statute that requires government agencies or corporations operating under government contracts or procedures to prepare an EIS—environmental impact statement— concerning any major construction project such as Storm King. Along the Hudson, environmentalists vowed they would never allow anyone to go back to sleep again with regard to their beloved river.

The organization formed to fight for Storm King, the Scenic Hudson Preservation Conference, survives to this day (after a merger and a name change to Scenic Hudson, Inc.). Appropriately, this was the non-profit group that played a key role in enunciating a greenway concept for the river—proposed in 1985 as a heritage corridor—as an outgrowth of its successful efforts in the Hudson Highlands. Under the leadership of Klara Sauer, a German-born planner with a steely determination to save "the American Rhine," Scenic Hudson organized a powerful coalition of 150 local, regional, and national organizations to support the greenway idea and to demand that the government of New York State take action.

Meanwhile, another cadre of Hudson River conservationists, under the leadership of philanthropist Laurance S. Rockefeller and Henry Diamond, a Washington lawyer and former commissioner of New York's Department of Environmental Conservation, had for some years, beginning in the late 1970s, been wondering how to frame a comprehensive concept for the protection of the riverway. At length, in the mid-1980s, it was Diamond who put the word *greenway* to a corridor conservation concept that had been hovering just beneath the surface. Working with Rockefeller and some of the Rockefeller family's conservation-oriented associates and colleagues, Diamond conducted a policy study of the prospects for a greenway approach and then published a booklet, written with the help of environmental freelancer Douglass Lea, to give substance to the greenway idea for the Hudson. The booklet, *Greenways in the Hudson*

River Valley: A New Strategy for Preserving an American Treasure (1988; see citation under "Published Reports" in the List of Principal Sources), was distributed to anyone and everyone with an interest in saving the valley. Most particularly, the booklet and the highly publicized research and analysis that preceded it put pressure on the governor of the state and the legislature to take quite specific action to adopt the greenway concept and to create a greenway council to carry it out.

The combination of a coalition of conservation organizations concerned with the fate of the Hudson River Valley and the Diamond-Rockefeller publication that put the idea into quite concrete terms did the job. Even before the booklet was published, the idea of establishing a greenway in the Hudson Valley was announced as a state policy objective by Governor Mario Cuomo. "I recommend," said the governor in his state of the state message to the legislature, in January, 1988, "that we create a Hudson River greenway, a chain of parks, open space, and trails from New York City to the foothills of the Adirondacks. . . . This cooperative public private undertaking will link the extraordinary environmental, cultural, and historical heritage of the Hudson River Valley—in the process, fostering a sense of regional identity while protecting a greenway of national and international significance." Later that year, the legislature followed up by appointing the Hudson River Valley Greenway Council to develop a draft action plan for the greenway by the spring of 1990. Named to lead the project as executive director was a Troy, New York, environmental lawyer named David S. Sampson, Hudson River born and bred and a participant in the work of both Scenic Hudson and Diamond's publication project.

Sampson has an enviable list of credentials as an environmentalist as well as solid connections with the Hudson River business community, but he is now facing the job of his life. Indeed, this project is as severe a test for the greenway idea as any in the country. As Henry Diamond and Douglass Lea put it in their booklet, the Hudson River Greenway project must, at once, be "plastic enough" to encompass a diversity of economic and environmental expectations, "and yet firm enough to provide a solid foundation for practical maps and plans and actions."

One difficulty that Sampson's new Greenway Council must face in producing practical maps and plans and actions is the sheer size of the project area—150 miles from Manhattan to Albany-Troy, with a corridor totaling one thousand square miles. There are thirteen counties here— ranging from urban Bronx to bucolic Greene—and untold numbers of municipal governments, civic groups, and business interests and associations. Another daunting problem is the pricey-ness of the land, a key factor. Although the river corridor is blessed with impressive public or quasi-public open space holdings along virtually all its length, these lands are discontinuous. Acquiring connecting linkages, in fee or easement, is obviously top priority but in the end may prove more daunting financially than political leaders have bargained for. Land within the New York City metropolitan area simply cannot be touched pricewise. But even in the rural mid-Hudson region, far from New York or any smaller city, waterfront prices have shot skyward in recent years. One crucial point of land extending into the riverway, a 102-acre parcel called Sloop Hill, long hankered after by park and open-space advocates, was appraised at $75,000 in 1974. In 1979 state park and recreation officials recommended that it should be acquired, but the legislature put off the purchase because of a serious budget crisis at the time. Finally, the owners sold the land in 1987 to a developer for $9.2 million. Then, after dithering yet another year, the state government took action in 1988. The price they paid for Sloop Hill was $13.3 million, an increase approaching 2,000 percent. And prices may be expected to rise even further in the future; the Hudson River Valley is now the fastest growing area in New York state.

There is a terrible double-bind implicit here. On the one hand, the corridor is too big and too politically diffuse to permit a coordinated regulatory approach to the protection of land resources in a way specific enough to create an actual greenway. Few local governments are willing to surrender their planning and zoning powers to a state commission that would bar development within, for example, the sight lines of the waterway. At the same time the direct purchase of land to create linkages among existing parks and open spaces along the waterfront is in many areas an economic impossibility, even if the land were available. In fact, much of it is not, since the direct waterfront along almost all of the east side of the river and some of the west is taken up by railroad rights-of-way, still in use.

Stalemate? Maybe not. It is true that many greenway proponents see the railroad as the ultimate barrier to a fully realized greenway—at least one in which continuous shoreline public access is a main feature. Some, however, believe that railroad land along the banks may be a blessing in disguise. Historically, it has been the railroad right-of-way that has kept much of the Hudson's shores on both sides free of residential development, which has in turn preserved some the visual charm of the river corridor, at least from a bit of a distance. It is the contention of Tony Hiss, a *New Yorker* magazine staff writer and consultant to Sampson's planning commission, that some of the right-of-way can be devoted to pedestrian use, sharing it, in effect, with the railroad. Hiss, well known for his nostalgic railroad pieces in the *New Yorker*'s "Talk of the Town," perhaps sees less conflict between uses than some, but the fact remains that over the long term, the old rights-of-way, especially where they are relatively wide and underused by trains, can perhaps produce a more or less continuous greenway corridor after all.

Meanwhile, Sampson and his staff are holding hearings in which they listen and citizens speak about the potentials for the greenway. They have held scores of hearings, in fact, which are invariably filled with enthusiastic people who sense that here, at last, may be a way to protect this beautiful, historic riverway. Sometimes, to be sure, Sampson feels his assignment is like a hobo's breakfast: If we had some ham we could have ham and eggs, if we had some eggs. There are a good many experts around the country who seriously doubt that the Hudson River Valley Greenway, the most ambitious river-based greenway effort in the nation, can ever be more than a paper project—a greenway by declaration as opposed to an organized effort that brings about a palpable change in land use throughout the river corridor by physically weaving the parks and historic areas together.

Then again, there was not a soul to be found who gave the riversavers during the Scenic Hudson-Storm King days even an outside chance to fight off the despoilers of the valley a generation ago. A pessimistic prediction as to the outcome of the greenway project would probably be a mistake. As Klara Sauer puts it, "I have faith that once the Hudson River Greenway becomes a tangible, identifiable element in people's consciousness, the rest will happen, almost inevitably. Until then, we just plow forward, one step at a time."

SAVING THE COAST THAT USED TO BE

The Big Sur Viewshed, San Luis Obispo to Monterey, California

Nothing is going to be left to chance in protecting the scenery along the most dramatic coastal road in America: California Route 1. Built in the 1930s, it runs from San Diego to well north of San Francisco. In the southern part of the state, the highway intertwines with U.S. Route 101, unlovely in this area. But finally, the highways diverge. While the federal road hightails it northward with its divided lanes and cloverleafs up the Salinas Valley, Route 1, born a two-laner and wanting to stay that way, chooses the sundown sea, winding through the breathtaking coastal cliff-faces from Morro Bay seventy miles north to Monterey. The White Knuckle Memorial Highway, some call it, especially along the northernmost part, where deep canyons cleave the steep mountains and dramatic concrete bridges link the headlands. Hundreds of feet below them, mountain streams lined with towering redwoods tumble into the sea, creating tiny beaches, often with small rock islands—called *sea stacks*—standing sentinel a few dozen yards offshore where seals alternately sun themselves and lift their sleek heads to bark for a mate. It is this section of Route 1—the Big Sur—that is the most beautiful of all. It is this section that has had conservationists in a flat panic for the past twenty-five years.

In the 1960s, afraid that commercial strip development, oozing southward out of Fort Ord and touristy Monterey and Carmel, might spoil the scenic route, Monterey County designated the highway and its surrounding landscape a conservation district, the width of the corridor depending on the terrain. This was, in fact, the second forward-thinking action the county had taken on behalf of Route 1. It had already enacted a tough law prohibiting billboards many years before—in 1941.

Despite the county's good intentions, however, many feared that a

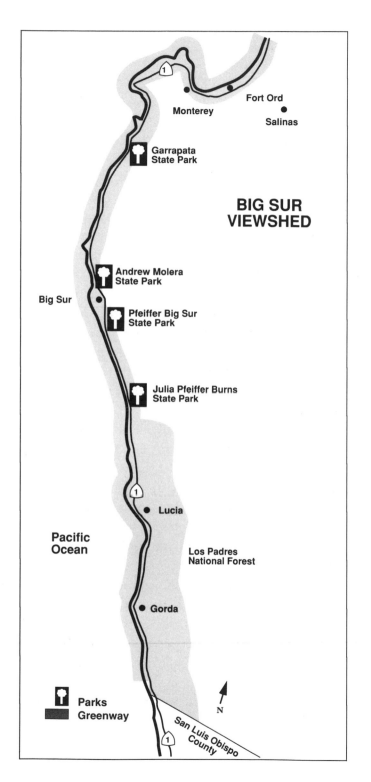

BIG SUR
VIEWSHED

Monterey

Fort Ord

Salinas

Garrapata
State Park

Andrew Molera
State Park

Big Sur

Pfeiffer Big Sur
State Park

Julia Pfeiffer Burns
State Park

Pacific
Ocean

Lucia

Los Padres
National Forest

Gorda

Parks

Greenway

N

San Luis Obispo
County

purely regulatory approach might be too weak. Accordingly, a number of philanthropic landowners banded together for the purpose of conveying scenic easements to the county government, perpetual deeded rights that would forever prohibit development on their lands, although the owners would retain title and rights of use. There were tax advantages for the donors, of course. Since real value had been stripped away from the property, an income tax deduction was possible, as were reductions in property taxes, which were levied on an ad valorum basis. The loss of a bit of property tax was no problem for the county, however. The trouble was that the county government believed it might not have the power, under state law, to accept anything less than full fee title to donated land. To remedy the matter, a local state legislator, Fred Farr, introduced enabling legislation in Sacramento, which not only permitted the conveyancing of easements but actively encouraged them. It was one of the first state laws in the country to do so. Later, when the California Highway Department started thinking about widening Route 1, Farr established a scenic-roads study that resulted in Route 1 being declared the first scenic highway in California.

Yet the battle for the coast had hardly begun. During the 1960s and into the 1970s, coastal development in the Golden State went on a rampage, threatening to wall off the Pacific shore completely with condos and roadside commerce. In 1972, a citizen-led ballot initiative called Proposition 20, officially known as the California Coastal Act, was enacted, which severely limited development all along the state's coastal zone. The conservationists of the Big Sur were among the leaders of the Proposition 20 initiative.

After passage, while the cumbersome processes of the Coastal Act were being put in place, Monterey County's government on its own did its best to reduce development by encouraging the cluster development of housing to limit the overall impact of residential subdivision along the Route 1 corridor and by inaugurating the transfer of development rights, wherein any residual right to develop a scenic property could be detached from it and subsequently attached to another, less visible parcel, in the form of a zoning permission to increase building density. But these were local remedies, however progressive and imaginative. What was needed, many Big Surians felt, was some sort of federal protection which could be relied upon, as perhaps local and even state government could not, in the matter of keeping the area scenically intact. Accordingly, in 1978, the Big Sur Foundation was formed by local conservation activists to advance land-saving policies for the scenic area. They immediately began working with the U.S. Congress to see if some sort of hybrid national park designation could be worked out which would retain existing landownership but greatly reduce further development.

Various concepts along these lines were advanced but were so unpopular locally—even the foundation was less than sanguine about some of them—that the effort finally petered out, failing to win the support of the congressional delegation, most particularly Representative Leon Panetta, who was highly regarded both at home and in Washington. Still, the federal government's concern, although legislatively unfulfilled, had its uses in stimulating state and local interest in a comprehensive means to protect the Big Sur coast.

The renewed interest was especially helpful in advancing the work of the Big Sur Land Trust. The trust, also founded in 1978, was meant to be a low-profile organization that would not engage in controversial policy remedies to protect scenic resources. Instead, it would work closely, and quietly, with landowners, encouraging them to donate land or scenic easements or, failing that, to offer land at a bargain sale price and allow the trust the time needed to mount a public subscription campaign to raise money for its purchase. Although the regulatory potential of the state's Coastal Act promised much in terms of protecting the aesthetic integrity of the Big Sur, it was still only a promise. So the trust went diligently about its business. Within ten years it had permanently protected some seven thousand acres of scenic open space, nearly 10 percent of all privately owned scenic land on the Big Sur coast.

As it turned out, it was not until 1986 that the local planning required by the Coastal Act was completed and officially adopted. As might be expected, it was, according to Monterey County Supervisor Karin Strasser-Kauffman, "among the most stringent in the nation" with regard to controlling development. The plan would permit building only in those areas out of sight of the Big Sur "viewshed," which is to say suitable spots not visible from Highway 1.

The coastal plan's viewshed concept is strong and would appear to be simple to enforce. Yet inevitable questions are raised. Can land that is part in and part out of the viewshed be developed? What if a parcel is in view only from a very small stretch of the road or is a very long distance away from the road? What about adding additional structures on already developed land in the viewshed? According to Brian Steen, executive director of the Big Sur Land Trust, the county government as well as the Coastal Commission managed to postpone dealing with such questions by simply not mapping the viewshed. Designating which properties were within the protected viewshed area, they felt, might lead to dozens of lawsuits brought by landowners wishing to escape the regulations altogether.

Sensing trouble ahead in the county's effort to carry out the land-use plan, Steen and his board of directors applied to the Packard Foundation for a research grant to help them determine exactly which parcels of land, owner by owner, actually *were* in the viewshed of the Big Sur. A consultant was retained to survey all properties. The survey would not only identify how much land was involved but would also give the trust an idea of priorities, ownership by ownership, for the acquisition of land or scenic easements. After eliminating all parcels with a thirty-degree or greater slope, which could not be built on under any circumstances, what remained were 110 properties that were both buildable and within view of the highway.

During this period, the land trust and the Big Sur residents, with the help of Leon Panetta, had raised a war chest of $62,500 to promote a *new* California ballot proposition, Proposition 70, which, like Proposition 20 fifteen years before, could have a great deal to do with the future of the Big Sur. In the state of California, if the legislature does not take up an issue to the satisfaction of the voters, the citizens have a right to place a proposition on a ballot—so long as they can collect 600,000 signatures on a petition for it. In the case of Proposition 70, that part of the work went fairly smoothly as a statewide grass roots effort. Passing the measure would be another matter.

In many ways, Proposition 70 was as bold a conservation measure as Proposition 20 had been. Entitled the California Wildlife, Coastal, and Parks Initiative, it called for a $776 million bond issue for the purchase of wildlife habitat, scenic lands, and open space throughout California. Usually, voters can easily be touted off any proposition involving new revenues. In fact, there was only one precedent for a bond issue proposition, and that was in 1914. Nevertheless, in a June, 1988, vote, Californians passed the initiative with a comfortable 66 percent majority. The payoff for the Big Sur is an earmarked $25 million that will be used to acquire scenic easements in the viewshed. It is no accident, of course, that the land trust is ready to swing into action—the research completed, the priorities set.

It would now appear that the work of a quarter-century to protect this nationally significant scenic greenway is nearly complete. For some, the combination of regulation through the Proposition 20 Coastal Act joined with the easement acquisition made possible by the Proposition 70 bond act might seem failure-proof. What the regulations do not cover, positive control through easement acquisition will. And vice versa. But it is hard to find anyone along the Big Sur coast talking that way. Land trust executive Brian Streen worries, "I just don't know how we're going to do it," he says. "We don't know if the money will go far enough, and we have so little time."

Is that Eeyore—the congenitally pessimistic old gray donkey in the Winnie-the-Pooh stories—talking, or is it the wisdom of a seasoned land-saver? Probably both. If anyone needs a reminder about what happens without eternal vigilance, they have but to travel a few hundred miles to the south, where that same Highway 1 is lined with condos, fast-food joints, office buildings, and shopping malls, disappearing into the taupe-colored distances of the Los Angeles basin. There is an ocean behind that mess somewhere, although it's hard to spot. Future generations will be thankful that the preservers of the Big Sur coast never rested on their laurels. They didn't in 1941 when the billboards were banned or in

1964 when the road was made a scenic highway or even in 1972 when the Coastal Act was passed. And so, in the future, if you want to know how the magnificent California coast used to be, try the Big Sur.

CLOSING THE CIRCLE

The 40-Mile Loop, Portland, Oregon

The year is 1903, and Frederick Law Olmsted, the great designer of New York's Central Park and much else that is green and good in America, has just passed away. He was eighty-one. But his nephew and (later) adopted stepson John, now the head of the Olmsted firm, travels to Portland, Oregon, to help the city beautify itself for the Lewis and Clark Centennial Exposition that will be held the following year. Later, he is joined by his young stepbrother, Frederick Law Olmsted, Jr., to devise a park plan. In it, they make a bold proposal to the Portlanders: Instead of parks here and there, how about a forty-mile-long system of interlinking parks all around the city, as FLO himself (as Olmsted signed himself and as his admirers were inclined to refer to him) often proposed to his municipal clients?

As the two landscape architects ink in the garland of parks on a map of the city, Rick raises his head from his work. "What shall we call this notion?" he asks his older brother.

"I dunno," John answers. "What *would* you call a forty-mile loop?"

"I can't think of anything," says Rick. "It's just a forty-mile loop." In fact, there is a tradition in the Olmsted firm, started by the old man himself, not to use fancy names. That was for the boosters, not the designers.

So there is a lull in the discussion. The brothers are probably thinking about their father's dictum. "Well," says John, wishing to turn to other matters. "Are we done?"

"Done and done," says Rick.

And that is the "Just So" story of how it came to pass that the Olmsteds' idea was given its name, the 40-Mile Loop—a name that it keeps to this very day as a modern greenway project. But there is a difference. The 40-Mile Loop greenway is no longer forty miles, but *one hun-*

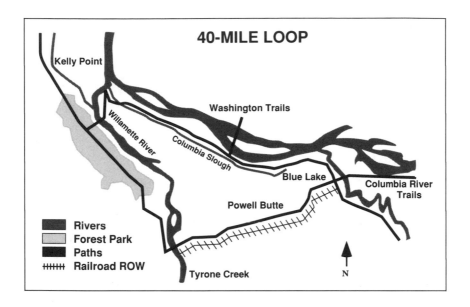

dred and forty miles, and is one of the most creative and resourceful greenway projects in the country, as befits its origins. "A connected system of parks and parkways," the brothers presciently wrote in their 1903 report, "is manifestly far more complete and useful than a series of isolated parks." Today that vision is about to be fulfilled but only after some very shaky and protracted beginnings.

Indeed, however compelling the Olmsteds' idea might have been in 1903, Portlanders were unable to act on the plan in any coherent way for three-quarters of a century, despite many attempts. A $1 million bond issue to create a key portion of the loop along a wooded ridge to the west which overlooks the city was passed by the voters in 1907, but the money went for developing old parks rather than for buying new land. Then, in 1912, a noted planner from Chicago named Edward H. Bennett was brought in. He recommended, again, that the ridge—hopefully called Forest Park by its proponents—be acquired. A $2 million bond issue was proposed this time, but it failed to achieve a majority of votes. Then, a bit of sheer luck came about. Much of Forest Park's land had been sold off for lots, but extremely high costs for road-building (due in substantial part to a fortuitous landslide) caused many of the land titles to revert to the city for nonpayment of road assessments. Meanwhile, in adjacent Multnomah county, additional forest land had been forfeited for taxes as well. There was no park yet, but at least a good bit of land was in public ownership. Then in 1943, famed New York City park-maker Robert Moses was called in. He also recommended that a forest park be established. But there was a war on. Finally, in 1948, the park came into being, made up of tax-delinquent land, gifts, and some purchases. At last the first leg of the 40-Mile Loop had been created.

Not wishing to violate the tortoise-like tradition of implementing the Olmsteds' plan, once the Forest Park dedication had taken place, city officials and civic leaders allowed several more decades to pass without thinking very much about the brothers' old-fashioned forty-mile loop. Other things were on their minds. The post–World War II boom brought stupendous growth to Portland, changing it from a compact little city to a sprawling metropolitan region. By the 1970s, the ability of a forty-mile loop to encircle the city was, to put it mildly, laughable. And yet, once again, in 1978, good fortune struck. At the request of the Oregon delegation, the U.S. Congress passed a bill declaring that the Columbia Slough—a key parcel in the Olmsted scheme—was no longer a navigable waterway, meaning that dredging could cease, and the land could be devoted in substantial part to open space and recreational use. Another segment of the loop was in place.

It was at that time, too, that Al Edelman, architect and state director for the Nature Conservancy, began to realize that federal money for the purchase of parks and natural areas was getting scarce. Some other means would have to be found to conserve and enhance the natural assets of the Portland region. What to do? Well, instead of trying to buy additional large parcels of land for which there was no money, how about dusting off the old forty-mile loop idea and building an open-space program around the parks that had already been established? So Edelman and his colleagues studied the old plans in the light of the new realities. What was needed, they found, was not 40 but 140 miles to create a loop around the urban area as it had grown to be. Yet the concept could remain the same: a string of parks linked by pedestrian and bicycle ways.

Everyone thought this new approach—the new 140-mile 40-Mile

Loop (only a literalist would insist that its name be changed)—was wonderful. The state parks people thought it was wonderful. So did Portland city officials, suburban governments, federal agencies, civic groups, conservationists. At last, seventy-five years later, Portlanders struck themselves collectively on the forehead, saying, "What a great idea! Why didn't we think of that before?" Today, as a citizen movement, the project appears to be on its way toward closing the circle that in the end will link thirty parks in the Portland metropolitan area.

As a means to maintain the focus in an increasingly fragmented governmental and civic arena, Edelman and his associates created a nonprofit body called the 40-Mile Loop Land Trust. This way, the scores of government agencies and departments at the federal, state, and municipal levels could be coordinated. The purpose of the land trust was not just to keep the pressure on, it was also to have a regional paragovernmental agency with the flexibility to raise funds, to acquire lands by donation (subsequently conveying them to the appropriate governmental body), and to provide planning standards and guidelines for constituent elements of the loop.

An early and crucial decision made by the land trust was to commission a new 40-Mile Loop Master Plan. This plan, Edelman says, provided the land trust with credibility as well as an ideal means to coordinate actions among thirteen key governmental entities whose decision-making powers could make or break the project. Accordingly, the land trust has become a "message carrier," as Edelman puts it, because government agencies "simply don't, or won't, talk to each other." They practice a kind of shuttle diplomacy borrowed from Henry Kissinger's techniques in the Middle East. So now when a satrapy such as the U.S. Army Corps of Engineers needs to work with, for example, the Multnomah County Planning Board sultanate, Edelman's group can get the players together. This is done on an ad hoc basis as well as formally in quarterly show-and-tell meetings on the state of the loop.

One recent challenge to the land trust's deal-making acumen involved converting a twelve-mile stretch of abandoned railroad right-of-way which can connect the loop along its southern edge, from the far suburbs to the heart of Portland. The railbed is owned jointly by the

Union Pacific and the Southern Pacific, who, as the Macy's and Gimbel's of railroading, are even harder to bring to the table than diverse public agencies. But the land trust managed to bring it off anyway. "It's a done deal," says Edelman.

All in all, since the reemergence of the forty-mile loop idea in the late 1970s, Edelman and his associates have presided over the establishment of over 70 miles of the 140-mile circuit, raising over $2 million in donations to the greenway, and leveraging ten, or fifty, times that much through their deal-making. Edelman hopes the loop will be completed by 1995. After ninety-two years of waiting, Rick and John will be pleased about the 40-Mile Loop, wherever they are. Even if they didn't know what to call it.

Big Sur Viewshed, Monterey County, California.

Greenways come in many sizes, have many uses, and are being created from one end of America to the other. In California, the magnificent Big Sur coast (previous page) is protected as a "viewshed" greenway along State Route 1. In Connecticut, rustic trails wind through the Redding Greenbelts, one of them leading to the locally famous "Great Ledge" (above). Landscape architect Bill Flournoy (right) is known as the "father of the Raleigh Greenways." The project, perhaps the earliest of the modern greenway systems in the country, began life as a master's degree thesis. Raleigh's goal is to create 200 miles of linked paths by the year 2000. The greenway is used for school outings (top right) as well as for simply strolling through the Carolina woods (lower right).

17

18

19

21

20

22

Volunteers work on a railroad trestle (above), a feature of Heritage Trail, an abandoned right-of-way that runs through Iowa's prairie landscape. Early opponents of the greenway burned nine such bridges; now the trail is host to thousands of hikers and bikers every year. At right, a user registry is provided at a country store along the route. Railroads are also an element in the long-range planning for the Hudson River Valley Greenway (although the rights-of-way are still in use, bottom left). Here, an ambitious greenway project may help to save the "American Rhine" (note castle, top left) from being overrun by development. Klara Sauer (top, near-left) organized over a hundred civic groups to support the project.

25

Al Foster, a St. Louis publicity man (shown, left, with planner Susan Sedgwick), saved his beloved Meramec River via "Operation Cleanstream," which led to the establishment of the 108-mile Meramec Greenway in Missouri. The project raises money at its annual "Great Raft Float" (below). Portland, Oregon's "40-Mile Loop," conceived in 1903 by the Olmsted brothers, John C. and Frederick , Jr., has become a 140-mile-long greenway taking in remote woodlands (top right) and urban parks (bottom right). In Tucson (overleaf), another multi-mile greenway is based on protecting the flood-prone desert washes that pattern the city.

29

Pima County River Parks, Tucson, Arizona.

4

Rivers through the City

*The great Mississippi, the majestic Mississippi,
rolling its mile-wide tide along, shining in
the sun; the dense forest away on the other
side; the "point" above the town, and the
"point" below, bounding the river-glimpse and
turning it into a sort of sea.*

—*MARK TWAIN,*
Life on the Mississippi

We are rediscovering the urban river. It doesn't really matter what part of the country it's in, or what kind of river it is, or even very much what kind of history it has had (although the worse, the better, as we shall see); we are rediscovering it with the round-eyed wonder and enthusiasm of a young Sam Clemens apprehending the Mississippi sliding past Hannibal. One result of the discovery—a quite tangible means we have to reclaim the rivers that run through our cities—is the urban river greenway. Such a greenway is, in the words of Denver's patriarch of the Platte River Greenway, Joe Shoemaker, a way of "returning the river to the people."

And the people seem to be delighted with the idea. In Tucson, for example, a greenway along the Rillito became the most intensively used park in the city within days of its opening. And that story has repeated itself across the country in old greenways and new. Shoemaker's own

Platte River Greenway has 150,000 users a year, to become the most heavily used recreational facility in Denver. In Sacramento, a costly lawsuit was successfully brought by the municipality and by conservation groups in behalf of the American River Parkway, a greenway project started in 1963, to keep the state water authorities from pumping out upstream water for agricultural purposes. The effect would have been to lower the flow of the river as it passes—most beautifully—through the city. State officials were stunned that anyone should care, but they did. Once an urban river *is* returned to the people, it tends to stay that way. In Casper, Wyoming, a city that was economically devastated by plummeting oil prices in the mid-1980s leading to a white-collar exodus totaling 30 percent of the population, the local greenway project—the Platte River Parkway—not only survived, but prevailed.

Permit me a small digression. When I went to visit the Casper project, a four-mile greenway through the heart of the city, I stayed at a nearby motel that was so large I mistook it for a complete shopping center when I drove up. Leaving the car at an elegant *porte-cochère,* I went into the lobby, which stretched away luxuriously for what seemed to be a hundred yards of inch-thick carpet and crystal chandeliers. Soft music played. Polished brass gleamed in the dim distances. There was such a genteel aura about the place that I figured I'd better cancel my reservation and head for the nearest Red Roof Inn or Motel 6 where they leave the light on for ya' (as the radio commercials have it) and don't mind too much what you might be tracking in on your boots. At the desk a very correct East Indian or perhaps Pakistani with a pure Oxbridge accent inquired after my wishes. I wished to know how much the room would cost. "That would be $28.50, sir," came the reply. There was a moment of open-mouthed silence as I reflected on the immediate and personal implications of the energy boom that had gone bust. In the boom days, that room went for $150, said the clerk, if you were lucky enough to have a reservation. If you didn't and a big international conference was on, maybe they would rent you a cot in one of the ballrooms for $40 a night.

What this story has to do with greenways is that the work on Platte River Parkway did not miss a beat throughout this dark period, regardless of the economic calamity. "All you could see," project executive

Kristi Akers told me while we toured the greenway, "was the back end of moving vans heading out of town." Nevertheless, funding for the project kept on coming. Under a local ordinance, a city sales tax (1 percent) is imposed for the express purpose of funding civic improvement projects, and a priority list is voted on every year. Many greenway officials (work is conducted by a private land trust that receives public money as well as donations and foundation grants) feared that after the glut and the disappearance of 20,000 people the project would just drop off the bottom of the funding list. Not at all. The parkway still made the cut and received a large donation from Amoco of money and land to boot, either in expiation or as a way of bucking up the community or both.

Casper's economic travails were poignantly illustrated when Kristi Akers conducted me to a segment of the greenway still under development. There we encountered a homeless man who had set up housekeeping under a bridge abutment at the water's edge. "I'm not going to tell anyone about that guy," said Akers, who got her job after everyone left town and a new board was formed. "He'll have to leave in wintertime anyway." In this part of Wyoming, civic leaders have developed a sense of tolerance about fellow humans caught in the meatgrinder of a global oil economy turned to sludge. It could have been you or me under that bridge. For my part, the homeless man's presence served to deepen my understanding of the astonishing degree of civic commitment greenway projects can engender, even in a devastated place like Casper. Although there were many pressing social needs in this city, the need for the people to have a sense of a bright civic future was thought to have a high priority. And the Platte River Parkway was, and is, elegantly emblematic of just that.

Rivers also have practical values, of course. Since human communities first began, rivers have conferred manifold blessings on those who settle along their banks: a source of water for households, crops, and livestock; a transportation route for people and products; a provider of food, from fish and shellfish to the game birds and animals drawn to a river's margins and shallows; and, yes, a river is the means by which a community can rid itself of its wastes almost effortlessly.

It is no wonder that great cities have arisen on rivers. It is also no wonder that cities have always had an uneasy relation to them. City-builders often forget that a river has its own logic that is not necessarily the logic of the urban economy. When a city crowds a river too closely and too intensively (the wont of city-builders for five thousand years), devastation and disease have followed from floods and the septic wastes the floodwaters carry. For most of urban history, such devastation and disease simply had to be tolerated somehow. In more recent times, however, the economic functions of rivers were replaced by railroads and highways and by alternative sources for water and food. Moreover, rivers could be dammed and channeled to reduce flooding so they could most efficiently carry out their sole remaining function: as a sewer.

Let us take for an example a medium-sized river that passes through a medium-sized city, far from Wyoming. The river is the French Broad, which rises on the flanks of the North Carolina Blue Ridge and runs northward through Pisgah National Forest, the first national forest in the country. The French Broad (so named in colonial times because it flowed toward lands under control of the French) then enters the great Vander-bilt estate, Biltmore, whose grounds were designed by Frederick Law Olmsted in his last major commission (1888–95). Directly upon leaving Biltmore, the river begins a five-mile journey through the city of Asheville, North Carolina, before passing on to join the Tennessee and then Mark Twain's Mississippi.

Long Man is what the Cherokees called the river, as Wilma Dykeman writes in a history of the French Broad—"whose head rested on the mountains, whose feet lay along the valleys, who was fed by the Chattering Children of all his tributary streams." The natural and cultural history of the upper French Broad is a rich one. But there is an urban history as well which is not so charming. For example, on September 15, 1951, the Asheville *Times* reported as follows: "Witnesses told [North Carolina Wildlife Resources Department] investigators that the small streams feeding into the French Broad were churned into a muddy froth last evening by fish fighting their way to clean water. Eighteen- and twenty-inch trout often failed to get over the miniature sandbars at the mouths of the streams and flopped back into the main river to die. . . . The big stream looked no different this morning than any other morning. It was its usual darkish color with flakes of foam floating aimlessly along on it. The only thing different was the number of fish flopping feebly on the surface." Later that year, a U.S. Fish and Wildlife Service scientist extracted a sample of the polluted French Broad River water for testing. He found that some of the fish he placed in the sample died in less than one minute.

Similar events followed on the French Broad over the next quarter-century. In that regard, this river was like many others in the United States. In 1967, for example, one million alewives were killed in the infamous Albany pools of the Hudson River. The pools were so loaded with sewage from Albany, Troy, and surrounding cities that the river in this area simply would not support life most seasons of the year. As reported by conservationist-journalist Robert Boyle, "The filth is incredible; during a state hearing on the problems of the pool, a press report had it that men 'gritted their teeth and women left the room.' " And who can forget the Cuyahoga River in Cleveland? It was so polluted with oil during the 1960s, according to author William Longgood in a contemporary account, "that it frequently catches fire and requires firebreaks and a fire patrol."

It is not surprising, during these environmental worst of times in cities, that the rivers were abandoned, spurned, disregarded. When the rivers had been sewers for a generation, or two, or three, the cities would turn away, leaving the river corridors to decaying buildings, solid-waste dumps, trash-filled industrial landscapes, and the ramshackle vacant-lot neighborhoods of those entrapped by poverty. While every place else in the metropolitan areas was on a new-development binge, the riversides lay forgotten.

For the greenway-maker, however, the spurning of a riverfront was sometimes the best thing that could have happened because when the rivers were cleaned up (courtesy of the federal Water Pollution Control Act Amendments of 1972, the so-called "Clean Water Act," along with state bond issues to improve water quality) there was something left to make a greenway *with*. Between Cleveland and Akron, there is now a unit of the national park system—the Cuyahoga National Recreation Area. The Hudson River greenway project (profiled in Chapter 3) proposes to weave together many urban waterfront open spaces along the entire length of the Hudson, including new urban cultural parks in Albany and Troy, near the infamous Albany pools. There, newly established riverside walks and promenades have been built and old buildings adapted to new purposes, including one huge Troy warehouse being used to recreate, in exacting detail, a full-sized replica of Henry Hudson's ship, the *Half Moon*.

The point is that greenways are possible on urban riverways because a goodly amount of passed-over, low-cost land and interesting buildings (for adaptive reuse) can be uncovered, if one looks hard enough, although the riverway as a whole may be almost invisible, even to strangers. When I learned about the French Broad project, I arranged for an interview with its leaders. I was given travel directions over the phone by Bob Kendrick, a Chamber of Commerce executive, who assumed I could easily find the chamber offices, where the meeting was to be held. I discovered, however, that Kendrick's street address could be on either the east or the west side of town. Naturally, I chose the wrong side, west, based on a now-exploded theory of the organization of cities having to do with prevailing winds. Back and forth along the interstate I went. Finally, I arrived and told Kendrick of my misadventure. "Well, anyway," he said, "at least you got to see the river."

"What river?" I replied.

It was, in a way, a kind of joke because until recently, *nobody* saw the river. Where the French Broad passes through the city it is sunken beneath the surrounding landscape in a canyonlike depression. The interstate passes fifty feet or more above it. You can stand on a high point in one part of town and look across to another high point and not see the river at all. So, as the city grew away from its sewer-river, everyone simply forgot about it. Kendrick said that even he was surprised at how green and lush, almost pristine, it was, hiding below the sight lines of Asheville. And that is why he and a small group of savvy Ashevillians smelled an economic opportunity while others remembered only the fragrance of sewage.

The idea for a greenway along the French Broad got its start when a Chamber of Commerce committee was asked to figure out how to get the tourists to spend one more night in Asheville. Visitors would come to the city to take in the house and gardens of Biltmore—western North Carolina's most-visited attraction—or to use the city as a base for touring the surrounding lakes and mountains of the Blue Ridge and Smoky Mountains. If, the Chamber of Commerce types reasoned, the tourists could find an in-town attraction, then maybe some one-more-night money might be made by local merchants. But the only attraction they had in town was the river. So they took a look. *Voila!* It wasn't bad at all. And then they did something brilliant: they invited all different kinds of civic groups in the city to take part on a planning committee. A key player turned out to be the French Broad River Foundation, which added a conservationist-oriented dimension that the earlier chamber-only group had lacked.

According to Kendrick, the project developed with "two conceptual threads running through it." One of them was "a strong environmental thrust. We are going to be drinking that river—it's our future water supply. Also, it's in a semi-pristine state in an urban area, and that has a benefit. But there is an additional benefit if there's a little bit of development activity—that's the other thread. So the attractions might include a symphony band shell, for example, or a river walk like the one in San Antonio."

The San Antonio River Walk seems to be everyone's favorite downtown riverside tourist development project. According to *Waterfront World,* a newsletter published by the Waterfront Center, Inc., a nonprofit consulting group concerned with such matters, the river walk was conceived in 1929 as a downtown festival marketplace along the San Antonio River, a place with "boats, shops, cafés, housing, greenery, lighting along the banks—an entertaining and romantic environment to delight residents and tourists alike." The initial development of the river walk took place during the 1930s, with redevelopment and vast improvement during the 1960s, after which it became a national model for waterfront planners.

Back in Asheville, everyone in town, when hearing about the greenway idea, had a different image of the river as it was to be. An eclectic approach, clearly influenced by San Antonio, was voiced early on by city councilman Walter Boland who enthused to an Asheville *Citizen Times* reporter, "We're looking at special lighting, signs, bike paths, jogging and hiking paths, indigenous trees, bushes, flowers . . . a promenade alternating on the west and east banks of the river linked by bridges across the water."

He went on: "An outdoor amphitheater could very well be considered for plays, musical performances, and so on in the summer. . . . Another idea is for a center for artists and musicians, perhaps modeled after the Campbell Folk School or the Penland School, with visiting artists and folk musicians making use of the existing buildings in the riverfront area. Another idea that strikes me as very interesting would be the creation of an Olympic training center for kayacking. . . . And there's also the possibility of a convention hotel on the riverfront." A fair amount of activity, one might say, for a river that is one hundred yards wide and runs for just five miles from one side of town to the other.

But was that degree of development that people wanted? Joining with the Chamber of Commerce in its work to get a greenway plan created was the conservation-minded French Broad River Foundation, heretofore concerned with the river as it passed through the countryside rather than the city. The foundation represented those interested in the fish and wildlife, in the way the huge willows arched out over the water, and in the patches of more or less natural open space remaining along the banks which could be converted into parks. As Jean Webb, president of the foundation, told me, "That's the appeal of the river to the historical and environmental organizations." So the foundation, along with the Junior League, set about to create Haywood Park, a small but highly emblematic beginning for the greenway. The land, which is only a few acres, was acquired from the railroad, cleaned up, and outfitted with a picnic area, a fishing pier, and a parking lot. As it turned out, that action, albeit a fairly modest one, was more expressive of the greenway's potential than any amount of planning theory or grand dreams of the future. "We found," said Webb, "that without a great deal of effort on our part, garden clubs and others will come forward with money and effort—because we were doing something instead of talking."

It fell to Karen Cragnolin to make something concrete come of the talking. Cragnolin, a lawyer, was appointed the executive director of the French Broad Riverfront Planning Committee, an unincorporated non-official consortium with loaned offices (from the Chamber of Commerce) and no mandate except the implicit one not to let the project fail because people could not agree on just what kind of greenway they wanted. Committee expenses and Cragnolin's part-time salary were to be paid out of grants that one or another consortium member would receive for the work.

The immediate job, as Cragnolin saw it, was to encourage even more talking, but in a directed way. The device she used to achieve this was to combine two pro bono professional-advice programs, the American Institute of Architect's Rural/Urban Design Assistance Team (R/UDAT) and a similar program of the American Society of Landscape Architects called the Community Assistance Team (CAT). The idea was to assemble a group of professionals drawn from various disciplines to work together over a four-day period and come up with a conceptual plan for the area in question. There would be no charge.

The R/UDAT-CAT team assembled to take on the French Broad included a professor of landscape architecture, a professor of urban design, a landscape architect specializing in greenways, a regional planner, an architect specializing in public facilities, an AIA official, a wildlife biologist, a general practice architect, and a general practice landscape architect. Team members were put through an arduous marathon of field visits and public hearings before they retired to do their planning. The plan had no ax to grind for none of the participants was from Asheville nor were they conducting current projects there. Instead, it represented the views of the citizens, the demands of the resource itself, and the best thinking of a talented group of people. A key feature of the plan, aside from the riverside greenway itself, was the use of greenway connectors that would link the riverfront with downtown areas and neighborhoods, plus a circular trailway around the whole of the city, something like the 40-Mile Loop in Portland, Oregon.

The combination of immediate action by Jean Webb and her colleagues counterpoised against the long-range R/UDAT-CAT planning orchestrated by Karen Cragnolin would appear to be effective in Asheville. The late New York regional planner Stanley Tankel once told me that "action drives out planning." And that is true. On the other hand, the reverse is true, too: planning drives out action, in the sense that while the community dithers, the opportunity for action may be lost. The trick is to plan and act at the same time—something instinctively understood by Kendrick, Webb, Cragnolin, and the others involved in creating a riverfront greenway for Asheville.

Clearly, making a greenway—especially along an urban riverfront—brings out everyone's most creative instincts, in Asheville and elsewhere, as the profiles in the World of Greenways chapters of this book tend to prove. In this regard, please allow yet another anecdotal digression. When I was preparing to visit the Yakima River Greenway in Washington State, I looked up the city in my AAA guidebook and found a motel that advertised itself as being "on the greenway." Obviously, it was impossible for me to stay anywhere else. When I got to my room, I drew open the ubiquitous floor-to-ceiling drapes that covered the ubiquitous motel sliding glass door. One might expect it to look out, ubiquitously, on other sliding glass doors. But not in this case. There, not fifty feet from a little patio outside the room, was a river—the Yakima River, flowing full and powerful out of the Cascades, cutting luminously through the basaltic ridges, fructifying this desert place. In the desert, even a modest-sized river like the Yakima is thrilling, especially up close.

The next day, I asked Dick Anderwald, planning director for Yakima County and current president of the Yakima Greenway Foundation, about the motel, telling him about the AAA write-up. Anderwald said that the plans brought to him for approval were for an ordinary, stock-design, low-priced motel with rooms facing the highway as they do practically everywhere else. "I told them about the greenway," he said, "and suggested that they turn the motel around and add the sliding doors, reorienting it to the river. It was not a difficult change; they agreed to it immediately and donated a permanent easement for a trailway. They are doing very well indeed." When I checked out of my room the next day, I said something to the lady at the desk about how nice the greenway was. "Oh yes, our greenway. Isn't it wonderful?" I agreed. Because it was.

Here is a final point. Beneath the details of the urban river greenway projects discussed in this chapter and profiled in the World of Greenways chapters there is, I believe, a message of major significance for any city or town lucky enough to have a river running through it. From Casper to Yakima to Asheville, greenways or greenway-like projects have been extraordinarily successful in restoring rivers to their former economic and cultural signficance. New jobs, new tax ratables, new recreational opportunities, the conservation of wildlife, and the maintenance and improvement of water quality are the tangible benefits of urban river greenway-making.

But there is another benefit that should not be forgotten. For a hundred years or more, urban rivers have been relegated to the ugliest of urban functions—sewage disposal, sites for heavy industry, a place to dump the refuse of the city. Inevitably, the river corridors became a kind of no-man's-land, dividing cities, economically and socially, rather than uniting them—the poor on one side, the rich on the other.

Today, many of the ugly functions have been replaced or have simply disappeared. Much of the heavy industry has relocated, and the dumps and sewer outfalls have (or can be) eliminated. When cities discover this, the impulse is strong to establish a greenway project along the riverfront. And then a kind of miracle happens. The river begins to join the people of the city together rather than separating them; what was once an open wound begins to heal itself and the city along with it. I cannot imagine a more persuasive justification than this for greenway action.

5

The Paths and Trails

When we walk, we naturally go to the fields
and woods: what would become of us, if we
walked only in a garden or a mall?

—*HENRY DAVID THOREAU*

T*here are some* who find a trailhead, or a path through the woods which curves invitingly out of sight, simply irresistible. Thoreau was such a person, and before him Wordsworth: And today it's me and probably you. It is a romantic idea, surely, a reaction to the organized spaces of an industrial age, with all its square corners and square lives and intentionality. Sometimes we need just to set out, afoot or a-bike, to go where a path takes us. This is, it seems to me, yet another aspect of the magic of greenways. Not all greenways have paths or trails, it is true; and not all paths or trails are greenways in the strict sense (which some insist on) that a greenway be based on a natural landform. But when a path and a natural scene are joined, the congruence can work powerfully on our imagination. Striding across a meadow, picking one's way along a ridge, or meandering down the banks of a stream makes even ordinary landscapes somehow wonderful. As Thoreau writes, "The walker in the familiar fields which stretch around my native town sometimes finds himself in another land than is described in their owners' deeds."

It was sentiments such as these which animated the authors of *Ameri-*

cans Outdoors (1987), the report of the presidential commission on recreation (discussed in earlier chapters) which has been so effective in coalescing a heretofore inchoate greenway movement. "We have a vision," confess the report-writers, who threw ordinary bureaucratic caution to the winds, "for allowing every American easy access to the natural world." They describe "fingers of green that reach out from and around and through communities all across America." The object is to use riversides and stream courses that have been floodplain-zoned against development, to use abandoned railroad beds and canal towpaths, to use high-tension lines and even sewerline rights-of-way, to use old roads untrod and new roads unbuilt, to use mandatory recreational land dedications by subdividers, to use pieced-together ridgeline open spaces—in short, to use anything linear they can lay their hands on to provide the green ways for a skein of paths and trails crisscrossing within and leading out of metropolitan America.

One of the earliest of the modern greenways, the Staten Island Greenbelt, has just this quality of creative assembly. It is based on the conversion of a public right-of-way, a characteristic of many if not most greenway-trail projects.[1] But most of all—and this too is a characteristic of greenway trailmaking—it demonstrates how a simple trail can amplify the utility and public value of all the open spaces it touches along its route. These spaces become, as transcendentalist Thoreau insists, something greater than mere property described in an owner's deed.

The Staten Island project got its start, as many do, with the threatened sale of a valued tract of secluded woodlands straddling the ridgeline of the low escarpment that rises at the center of Staten Island. In 1963, this acreage, called High Rock, was put up for sale by the Girl Scouts of America to cash in on real estate prices that had inflated by 3,000 percent in the twelve years that the scouts had owned the land. A successful campaign was mounted to induce the city of New York to buy High Rock

---

1. The Staten Island Greenbelt in New York is not really a greenbelt, as I point out in an earlier discussion of nomenclature. In this case, the name *greenbelt* was attached to the project in 1963 by Richmond County (Staten Island) Borough President Albert I. Maniscalco, who heard it at a cocktail party and thought it had an authoritative ring. A rose by any other name. . . .

Camp and to convert it to the High Rock Nature Center, an educational facility for all the children of greater New York. But scarcely was the deal done than the High Rock land-savers learned that a Robert Moses highway project, the Richmond Parkway, was planned so that its southbound lanes would run right along the edge of the new facility. Somehow the idea of a nature center did not comport well with streaming traffic.

Then the High Rock advocates looked at the situation in another light. Suppose, they asked themselves, we could not only stop the road from being built *but also* use the right-of-way as a linchpin to preserve the entire ridge? Thus it was that a remarkable congeries of Staten Island conservationists began the process of turning a 4.7-mile-long, 300-foot-wide strip of natural woodlands, ponds, wetlands, and bouldery glades originally acquired for a highway into an open-space corridor that could link other major open spaces such as the proposed site of the Staten Island Arboretum, Kaufmann Campgrounds (for underprivileged Jewish youth of the city), the William T. Pouch Boy Scout Camp, the Richmond Country Club, the Moravian Cemetery, the new High Rock Nature Conservation Center, and La Tourette Park. The effect would be to nail down one of the largest undeveloped natural areas in New York City. At three thousand acres it would be four times the size of Central Park.

The highway-versus-trailway issue was dramatically joined early in 1966 at a meeting held to celebrate the opening of the High Rock Nature as a city-owned facility. The governor, the late Nelson Rockefeller, was affably presiding over the formal ceremony at which many dignitaries of New York, both state and city, were in attendance. Also in attendance was Robert Hagenhofer, a Staten Island graphic artist and amateur actor with a commanding Shakespearean delivery and a keen sense of irony. When the governor had completed his speech, Hagenhofer boldly rose to protest. "Mister Governor," said Hagenhofer, projecting to the farthest seats, "it is *proposed* that a state highway be built immediately adjacent to this beautiful area so many of us here have worked so hard to save." He paused, waiting, as a shocked stillness fell upon the room. Then with a flourish he pointed an accusing finger at the High Rock map, set upon an easel near the podium, which also illustrated the offending right-of-way. "Mister Governor," he intoned, finger aloft, "my question is—is there *any good reason* why a *road*—a road!—should be built through these magnificent woods?" Whereupon Hagenhofer turned his palms upward, as if in supplication of divine agreement on how utterly insane the idea of it was, and took his seat.

As it turned out, Mister Governor was stumped and suggested that Hagenhofer ask the state highway commissioner, which Hagenhofer did, but he and his associates already knew that the real power behind the highway was Robert Moses, who would brook no interference. Even after Terry Benbow, lawyer for Hagenhofer's citizen group, the Staten Island Citizens Planning Association, brought suit to stop the highway from being built, Moses failed to take the protest seriously, belittling their effort to save the ridge. He asserted archly that without the civilizing influence of the road, the parklands would harbor all sorts of lurking cutpurses, arsonists, and hoodlums. "There are," wrote journalist and author John G. Mitchell, himself a leader in the greenbelt project, "people who actually regard the greenbelt as a fire hazard, and the parkway an effective fire-break; who truly feel (as Robert Moses said he did on June 29, 1967) that preserving the greenbelt as a natural area might somehow turn it into 'the most dangerous place in New York,' and who, like Moses, cannot conceive of any valid form of outdoor recreation unless it is played out within earshot of moving pistons."

Hagenhofer, Benbow, Mitchell, and many others including Dick Buegler, a civic leader who worked on the project longer than almost anyone else, brilliantly warded off the highway for nearly twenty years—work that continued even after some of the original cadre of greenbelters had passed away (Gretta Moulton, the savior of High Rock, and Frank Duffy, another lawyer for the group) or moved away (Mitchell to Connecticut and Hagenhofer to New Jersey).

One key figure in the piece, however, had been dead for sixty years (and removed for ninety) even before the project started: Frederick Law Olmsted. Bradford Greene, a landscape architect and greenbelt activist, found that Olmsted had proposed a linear park for the ridge in 1871. It followed then that the way to call attention to the need to save the greenbelt from the highway-builders was to establish the Olmsted Trailway along the proposed alignment of the hated Richmond Parkway. The technique was to stage frequent greenbelt hikes along this trail, to which dignitaries and celebrities would be invited who would help to draw the crowds and, importantly, the press.

The ceremonial-hike approach has had a long and honored tradition, most effectively expressed by Supreme Court Justice William O. Douglas who, beginning in 1954, conducted a number of walks along the Chesapeake and Ohio Canal between Washington, D.C., and Cumberland, Maryland, leading to its designation as a national monument in 1961 and a national park in 1971. The Olmsted Trailway hikes were not so august, but according to a 1988 retrospective article about the greenbelt in the *Staten Island Advance,* the walks "drew support from national environmental groups like the Sierra Club, Audubon Society, and the Appalachian Mountain Club, and were led by such notables as U.S. Secretary of the Interior Stewart Udall, Senator Jacob Javits, and New York Mayor John Lindsay." As a very minor participant in the project, I went on some of these hikes myself. The greenbelters, for some perverse reason, liked to organize them in the winter, and yet, despite the season, hundreds of people would show up—strung out along the Olmsted Trail for a half-mile or more, feeling noble and healthy in mind and body. One time, there had been a January thaw—common on Staten Island—and it had rained lightly, a misty rain, in the small hours of the hike day, Sunday. And then a sudden arctic front came through, freezing everything hard. By the time the hikers hit the trail at midmorning, the cold snap had not only sheathed the branches of the trees and bushes in bright ice but also had created a jeweled arbor for the trail: tiny diamond droplets had frozen along the vinestems of catbriar and fox grape, transforming them into glinting garlands that lighted our way. It was a magical moment for us all.

Today, the Staten Island Greenbelt is laced with trails, and the opportunistically named Olmsted Trailway is no longer much mentioned. But it is my view that it was this trailway idea, and the trail walks, that made all the difference to the success of the project—and it did most assuredly succeed. In 1984, the greenbelt became a city park, and the parkway that would have skewered it was officially demapped in 1989. Looking back on it, the achievement seems almost impossible. It is as if Harold had won the battle of Hastings, after all. Surely, the Norman invader was no more forbidding a foe in 1066 than was Robert Moses in 1966 who, in terms of public works, possessed more raw power than any other person in both the city and the state of New York. He did not lose many highway battles. But this one he did.

There must be a message in there somewhere about the raw power of trails.

A more recent example of the power of a greenway trail to connect and therefore multiply open spaces, although no battle royal was needed to secure it, is also in New York City. It is the Brooklyn-Queens Greenway that runs almost uninterrupted through forty miles of parks and park-ways, cemeteries, arboretums, zoos, museum grounds, golf courses, and other public and quasi-public open spaces imaginatively linked together by planner Tom Fox of the Neighborhood Open Space Coalition of New York. (See the profile, Chapter 9.) Such an assembly is also illustrated by the 40-Mile Loop greenway in Portland, Oregon. Here, Al Edelman and his colleagues in the 40-Mile Loop Land Trust (as described in Chapter 3) were able to organize a large number of government agencies, utilities, and corporations to create what has turned out to be a *140*-mile loop— one hundred miles longer than the original plan, proposed in 1903 by the Olmsted firm but never fully implemented. Here a trailway connects Forest Park, originally acquired through the reversion of building lots to city government for nonpayment of taxes, some valuable federal land along the Columbia Slough, where the trail is located atop dikes no longer needed by U.S. Army Corps of Engineers for river dredging, plus various suburban parks, preserves, and developer-dedicated open spaces in the suburbs, with a final leg, just recently negotiated, created from a ten-mile stretch of abandoned railbed.

Such a diversity of linear land sources is not always required for a successful greenway. Sometimes, trailways can be fashioned from the donation or purchase of private lands, as is the case of the Stowe Recreation Path in Vermont. In this popular ski resort, former fashion model and indefatigable civic leader Anne Lusk assembled a trailway out of "back land," away from the main road passing through Stowe, creating a pedestrian and bicycle bypass for the people of the village in this narrow Green Mountain valley.

In large part, however, trail-based greenways tend to capitalize on public rights-of-way originally created for nonrecreational purposes. In the case of the Staten Island Greenbelt, it was a stretch of land initially intended to be a highway. For the Brooklyn-Queens Greenway, the main connecting links are the wooded margins of parkways, some built by Olmsted and some by Moses. In Portland, the completion of the 40-Mile Loop depends in substantial part on the federal dikes along the Columbia Slough and the abandoned railroad right-of-way.

The many riverside or streamside greenway trails in the United States owe their provenance to a right-of-way, too—at least of a sort. The public exercises its rights in this case by zoning the floodplains of watercourses against development, for quite practical reasons pertaining to public health, safety, and economic considerations associated with flood insurance. As recounted in the profile on the Meramec River Greenway (Chapter 3), federal flood insurance is unavailable to municipalities that permit severely flood-damaged structures to be rebuilt. As commonly practiced in most jurisdictions, the regulated corridor consists of the land that would be inundated in a hundred-year flood occurrence (1 percent probability), although in some cases it may be even wider. In New Jersey, for example, floodplain ordinances are being considered which would regulate the hundred-year floodplain plus one hundred feet on either side. Moreover, many localities will not permit development on steep slopes or within a fair distance from their top edges. When such slopes are associated with a streamway, this adds further land to the hydrological "right-of-way."

Although the regulation does not imply public access, the land has limited value for any use other than to serve as a floodway. Accordingly, privately owned floodplains are prime candidates for the greenway trails, since a trail easement can often be secured at reasonable cost because the land it would traverse retains only marginal value as residential or commercial real estate. In many developing areas, builders will dedicate trailway easements to the public along a streamway under regulations providing for a mandatory set-aside of recreational or open-space lands.

For sheer romance, the rights-of-way that take first prize for conversion to a greenway trail are clearly those of the old-time canals such as the Delaware and Raritan in New Jersey, the Chesapeake and Ohio in Washington, D.C., and Maryland, the Illinois and Michigan Canal in northern Illinois, and the Blackstone Canal in Rhode Island, among others. Not only are they historic, with their locks and lock-tender's houses, they often, if not usually, parallel a major waterway, thus protecting a quite wide swath of riverine open space. The building of a trail is also relatively simple since it is already in place, however neglected, in the form of a towpath. Usually, the surfacing is smooth enough for bicycling, even without paving. Today, Justice Douglas's C & O towpath along the Potomac is literally thronged with cyclists on fine weekends. The same is true of the D & R along the scenic Delaware River. Many of these old canals are state or federal parks already. The C & O is a national park, the D & R a state park, and the Illinois and Michigan Canal (profiled in Chapter 9) is a kind of hybrid—a state-administered national historic corridor, a category I shall discuss in a later chapter. Those canals that remain to be converted, such as the Delaware and Hudson Canal in New York state, are a relative handful but are clearly top priority.

Another public right-of-way that can almost as readily be converted to a greenway trail is the abandoned railroad line. The national movement to convert abandoned rails to trails began in the 1960s.[2] An early proponent was the beloved Midwest naturalist May Theilgaard Watts (author of the classic nature guide, *Reading the Landscape*), who proposed, in a 1963 letter to the *Chicago Tribune,* the establishment of the

2. Obviously, abandoned railroad rights-of-way have been used for foot traffic since the beginning of the age of rail. As a significant nationwide component of recreational policy, however, it is difficult to trace the beginnings of rail-to-trail conversions much before the 1960s, when railroad abandonments rapidly increased with the loss of passenger and freight traffic to air travel and the new network of interstate highways inaugurated in 1956.

Illinois Prairie Path. Here, along an abandoned right-of-way of the Chicago, Aurora, and Elgin Railway, May Watts found the botanic remnants of the original tall-grass prairie ecosystem—a rarity in Illinois where the deep, black soils had long since been plowed out to grow corn and soybeans.

The upper Midwest is, in fact, a hotbed of rail-trail projects, as they are now called. Another early conversion, the Elroy-Sparta Trail, established in 1966, traverses thirty-two miles of the old Chicago and North Western trackbed through the southwestern Wisconsin countryside and has become nationally known for its beautiful railway tunnels. The longest of them (there are three) is 3,810 feet. At this writing, Wisconsin has the greatest mileage of rail-trails (444 miles). Other top-mileage Midwestern states are Minnesota (296), Illinois (203), and Iowa (164). On the West Coast, Washington is the leader (in miles—299—although California has a greater number of projects); in the East, Pennsylvania ranks first, at 167 miles. As of 1989, the total mileage of trails developed from former railroad rights-of-way was 2,701. These impressive statistics—and many more—are compiled annually by the Washington-based Rails-to-Trails Conservancy, a 55,000-member national organization established in 1985 by conservationists and outdoor recreation leaders around the country to serve as an information clearinghouse and advocacy group for rail-trail conversions. Indeed, the resource base for greenways offered by unused railroad rights-of-way is immense—some three thousand miles of tracks are abandoned every year. Nationally, railroad trackage reached its zenith in the 1920s, totaling 272,000 miles. Only a third of that is expected to remain by the beginning of the twenty-first century.

The great potential for thousands of miles of trails everywhere in America is exciting to contemplate, although the rail-trail conversion process is expensive, legally tricky, and fraught with controversy. If railbed land is owned outright by a railroad company (as opposed to a right-of-way over land owned by others) and is located in a prime urban real estate market, the cost of acquisition for trail use can be prohibitively high. Even if the land is affordable, there have been scores of cases in which trailmakers have not learned about the sale of the railbed land until it was too late. In general, when a railroad wishes to sell off an unused rail corridor, the Interstate Commerce Commission allows local or state governments 180 days to make an offer for the railbed for trail use. After that, presumably, it is up for grabs. However, the grace period applies only to land on which the trackage is used in interstate commerce. On certain spurs and sidings, railroad companies have asserted their right to sell off such land privately and without public notice.

A no-public-notice sell-off such as this happened in 1988 to some key pieces of the famed Burke-Gilman Trail, a twelve-mile jogging and biking path through a residential area of Seattle and the campus of the University of Washington. More than 750,000 people use the trail every year for exercise, commuting, and shopping, but the Burlington Northern, on whose land the trail is constructed, suddenly announced it had sold some parcels to a developer. It was, wrote reporter Timothy Egan in a *New York Times* story, "as if the Space Needle had gone condo." The rail-trail people knew their law, however, and successfully argued that the land in question was indeed subject to the ICC rule and that its sale had been conducted improperly. The case was settled out of court, and the trail not only stayed intact but was extended four miles to the shoreline of Puget Sound. The larger effect of the Burke-Gilman case was to put increasing pressure on all private railroads to provide public notice of their abandonments and to give public agencies an exclusive first option to acquire the corridors for alternative uses before the land can be offered for sale as real estate.

In places in which railroad companies acquired a right-of-way as opposed to full fee title, the legal rules of the game are entirely different. Although a right-of-way acquired by a railroad company precludes all other use as long as the trains are still running on the track, if the right is abandoned, then the full use of the property can return to the original owner of land or to his or her assigns. The sticky wicket here is what exactly constitutes legal abandonment of a right-of-way. After abandonment, a good many landowners are inclined to claim that their rights to the land take precedence over any public rights that might be asserted by rail-trail advocates. The trailmakers argue that the right-of-way is a public transportation right that is not extinguished just because the trains are not running.

In 1983 the National Trails Act[3] was amended to take up the right-of-way/abandonment issue in a manner that would obviate the problem of abandonment altogether by providing a means for railway corridors to be "railbanked." Under this provision, the right-of-way is retained by the railroad (or by a public agency to which it may be transferred) for possible transportation use in the future, even though the railroad has long since ceased running trains. A government agency then takes over the maintenance of the corridor from the railroad. One way to maintain it, obviously, is to use it for a recreational trail. The legality of railbanking has been repeatedly challenged by adjoining landowners who wish full use of the land to revert to them. So far, the railbanking law has been upheld, although at this writing, one suit is destined to be heard by the U.S. Supreme Court.

I have compressed some quite complicated legal matters into a few paragraphs here, when indeed millions of words in legal briefs, opinions, congressional testimony, and scholarly papers have been printed in an effort to deal with the complexities of rails-to-trails conversions over the past quarter-century. Now, thanks in good measure to the coordination of effort provided by the Rails-to-Trails Conservancy, the "killer" issues, as RTC president David Burwell calls them, appear to be getting themselves settled. These days, trailmakers will encounter fewer of the kinds of heart-stopping contretemps faced by the city of Seattle with regard to the Burke-Gilman Trail or those encountered by the leaders of Iowa's Heritage Trail (profiled in Chapter 3), who had to contend with railroad

3. An influential Interior Department study, *Trails for America,* published in 1966, led the Congress (in 1968) to authorize the National Park Service to develop a system of long-distance scenic and historic trails. There are presently six interstate scenic trails—although none except the two thousand-mile Appalachian Trail is fully completed—and seven historic trails, such as the Lewis and Clark Trail from St. Louis to the Oregon coast, which tend to parallel highway routes. Congress has also authorized federal involvement in two state-level scenic trails: the Ice Age Trail traversing the terminal moraines across Wisconsin, and the Florida Trail which runs down the middle of the state. Other states have non-federal long-distance trails. Colorado, for example, has a lottery-financed statewide system traversing the Rocky Mountains. Although these long-distance recreation trails can augment greenway programs, they are not generally considered to be greenways themselves.

bridges being burned by those objecting to the trail and wanting the land to revert to adjoining owners. This was no isolated attitude, either. In another Iowa case, the Cedar Valley Nature Trail, one farmer persisted in plowing up and destroying a bikepath that passed by his property.

Thinking back, it is a wonder there have been any rail-trail conversions at all, considering the kinds of problems the pioneer projects had to face. Even without the killers, almost any rail-trail project is a huge challenge, given the large number of jurisdictions and adjoining land users any railroad right-of-way encounters in just a few miles, never mind the typical twenty- to thirty-mile length (or more) of some of the major projects. Morever, the cost of land purchase and trail construction and maintenance can be steep, particularly in high-use areas, even without the lawsuits. RTC's Burwell likes to quote open-space authority William H. Whyte, who said that "it takes a hard core of screwballs to tackle a rail-trail conversion."

Possibly so. But the screwballs are pleased to report that they have completed 215 projects as of mid-1989, with a new project begun "literally every day," according to Peter Harnik, RTC's director of programs.

The question remains, how do the rail-trails relate to the larger greenway movement? Thoreauvian greenway types, given to ruminative country walks, would have a hard time feeling at home on the Burke-Gilman Trail with light-weight racing bikes zooming by at twenty miles an hour. Indeed, many of the rail-trails are so single-mindedly recreational that even their sponsors do not consider them to be greenways—although RTC's Burwell maintains that virtually all rail-trails *are* greenways, at least potentially. My own view is that this is not a terribly useful argument. Most of the rail-trails provide multiple benefits, including ecological ones, since many rail lines parallel water courses or otherwise present the natural scene to us in fresh new ways, such as the Illinois Prairie Path. As Aldo Leopold counseled, "recreation is not the outdoors, but our reaction to it." And when we have no less of a naturalist at our side than May Theilgaard Watts, we may be sure that our reaction to the out-of-doors is of the most profound and beneficial kind, for it and for us. Here, on a beloved old prairie railroad right-of-way or on some other patch of rail-trail elsewhere in the country is where Leopold's idea of a land ethic might well take hold in minds that otherwise would never consider such a thing.

There is one final point to make about rail-trails—the one great benefit they have in terms of the overall greenway movement. They can, especially in combination with the long-distance trails of the national trails system, provide the long-distance linkages between one metropolitan system of greenways and another system in the next metropolitan area down (or up) the line.

In talking about this aspect of the rail-trails with David Burwell, I asked just how far afield I could get on a greenway hike from my house, which is located just outside of Washington, D.C. He told me to walk on over to a part of Rock Creek Park (itself a greenway progenitor as a prime example of stream valley linear parkland) only two blocks away, then walk south to Georgetown, at which point I could either go across the Potomac River and get on the Washington & Old Dominion Trail and slope off toward the Blue Ridge Mountains, or stay on the Maryland side via the C & O. Using the W & OD route, Burwell said, I would have to walk about a mile through the town of Bluemont, Virginia to get to the Appalachian Trail. "Then hang a right on the trail," he said, "till you get to the canal, then hang a left and go into Cumberland [Maryland]."

"What about taking the C & O Canal direct?" I asked.

"Well then, just stay on it till Cumberland. Then take the Potomac Heritage Trail from Cumberland to Connellsville, Pennsylvania. And if you'll give us a few years, you can take a rail-trail link we're working on clear into Pittsburgh. From there, you can walk over to Ohio, up through Michgan and into North Dakota via the North Country Trail [a national scenic trail], which one day may connect with the Lewis and Clark Trail [a national historic trail] and then you can walk all the way to Portland."

"Wow," I said. "Portland, Oregon?"

"You want Portland, Maine?"

"No, no," I said hurriedly. "Oregon's fine. Once I'm out there I might as well walk around the 40-Mile Loop."

"It's actually 140 miles, you know," said Burwell.

"I know, I know," I said. "But at this point, who's counting?"

6

Nature's Corridors

*When we try to pick anything out by itself,
we find it hitched to everything else in the
universe.*

—JOHN MUIR

*H*omo sapiens is not the only creature needful of greenways. In
fact, some greenways are concerned more with the economy of nature
than with the economics of redevelopment or the statistics of recreational
demand which are of such moment in urban or trail-based greenways.

It was Kenny King who put me in mind of this ecological view of
greenways while he was maneuvering the Willamette River in a driftboat, which is a high-freeboard, exceedingly lithe, double-ended rowboat specially designed for salmon fishing on the Oregon rivers. What
one does in an Oregon driftboat is row against the current, and that is a
fair metaphor for Kenny King's life. King is a professional river guide,
providing (for those who can afford it) arguably the best trout, salmon,
and steelhead fishing in the world, and he has done so since the 1930s
when he would take his "business executives," as he calls them, down the
McKenzie for five dollars a day. Except for a brief stint in the merchant
marine and as a baseball player for a Cincinnati Reds farm club in Bir-
mingham, Alabama, King plied his trade for fifty years before semiretir-
ing in the mid-1980s. After half a century you get to know every salmon
hole there is in a river like the Willamette and every inch of shoreline,

too—even though the Rogue, the McKenzie, and the Umpqua are better salmon streams. On my trip, we were not fishing anyway, at least not very much. Mainly, King was muttering about the "ridiculous" idea of having a trail down the banks of the what is now the Willamette River Greenway, running 225 miles from St. Helens, north of Portland, to Cottage Grove, south of Eugene. "Look at that," he would say, between pulling on the oars of the driftboat to slow our descent. "See where that creek comes into the river? See how wide it is? Now, how would they get a trail across there without an expensive bridge? Ridiculous." Then he would pull heavily at the oars again, reversing the drift of the boat, defying the downstream force of the river.

He is a small, wiry man, Kenny King, with close-cropped gray hair. He weighs 145 pounds soaking wet. He is seventy. On a two-hour trip down a short stretch of the Willamette, he spotted a dozen ospreys for me and as many great blue heron and, in one case, a display of aerial combat between an osprey and a heron. We saw a beaver. We saw a fawn. We saw four bucks lined up along a gravel bar, having an early morning drink, like dissolute gents in a saloon. We saw salmon flopping around at the base of a dam. We saw innumerable songbirds, too many kinds to list here. We saw, in sum, one of nature's corridors operating exactly the way its legislative sponsors intended.

The fact is, the idea of a trailway along the Willamette was only a fleeting notion in the mid-1960s, after Oregon's 1965 Clean Water Act had done much to clean up a river described by one state official during the 1950s as the "filthiest waterway in the Northwest." The river is the organizing physiographic feature of the Willamette Valley, where some 70 percent of Oregonians live. Portland, Eugene, and a half-dozen smaller cities are located along the river. Even so, more than 90 percent of the Willamette's length is through rural land.

In 1967, the Oregon legislature enacted the first of two greenway statutes (the Willamette project was perhaps the first in the country to be legally designated as a *greenway*) that provided for the protection of the river corridor and for the expansion and enhancement of river-oriented recreational opportunities. In 1970, five regional state park sites were selected along the river, and in 1971 and 1972, the state's Department of Transportation began to acquire some of these lands. But as James Knight, a state official with the Land Conservation and Development Commission, later told me, the effort was unfocused. "No one really knew what a greenway was," he said. "Was it supposed to be a series of trails and bikepaths? A string of parks? What?" In any case, the state parks division acquired land for the parks and established some forty-three other sites along the river for picnicking and boat launching, a couple of which Kenny King used (one for putting in, another for taking out) on the driftboat trip. But that was about it. There was no official intention to protect the river by acquiring a continuous strip of land along the length of the corridor.

The best way to protect the Willamette, the legislature finally decided, was through land regulation, courtesy of Goal 15 of Oregon's statewide planning program, enacted in 1973. (Other goals have to do with such matters as farmlands, housing, and coastal lands.) Goal 15 says:

—Farmland uses shall be preserved along the river corridor as an effective means to carry out the purposes of the greenway.

—Recreational facilities shall be provided so long as they are consistent with the carrying capacity of the land.

—Fish and wildlife habitats shall be protected.

—Scenic qualities and views shall be preserved.

—Private property shall be protected against vandalism and trespass to the maximum extent practicable.

—The natural vegetative fringe along the river shall be enhanced and protected to the maximum extent practicable.

—Timber harvesting beyond the protective fringe shall be regulated to ensure that the natural scenic qualities of the greenway will be maintained.

—Aggregate extraction shall be subject to regulations that minimize adverse effects on water quality, fish and wildlife, vegetation, bank stability, streamflow, visual quality, noise, and safety—and the extractors must guarantee reclamation.

—Development shall be directed away from the river to the greatest possible degree, excepting existing urban uses, and the lands and facilities needed for ports and navigation.

—A greenway setback line shall be established to keep structures separated from the river in order to protect, maintain, preserve, and enhance the natural, scenic, historic, and recreational quality of the Willamette River Greenway.

After an exhaustive inventory of the river corridor was conducted, reflecting the foregoing paraphrased elements of Goal 15, a map was prepared, and a basic policy decision was made pertaining to the "setback line"—the line within which any change of use of the riparian land was to be largely forbidden (in cities an "extraordinary exception" can be made). The map also defined the remaining land within the greenway corridor. The *corridor* is that area, sometimes several miles wide, in which special planning considerations are to be taken into account by local jurisdictions. In general, the way the planning law works in Oregon is to require local planning to conform with the intent of the statutory goals and guidelines that concern themselves with land uses and land areas of statewide significance. The Willamette River corridor, now greenway, is one such area. Local plans are submitted to a state agency—the Land Conservation and Development Commission—which approves them, suggests changes to bring the plans into conformity with the goals and guidelines or (in the case of recalcitrant or impecunious jurisdictions) imposes its own plan. There are, of course, innumerable advisory committees, appeal processes, and similar bureaucratic paraphernalia; the law is a tough one to administer. And yet, having been tested for some fifteen years, it seems to be holding up well, despite many attempts at repeal. Like any comprehensive social legislation, whether it has to do with health care or education or land use, Oregon's planning laws leave much to be desired from almost any standpoint. Nevertheless, the state-enforced goals-and-guidelines approach appears to be sensible, effective, and enforceable. In this regard, Oregon is virtually alone. Indeed, most states have *no* approach or, at best, an extremely narrow area of influence over local land-use decision making, which almost invariably is driven by short-term economic considerations in the nation's 39,000 townships, municipalities, and counties.

On the Willamette, the key feature, beyond overall corridor planning, is the setback line. It has been established at a minimum of 150 feet from either bank and, according to James Knight, an LCDC official, might extend as much as a quarter-mile or more "where there are sloughs and backwaters." In the cities, the setback does not have much effect, since so much of the land is already developed. In the course of urban riverfront redevelopment, however, it encourages park and recreation use (and in both Portland and Eugene there are beautiful riverside parks and paths) as opposed to more economically oriented projects. This has become a somewhat controversial feature of the state's planning guidelines. The economic base, always shaky in this low-population state, has been especially beset in recent years because of the decline of the forest products industry, most significantly in processing, such as plywood manufacture and structural timber milling. Even the sale of old-growth timber in the form of whole logs to Japan at cut-rate prices—an outrageous policy that not only destroys two-hundred-year-old trees but also exports processing, marketing, and distributive jobs along with them—has declined in recent years as the remaining patches of old growth are depleted. Says Nina Lovinger of the Oregon Natural Re sources Council, "There's a big push for economic development because Oregon is so depressed. When timber prices were better it was easier to protect the land." In Eugene, where Lovinger lives, riverfront land is seen (by some) as a way to make up for economic decline in other sectors of the economy by using the scenic Willamette for high-rises and office buildings. So far, Lovinger and others who are determined to protect the natural integrity of the river have been able to discourage any changes in the conservationist spirit of the law. Nevertheless, according to Robert Rindy of the LCDC, some state officials are beginning to wonder if a certain amount of river-oriented economic development might be wise. In the rural areas, though, which comprise all but a small fraction of the river's corridor, the setback has made a profound difference in maintaining natural processes more or less intact along the corridor; it would appear to be a permanent fixture.

I mentioned some of this to Kenny King, only to discover (amid more muttering) that the only thing he hates worse than the idea of trails is land-use regulation. I resisted pointing out how wrong-headed he was about this, of course, for reasons that relate exactly to the fortunes of his own profession as a river guide for wealthy fanciers of salmon fishing. King is obviously a man of principle, not to be swayed by base appeals to self-interest. Anyway, he was wrong for larger salmonid reasons, for the Willamette River Greenway protects the corridor for the welfare of the species for its own sake not just for the fishers of it. Oregon's late governor Tom McCall believed the ecological health of the salmon and steelhead was emblematic of environmental quality generally. "If the salmon and the steelhead are running," McCall told me in an interview I had with him in the early 1970s, "then as far as I'm concerned, God knows that all is well in His world." He went on: "These fish are beautiful—just to know that they are there, whether you've caught one or not. Because the health of your environment is good if the salmon and the steelhead are around. It is that simple."

Almost true. The beauty of the salmon and the steelhead might be just a teeny bit more impressive if you have one on the end of your line— for God loves the salmon fisherman as well as the salmon, which means that He has taken the wonderful Tom McCall, defender of the Willamette and of "the beautiful Oregon country," into His embrace. And He surely maintains a warm regard for Kenny King, too, although, there in the driftboat, King was muttering profanely about the land-use regulation that McCall championed as governor. I decided to interrupt, asking about the trees along the banks. "That's Oregon white oak," King said, pointing, "over there's cottonwood, plenty of alder, fir, cedar." In some places, the setback line has worked so well along this river—which, after all, passes through the industrial and residential centerline of the entire state—that a two-hour driftboat trip not far from the city limits of Eugene can seem almost like a wilderness outing. I sent silent congratulations to the far-sighted politicians of Oregon, for it is also against the law to disturb the riparian vegetation. Meanwhile, Kenny King was keeping his eye out for salmon boils. And muttering.

It is true that virtually all greenways protect natural processes to one degree or another. Elaborately developed urban river greenways such as Denver's Platte River Greenway (profiled in Chapter 9) or the asphalted bikeways along abandoned railroad rights-of-way, which seem so resolutely oriented to recreation, produce benefits for the natural environment. Nevertheless, greenways established *primarily* to provide natural corridors for the benefit of wildlife, native plant associations, and the preservation of historic landscapes are still relatively rare—although such projects are among the most interesting of all.

Take the Oconee River Greenway, for example, which was begun in 1973 strictly as a nonrecreational project to protect the natural corridors of the north and middle forks of the Oconee and its tributaries north of Athens, Georgia. Within the city, which is where the University of Georgia is located, the greenway has recreational uses, but there is no continuous trailway. Along the upper reaches of the two branches, there are some large open-space holdings, including a nature sanctuary used by the university and local schools for teaching. But when I asked Charles Aguar, the landscape architecture professor who developed the first greenway plan as a class project, whether there were any future plans for a trailway, he was puzzled by my question. To him and to nearly a whole generation of students who have worked on the planning of the thirty-five-mile greenway corridor, the idea is to maintain environmental quality, including indigenous wildlife and plants, not simply to build a trail. "The river itself is the trail," said Aguar. And in that respect his project is much like Oregon's Willamette, although without the benefit of a rigorous state law.

In the case of the Oconee, the one hundred-year floodplains of the two branches are protected under local regulation, as is usual in most parts of the country. What is different about Aguar's plan is that it calls for a preservation district overlay, providing a means for government jurisdictions along the Oconee's branches to have their planning and zoning decisions comport with the environmental qualities of the corridor as a whole. The width of each corridor is two miles—a mile on each side of the riverway. "It's not completely a preservation plan," Aguar told me, "but proposes land uses that are consistent with maintaining the ecological integrity of the river corridors."

The emphasis in recent years on protecting riparian corridors, exemplified by the greenway projects such as the Oconee, may derive indirectly from the long-term federal government commitment to preserving undeveloped river corridors under the Wild and Scenic Rivers Act of 1968. This program provides for inventory and river studies by the National Park Service preparatory to inclusion of a candidate river in a national system which then leads to protection from the depredations of other agencies of the federal government which might destroy its wild and scenic qualities by building bridges or dams or otherwise modifying the riverway. Although the program produces only a modicum of enforceable protection for a limited number of rivers, it does supply a patina of legitimacy for river conservation actions in general by state and local governments and civic groups. Accordingly, the Wild and Scenic Rivers Act has spawned a number of local and state-level river conservation statutes that are less choosy about the rivers they would protect and which can work well with greenway programs. In recognition of this, the federal government, via a special unit of the National Park Service (see Chapter 10 for details), will assist localities in river studies and action plans for their protection.

Although the emphasis over the years on statutory river corridor protection is generally useful to greenway-makers around the country wishing to justify their projects to the general public, there is a new (at least to most of us) and quite specific scientific concept that has emerged which pertains directly to the crucial role that natural-corridor greenway planning can play in the protection of wildlife. This is the growing emphasis biologists and ecologists are placing on the problem of "island populations" of wildlife and plants in isolated reserves and the need for natural corridors to provide for species interchange so that the island populations will not die out. Lately, in fact, a new academic specialty has emerged to deal exactly with such matters—"landscape ecology." Here is where the science of ecology can be applied in quite specific ways to the presentiments during the 1960s of the pioneer environmental landscape architects and planners such as Philip Lewis and Ian McHarg.

One of the new breed is a University of Florida ecologist named Larry Harris. Despite the fact that a goodly number of wildlife habitat areas have been set aside as parks, reserves, and sanctuaries over the past one hundred years, many of these areas have been rendered ineffective by surrounding development. "Now," Harris writes, "decades of land development around our conservation areas and the isolation of remant populations [of wildlife] by gigantic systems of roadways, powerlines, pipelines, and strip development are increasing the [ecological] problems with which we must deal."

Harris maintains that such fragmentation, not simply the lack of wildlife refuges, is what is now taking such a toll on wildlife. Although in many cases additional large preserves still need to be established, by far the greater ecological problem is the dismemberment of the natural landscape. There are, Harris says, four major consequences of such fragmentation. The first is the loss of species that require "deep woods" for breeding—a category that includes many kinds of birds. A second consequence is the local extinction of larger species such as bear and the large cats, most of which travel long distances for feeding and breeding. Under ordinary circumstances, Harris says, a single Florida panther needs at least a 50,000-acre range. Third, fragmentation leads to a "human subsidy" for certain adaptive species such as English sparrows, raccoons, and deer, which can overpopulate and degrade habitat areas, making them less hospitable to species that are less adaptive. The fourth consequence is inbreeding, which weakens the genetic integrity of a species in isolation, sometimes leading to local extinction.

But there is hope. The fragmentation and isolation of habitats, Harris continues, "can be largely alleviated through a series of greenbelts, habitat linkages, wildlife corridors, and riparian buffer strips connecting key parks, refuges, and habitat islands."

Harris makes a special plea for "the junction between land and water" as the best location for wildlife corridors. He writes: "Numerous species of fish, amphibians, reptiles, mammals, and birds not only live there, but they also use these riparian or streamside woods as *landscape thoroughfares* [my emphasis]. Thus, even if rivers and riparian woods had no fisheries value, no recreational value, no hardwood forestry value, or hydroperiod regulation or water recharge or cleansing value, we would still choose them as priority wildlife conservation areas. Even if humans were not involved at all, rivers, streams, and drainageways would still portray nature's own energy signature to be read as a resource management template." To illustrate his point, Harris has proposed a natural corridor along the Suwannee River drainage in northern Florida and southern Georgia which would provide a landscape thoroughfare for wildlife, linking twenty habitat areas totaling nearly one million acres.

Another leading landscape ecologist, Richard T. T. Forman of Harvard University's Graduate School of Design, has studied the relationship of natural corridors to what he calls "remnant patches" in a "disturbed matrix" (such as farmlands or suburban development). The patches contain what remains of the original natural community in a given landscape; corridors can provide a means for species to move between patches in order to retain biological diversity and ecological balance. There are, Forman says, four different kinds of corridors: the *line corridor*, such as a hedgerow or drainage ditch; the *strip corridor*, which is a wider band of land ecologically similar to the patches it connects; the *stream corridor*, which borders a water course; and a *network*, which can consist of manmade corridors such as paths and roadsides as well as natural corridors.

In the Sourland Mountain region, an area of central New Jersey between Trenton and New Brunswick (and familiar to Forman who, before Harvard, taught biology at Rutgers University), an understanding of patches and corridors may help to reconnect remnants of the original landscape and restore, after a fashion, some of its original ecological functions. In this case, three greenway-type projects are coming together to create an ecological *connectivity*, as Forman would call it.

The mountain itself is not really a mountain but a low, lozenge-shaped upthrust escarpment of diabase and argillite—a bouldery place not amenable to farming, unlike the patterned fields that surround it.

Sourland Mountain, about ten miles long and four miles wide, has also been somewhat inhospitable to residential subdividers who have long since invaded the farm flatlands below. So far, the homebuilders have pretty much let the mountain be (although that may be changing), since site preparation work is difficult, and water supply and percolation (for septic fields) are a problem owing to the underlying rock. The upshot is that this forty-square-mile area is a remnant patch, a relatively unbroken woodland that can harbor many, if not all, of its original animals and plants because of its size. According to Forman, the Sourlands, as the area is called, are big enough as they stand not only for fox and deer and hawks and owls, but bear as well—although none have been sighted there for a generation.

Sourland Mountain, as a small outpost of natural landscape in the path of a massed charge of oncoming urban development, has its citizen defenders, as do most such places. In the case of the Sourlands, though, the challenge is an especially difficult one. Since the mountain is neither high nor much traversed or visited by residents round about, it tends to be forgotten. This invisibility is further reinforced by the historic circumstance that the Sourland area is divided among three counties and four townships and thus only marginally significant to any one of them. Even though the mountain is ecologically intact, its political structure is fragmented.

Because of this situation, a civic organization called the Sourland Regional Citizens Planning Council was established in 1986 by a group of Sourland residents, among them Robert Hagenhofer who, twenty years before, was such a decisive figure in the battle to save another escarpment—the Staten Island Greenbelt, which I discussed in Chapter 4. As with the greenbelt, one focus of the council's program is to establish a trail system on the mountain. Unlike the Staten Island situation, however, the Sourlands have had no Robert Moses Parkway to concentrate the mind—only the slow fragmentation of the woodlands, a few houses at a time. Accordingly, it has been difficult to suggest the larger significance of the Sourlands to the general public—except in one respect: it is a crucial patch in the attenuated ecology of central New Jersey. On a topographic map of this part of the state, Sourland Mountain is embraced by an inverted triangle of rivers. To the west is the Delaware; to the east, the Millstone; and to the north, across the top of the triangle (at least part of it), is the south branch of the Raritan. The land along most of the riverine lowlands is protected open space, a greenway, courtesy of the Delaware and Raritan Canal, now a state park.

Connecting the riverine-and-canal park lowlands with the wooded uplands of the Sourlands are a number of streams coming off the mountain whose margins are relatively undisturbed. Many of these streams have been the focus of another citizen-led conservation effort called the Delaware and Raritan Greenway Alliance, organized by the Stony Brook-Millstone Watershed Association. The first project of the alliance, the Stony Brook Greenway, it is hoped, will be a model for all the other streams. According to Maude Backes, the project's director, the alliance wants to convince local governments to prohibit land development along stream corridors via a hundred-foot setback beyond the hundred-year floodplain and to encourage private donations of lands and easements along streamways. There is no plan at present for recreational trails.

Given the protection of the streamway corridors, the unbroken woods of the Sourlands can escape becoming an island, for permanent wildlife corridors would connect it with the riverine lowlands, which themselves are wildlife corridors to other woods, often at great distances. The three different greenway-type projects—the Sourlands with its ridgeline trail system, the streamway protection, and the rivers with the already established canal park—could produce in total a dynamic mechanism for retaining a kind of skeleton ecosystem for the long-settled Jersey midlands. If all the various elements are brought together, the greenways of the Sourland Mountain area could become a useful model for ecological greenway planning, taking advantage of remnant patches and corridors in other locations beset with the inexorable advance of urbanization.

7

Scenic Drives and
Historic Routes

You road I enter upon and look around,
I believe you are not all that is here,
I believe that much unseen is also here.

— WALT WHITMAN,
Song of the Open Road

Although Henry Ford succeeded beyond his wildest dreams in turning the automobile from a purely recreational vehicle into a necessity, "driving for pleasure," as the recreation researchers put it, is still near the top of the list of all outdoor recreational activities. In the early 1960s it was a clear winner, according to the Outdoor Recreation Resources Review Commission, but even now, after a generation of interstates and gridlock, more recent research shows that DFP (driving for pleasure) comes in second, just behind walking for pleasure, which doubtless is some sort of landmark in American social history.

In either case, it seems logical that scenic and historic automobile routes (sometimes they *are* both scenic and historic) might be prime candidates for greenway-makers. Although purists may argue that greenways and roadways are incompatible, to eliminate road-based greenways would be to miss some significant opportunities for first-rate projects. Here, the idea is not to displace automobile use, as a rail-trail displaces a train, but to add something to the experience of a Sunday drive, for we still take them, even on Sundays, loading up the kids and setting off. One of the most constructive additions to the Sunday drive is the potential for such greenways to get the family out of the car and into the landscape the greenway preserves.

Consider, for example, the 31st Street Greenway outside Chicago, Illinois. The stretch of road in question begins ten miles southwest of the Loop, at Riverside, which is just beyond Cicero, and crosses the Cook-Du Page County line, ending at the village of Oak Brook. Just another suburban thoroughfare, you might say. Except that crammed into the last eight miles of 31st Street is enough prairie heritage—natural and cultural—to warm the nostalgic cockles of even the most urbanized denizen of southside Chicago, who might otherwise think that after Cicero, the known world more or less stops.

In fact, 31st Street is where an understanding of the history and ecology of the Middle West can begin for those willing to seek it out, which is exactly what Valerie Spale did shortly after she took on the job of executive director for the Save the Prairie Society, set up to protect some of the last remnants of true Illinois black-soil prairie. The remnants are located at Wolf Road, about halfway along the eight fascinating miles of 31st Street.

Beginning at Des Plaines Avenue, in Riverside, Illinois (as Valerie Spale describes), are the spacious, elm-lined parkways, designed in 1868 by Frederick Law Olmsted, dotted with distinctive residences, one of them the work of Frank Lloyd Wright. Surrounding the village is park land, administered by the Cook County Forest Preserve, which offers hiking and biking trails along the Des Plaines River and Salt Creek, both of which are crossed by 31st Street. Moving west, on the south side of 31st Street, is the Brookfield Zoo, which attracts a couple of million visitors a year.

Next, crossing over Salt Creek again, is the Wolf Road Prairie, containing eighty protected acres of the original native landscape in these parts. "A blend of oak savanna, mesic prairie, and prairie marsh which hosts a number of rare and endangered species," writes Spale. She would urge you to search for a rare white-fringed orchid. Back in a way, you can find some ancient cemeteries serving an agricultural community called Franzosenbusch. Also in the general area is the 1852 House where Charles Lindbergh—Lucky Lindy—rested up between his biplane airmail runs to Chicago during the 1920s. The house has been relocated from the village of Westchester to the Wolf Road Prairie to serve as a museum and visitor center.

Hard by the prairie, on the west, are sizable private estates along Hickory Lane. "Gentle country living continues here," as Spale poetically describes the place, "where deer and great horned owls travel with ease past lovely homes and stately trees." Nearby are the two remaining Indian Trail Oaks, whose bent branches were used as markers by the Potawatamies. Indian mounds and relics discovered in the vicinity indicate that settlement dates back eight thousand years.

One favorite attraction, a bit further along 31st Street, is the Oak Brook Polo Club whose members want you to know that fellow-player Prince Charles went a few chukkers here. Then a short detour down York Road to Spring Road leads to the heart of historic Hinsdale and Oak Brook itself where, says Spale, "the restored 1850s Graue Mill perches beside a tumbling waterfall." During the Civil War the mill was an underground railroad stop, and it is thought that Lincoln himself visited the area as a circuit rider. The mill is open to the public. Nearby is the Fullersburg Nature Center with trails through the woods and along Salt Creek. Back on 31st Street is the Mayslake Retreat, owned by the Franciscans. On the property is a 1919 Tudor Gothic mansion built by coal magnate Frances Stuyvesant Peabody, together with a reproduction of the original Italian Portiuncola Chapel of St. Francis of Assisi, constructed in 1926 as Peabody's tomb.

The greenway ends further down the road with the recently preserved ninety-acre Lyman Woods and Marsh, a natural area that protects, says Spale, "a rare combination of diverse upland forest dating back to the last glacial age, and a vital wetland area."

The rich collection of the features along the 31st Street corridor which Spale discovered and so persuasively describes in her articles and booklets did in fact capture the imagination of civic leaders and municipal officials, especially in regard to creating pedestrian linkages among

the features on the western end of the corridor, which augments the automotive route. To promote a pedestrian plan, Spale won a grant from the
National Trust for Historic Preservation to hold a workshop to which all
municipalities, county park agencies, and conservation organizations and
civic groups were invited. Renaming the project the Salt Creek Greenway, Spale and company began working with private landowners—some
of them quite dubious—on a trailway to be established along Salt Creek
which would provide a connection for many of the nonautomotive features in the 31st Street corridor. Thus did the emphasis shift gradually
from roadway to trailway, with both routes now integral to the project as
a whole.

To date, seven miles of trail have been pieced together. But there are
other connections this project has made, too. By joining the various
features along a corridor unassumingly named *31st Street,* a sum greater
than the parts has been created by the project which can keep a piece of
Illinois heritage permanently intact for the generations of the teeming
metropolis.

As Valerie Spale discovered, a scenic/historic auto route has a way of *becoming* a greenway, as a sort of organic process that takes place once people understand the value of a corridor. Mad Dog Mitchell, Broward
Davis, and the others working on the Canopy Roads project in Tallahassee (profiled in Chapter 9) are expecting the same result for their project. The end-state vision for these historic north Florida dirt roads is that
they be bracketed by hundred-foot-deep green strips on either side of the
roadway, with bicycle and pedestrian paths as well as setbacks here and
there for picnicking or resting. But the end state is a way off: present
landowners simply are not interested in opening their land to the public
in this way. Accordingly, the present effort is to seek scenic easements
along the Canopy Roads corridors so that trails and setbacks will one day
be possible.

Although most of those working on greenway projects that involve
or require automobile routes might one day like to see continuous footpaths or bikepaths along their scenic and historic corridors, the lack of
them at the outset does not make a project any less significant or exem-

plary as a greenway. In the case of the Bay Circuit, Boston's famed suburban loop of interconnected open space, the development program is based on providing three different modes of "making the circuit"—afoot along pathways, in a canoe or rowboat down streams, or by auto along a route that is to be specially marked for this purpose, with parking areas indicated where motorists can alight to explore one feature or another: Thoreau's Walden Pond, for example, or the Old Manse in Concord. Those who lead projects such as these see the auto routes as valid in their own right as well as being a means to an end—a way to acquaint as many people as possible with the scenic and historic features that their greenways connect.

For the history-oriented greenway-maker, there are a good many organizations, agencies, and statutes that may be of help. The most significant statute is the National Historic Preservation Act of 1966, which provides funding to state historic agencies and to the National Trust for Historic Preservation. Grants for researching areas of interest are sometimes available from the trust and the state agencies to determine if sites or districts should be included in the national or state registries of historic places. Listing on the national register, as well as on state-level counterpart registries, affords protection from government-sponsored development that might adversely affect historic properties, including those that are privately owned. For the owner, listing can add a good deal of cachet to a property, plus the ability to deduct certain renovation costs. A greenway can link such registered places or add to their public and private value along a historic corridor.

Old-time canals are a clear favorite as the basis for historic route greenway projects, some of them already units of the national park system. In recent years, Congress has established new heritage-corridor legislation, with the first two projects both canals—the Illinois and Michigan Canal (profiled in Chapter 9) and the Blackstone River in Rhode Island and Massachusetts. As with much else in Washington, D.C., these days, the recognition is mainly honorary. The federal government provides for studies, public relations, and "interpretation," but leaves the pricey part—the acquisition, development, and maintenance of recreational and historic features—to others. At the state and local levels, there are over a hundred canal-based greenways in place, with a number of historic canal societies, including the American Canal Society, headquartered in York, Pennsylvania, anxious to help bring others into being.

As for scenic-road greenways, nothing much beats the nationally famous California Route 1 (profiled in Chapter 3), notched into the mountainsides along the Big Sur coast. The most original scenic project, however, may well be the effort by Robert Myhr, a Ph.D. economist who formerly worked for the Weyerhaueser Corporation in Seattle, to establish a "San Juan Islands Ferryboat Corridor Greenway" under the aegis of the San Juan Islands Preservation Trust. The San Juan Islands lie in Washington's Puget Sound. At low tide, there are 788 islands, and at high tide, 456. Only 175 are large enough to be named; fifteen have year-round residents; and four (Lopez, Shaw, San Juan, and Orcas) are ports of call for a ferryboat that runs between Anacortes, Washington, on the U.S. mainland to Sidney, British Columbia, on Vancouver Island, not far from Victoria.

The islands have marvelous views of the water, half the rain of Seattle, and all the natural beauty any self-respecting northwesterner would want. With new people and new money pouring into the Seattle region as a burgeoning financial and trading center of the Pacific rim, the seemingly remote San Juans were (and are) extremely vulnerable to what hereabouts is generally called *Californication*. Once the shorelines are packed with houses, the striking scenery will be gone forever.

And Bob Myhr knew this was coming. A long-time summer resident of Lopez Island—the first stop on the ferry out of Anacortes—Myhr participated as a volunteer conservationist in the vital work of the San Juan Preservation Trust, established in 1979. When, in the early 1980s, the trust decided a part-time executive director was needed, Myhr, with an insouciance impressive even in the Pacific Northwest, resigned from Weyerhaueser, sold his house in a desirable Seattle suburb (where real estate prices had escalated wildly), and became a full-time land-saver at a small fraction of the salary he had been making as an internationally known expert in his field. Now, with his wife (who runs a reservation service for bed-and-breakfast places throughout the islands), Myhr has set up shop in a small but handsome glass-walled house snuggled in a rocky cove on the south shore of Lopez.

A well-spoken, scholarly looking man of middle years, Myhr told me during my visit to Lopez that although the San Juan Preservation Trust is set up to work with all the land on the islands, he did feel that the waterfront property was more crucial, and that strategically the most crucial of all was the land that could be seen from the deck of the ferryboat. "That's not only the scenery the tourist sees," said Myhr, "it's the scenery that islanders see. And they see it repeatedly, every time they ride the ferry back and forth to Anacortes. It's the route of private craft, as well. If we can make a kind of greenway out of it, then we'll have not only protected the visual integrity of the ferryboat route but provided significant momentum for the preservation of other key parcels, whether they're on the route or not."

To carry out his plan, Myhr works closely with landowners along the corridor, many of whom have substantial acreage, to enter into agreements with the trust—in the form of deeded development right easements—to maintain the view from the ferryboat, just as it is. In one project, Myhr worked out a deal with the owners of a forty-one-acre property at the top of Mount Woolard, a landmark dramatically visible from the waters of the ferry lanes. According to Myhr, "under the terms of the agreement, all but four of the forty-one acres will be conserved in their natural state. Along with the existing two-and-one-half-acre homesite, one additional home may be constructed on a hidden one and one-half acres, provided it is constructed in a manner to preserve the surrounding land and natural vegetation. Further land division, additional building, clear-cutting of timber, road-building, or extraction of minerals will not be allowed on the remaining thirty-seven acres."

In all, there are about five hundred miles of shoreline along the ferryboat corridor. As of 1989, Myhr had nailed down only about 5 percent of it, although the momentum was beginning to build for his greenway as the economic and aesthetic implications of his strategy become more widely recognized by islanders as well as by conservation leaders in the Northwest.

To be sure, the San Juan Islands Ferryboat Corridor Greenway is scarcely a typical scenic drive, but it does nevertheless suggest a broadly applicable strategic possibility for virtually all greenway projects of this kind—a means to deal with the increasing rate of landscape blight along nearly all the thoroughfares of what was once called America the beautiful. Let me explain.

In 1964, an eminent architect and scholar by the name of Peter Blake published a book whose first lines were: "This book is not written in anger. It is written in fury—though not, I trust, in blind fury. It is a deliberate attack upon all those who have already befouled a large portion of this country for private gain and are engaged in befouling the rest." What followed, after an introductory essay expanding on this point, were several hundred pictures, with a minimum of text, for little exegesis was needed, of America the ugly. The title of the book is *God's Own Junkyard,* and it ought to be on the library shelves of every patriotic citizen.

Now, a quarter-century has passed, but nothing much has changed in God's own junkyard. If anything, it has gotten junkier. High-tension wires, auto graveyards, billboards, cookie-cutter subdivisions, strip development, and bulldozed desecrated land assault the eye at every bend in the road. What is so terrible and moving about Professor Blake's book, from a vantage point twenty-five years later, is not just that it confirms reality but that we have evidently become inured to reality—especially along those roads that lead out of cities through the suburbs and exurbs, the *roads of ruin* a friend calls them. Here, it would seem, uglification has become a national cooperative effort, like war.

How did it happen? During the 1960s, because of the work of Peter Blake and many others, most notably Lady Bird Johnson, the U.S. Congress passed the Highway Beautification Act, an antibillboard law that was hailed at the time of passage but nevertheless turned out to be a blatant bit of legislative legerdemain. Historically, billboard interests routinely claimed that any regulation would be an unconstitutional infringement of the economic use of the property on which the billboard was placed. But the courts routinely held that this particular economic value of the land had nothing to do with the land's inherent worth—such as for crops—but existed only because of the use of the land adjacent, the public road. This was the so-called *parasite principle*. Take away the host —the road—and the parasite—the billboard-use value—would die. Therefore, ordinary, fair-minded local regulation, which usually allowed an amortization period before signs had to be removed, was held to impose no infringement on constitutional rights. That is the way things stood until the 1960s, and that was the basis on which a state like California, for example, could ban billboards along Route 1, as they did in 1940.

Then, Congress got into the act, feeling that the new interstate highway system needed special controls all its own. "That's okay," said the billboard lobby, round-eyed with innocent cooperation, and they made nary a peep about the issue of regulation being a form of taking without just compensation. In the Federal Highway Beautification Act of 1964, Congress cut a deal with the billboard lobby to the effect that, in exchange for being allowed to regulate the billboards (an authority they had anyway), they would eliminate the amortization period. Now, under federal law, it was necessary to provide cash compensation to billboard owners required to take down their signs, which event so weakened the court-approved principle of amortization that many localities found it impossible to afford to regulate billboards any longer.

There is more. The new law permitted giant signs, called *monopoles,* which could be seen a half-mile away. It permitted tree cutting to clear vegetation away from signs that were not removed under the program. It exempted signs associated with business use of a property. Its provision for scheduling the removal of noncomplying signs left up to the billboard companies the question of which signs were to be removed—the result being that only money-losers would be taken down, which would have happened anyway. The upshot, according to author James Nathan Miller, writing in the June, 1985, issue of *Reader's Digest,* was that "in fiscal 1983 the government paid for the removal of 2,235 old billboards—while the industry added about 18,000 new ones. Most of the removed signs were small ones on low-traffic roads. The new ones were bigger, taller, and located on heavily traveled stretches." There is even worse news. The program is now out of money to compensate owners of signs that ought to be banned, and so, effectively, the billboard interests have free reign along the interstates and, by extension, other highways as well.

This is, in my view, a serious matter, with significant implications for the whole American landscape. Nationally, the billboard is to the advertising business what the AK-47 is to the sporting arms business, a rogue product that too many people make too much money on to permit a straightforward legislative remedy to be easily enacted. I speak here as a former Madison Avenue advertising man who consistently recommended against outdoor advertising for clients on the grounds that it was an antisocial act, which it is.

But there is some good news, too. If the billboard battle went badly at the national level, states and localities have been making solid progress, according to Edward McMahon, executive director of the Coalition for Scenic Beauty, a Washington, D.C., lobby established in the early 1980s to carry forward the antibillboard work of the National Roadside Council. In Bob Myhr's native state of Washington, for example, the legislature of Kings County (Seattle and environs) has enacted a law requiring the removal of all billboards blocking views of Mount Rainier, Mount Baker, the Olympic Mountains, Puget Sound, lakes and rivers, and creates a "billboard-free zone within six hundred feet of all parks, historic sites, open space, and scenic resources." That pretty much covers most of the road miles in the Evergreen State. In Vermont, billboards along state highways have been replaced by tasteful signs describing commercal facilities. According to the coalition, a good many localities have also enacted stiff regulations recently. These include local jurisdictions in California, Colorado, Florida, Indiana, Massachusetts, Mississippi, New York, North Carolina, Pennsylvania, and Virginia.

Now here is where the scenic-road greenway strategy comes into play. Although the average citizen may find it difficult to notice the effects of this ground swell of reform, there are nevertheless some heartening evidences that the roads of ruin are being recognized for what they are: one of the most demoralizing features of all in God's own junkyard. Even the Federal Highway Administration has gotten into the fray. In 1988, the agency published a first-rate, citizen-oriented report called *Scenic Byways,* which provides a rationale, design standards, and financing techniques for establishing what might be called *scenic-road greenways—*

including how to tap into the FHWA's multibillion-dollar federal aid program. Significantly, the report focuses not only on what can be seen from the road but also on how the scenery can be permanently protected. Their recommendations include:

—Condemning a wider than normal right-of-way, in the case of new scenic byways.[1]

—Outright land acquisition within existing corridor areas for scenic and recreational purposes.

—Fee acquisition of land needing protection, with subsequent leaseback to adjacent owners.

—Acquisition of scenic or conservation easements or the placing of restrictive covenants in deeds.

—Local land-use zoning.

—State-level land-use restrictions along scenic corridors via special planning districts or other means.

The approach suggested here is much like that used for the Canopy Roads project in Tallahassee (profiled in Chapter 9). The idea is not simply to designate a scenic road but to build a greenway *around it,* using all the legal and financial tools that come to hand.

Encouraged by these quite-recent events, the Coalition for Scenic Beauty is solidly behind a 1989 congressional bill (H.R. 1087) to direct the Secretary of Transportation to "identify scenic and historic roads [throughout the United States] and to develop methods of designating, promoting, protecting, and enhancing [them] as scenic and historic roads." If the study is carried out, the key elements that scenic-road greenway-makers will want to look for are recommendations (including federal funding assistance) leading to the permanent protection of the scenic corridors. In this way, scenic-road greenways can begin to preclude the roads of ruin.

The strategic potential of such a policy derives quite directly from

---

1. Let us hope, however, that the interest of greenway-makers in scenic roads does not encourage the building of many more highways. As Aldo Leopold has written, "Recreational development is a job not of building roads into lovely country, but of building receptivity into the still unlovely human mind."

what might be called the Myhr Theory of Landscape Aesthetics—that aesthetic standards imposed in some places will produce a demand for similar aesthetic standards in other places. Certainly the theory operates in the negative. The reason is a kind of civic anomie born of demoralization: if there are twenty billboards, what's the matter with twenty-one? And if there are twenty-one billboards, what's the matter with commercial strip development? And if there is commercial strip development, what's all this business about preserving historic areas and scenic beauty? The befoulment feeds on itself until at last we have created America the ugly from sea to shining sea.

But what if there are no billboards, no golden-arch artifacts of strip development *at all,* along *this* road? Then, would we not wish for such an outcome elsewhere? If ugliness begets ugliness, perhaps beauty can beget beauty, inspired by a public will to make it actual. This is the Myhr Theory—by saving this stretch of shoreline from despoilment, we are emboldened to save another, and then another, until at last we reach some sort of parity with those roadside pornographers who so obscenely profit from turning God's country into God's junkyard.

History and scenery: unfortunately these seem to be such small issues in the welter of crises that face our nation that we sometimes forget how much they really count in our daily lives. If the greenway movement can help us get back a bit of honest natural beauty and our heritage of historic places, we shall owe it much.

8

Networks of Green

> *Town and country* must be married, *and out of this joyous union will spring a new hope, a new life, a new civilization.*
>
> —EBENEZER HOWARD

In the preceding chapters, I examined four of the five principal greenway project categories: the urban river greenways, which help humanize cities; the paths and trails, which provide people with access to the natural world and might, in time perhaps, lead to a greater understanding of the land ethic; the ecological corridors, which, in a landscape fragmented by modern development, can reconnect remnant wildlife habitats to maintain biological diversity and ecological balance; and the scenic drives and historic routes, which may help mitigate the demoralizing uglification of the American view-from-the-road and the destruction of our cultural landscape.

In a sense, the fifth category, local and regional greenway systems, with which this chapter deals, might simply be described as *all of the above.* I should emphasize, however, that the networks of green I refer to express an idea much more complex than connecting various kinds of greenways end to end, such as the attenuated linkage of rail-trail projects or even the linking of parks and cultural features such as the Brooklyn-Queens Greenway or the 40-Mile Loop in Portland, Oregon. For the greenway-makers committed to real networks of green, such linkage projects are only the beginning. What the networkers are interested in is nothing less than establishing a fully elaborated and ramified greenway infrastructure based primarily on regional landforms within a particular geographic area.

Networks such as these come about mostly in areas in which a good start on greenways has already been made and in which the natural lay of the land seems to demand expansion. In central North Carolina, for example, the Capital Area Greenway served as an effective model for a much more comprehensive regional effort to create a greenway network in the Research Triangle cities of Raleigh, Durham, and Chapel Hill along all major (and many minor) waterways, which are the dominant landform of the Carolina Piedmont. The network protects this large regional waterway system by superimposing a greenway framework upon it. But even in quite small areas such as the town of Redding, Connecticut, greenway infrastructure networks can be created. The Redding Greenbelts emerged as an outgrowth of a number of discrete trail projects. Based on regional ridge and valley geomorphology, the greenbelt corridors now constitute more than 50 percent of the land area of the town.

Most network programs tend to operate on a local or, most extensively, a substate regional level such as the interlocking greenways that connect the Front Range communities of Colorado or the linking of open spaces in the Hudson Valley in New York. In Maryland, however, an effort has been mounted to create a full-blown, integrated greenway network on a statewide basis. It is the first state to try to develop an elaborated greenway system based on the ecological and geological imperatives of the region of which it is a part. In this regard, Maryland's is a far more ambitious effort than a simple opportunistic aggregation of linear open spaces of various kinds.

Looking at a map, Maryland might seem like too much of a Duke's Mixture kind of a state for the establishment of a coherent greenway network to be possible. Baltimore is an East Coast-style "gritty city," though improved somewhat by the elegant Harborplace downtown with its shops and restaurants and promenades and the famous National Aquarium. Then, too, there are the Washington, D.C., suburbs and exurbs with their mansions, malls, and condos-in-the-cornfields. To the west, the Appalachian mountains; to the east the famed Eastern Shore; and in historic southern Maryland, an Old South tobacco economy still survives.

What this description excepts is the great geographic feature that the state of Maryland surrounds and that has organized its history, culture, and economy—the Chesapeake Bay. Beltways and interstates and heavily traveled highways of every description knit the commerce of the separate regions of the state together, of course. But a natural linear structure pulls it together, too: the rivers, and their tributaries, that run to the bay. This is to be the foundation for what may well be the most elaborate statewide greenway system plan in the country.

Luckily, Marylanders are not starting from scratch. Recently, and to their great delight, state officials realized that a greenway network along these rivers was already partially in place. Due to the foresight of many generations of state officials, most recently and most notably Torrey Brown, the present commissioner of the state's Department of Natural Resources, a large number of linear parks has been established along major rivers over the years, now totaling nearly eight hundred miles in length. This greenway network has been a-building, however unconsciously, since 1906. Much of it was acquired via the Capper-Crampton Act, which provided funds for the purchase of parklands in the national capital area. In recent years, riverside parkland has been acquired through Maryland's Program Open Space, a land preservation and recreational development fund financed through a real estate transfer tax. At this writing, the allocation is about $30 million for parks, recreation, and open space altogether, with a significant fraction to be applied to the greenway program. The approach the state legislature is considering would be a grant-in-aid program to encourage local governments and nonprofit groups to take the initiative in piecing a statewide system together, river by river, under a comprehensive set of state guidelines.

It was, in fact, a small stretch of river—a missing link in the system called the Patapsco Greenway—that led to a general understanding that there was, indeed, a system to begin with and that it related to the Chesapeake Bay as the state's dominant physiographic feature. By itself, the Patapsco project is unremarkable. The idea is to rehabilitate a twelve-mile-long degraded urban stretch of the river, where gravel mining had taken place for over a century, and thereby create a link between downtown Baltimore (and Harborplace) with Patapsco State Park upstream, making the crucial connection with the bay as well as with the state's greenway network as a whole. According to William A. Krebs, director of the Maryland's Program Open Space, the role of the Patapsco Greenway is emblematic, for it finally connects the largest urban population in the state with the vast natural greenway system accumulated over the years, which in turn provides the broadest possible constituency for acquiring and developing other missing links to provide public access to and through the entire network of rivers and tributaries flowing to the Chesapeake.

In an effort to move beyond the emblematic to the actual completion of a bay-oriented statewide greenway network, Maryland has retained the Conservation Fund to help develop a program for the comprehensive state system. According to Douglas Horne and Loring Schwarz, who lead the project, a team of experts will first inventory and map all existing publicly owned (or quasi-public) open space along natural corridors— primarily the stream and river valleys leading to the bay—to produce a fully articulated system of greenways to the bay. Then, the team will overlay a map of lands not in public ownership that have high resource value along these corridors, as well as lands that might be especially useful in elaborating the riparian greenways with overland linkages—utility rights-of-way, abandoned railroads and canals, and the like. The most significant linking features for the network are two federal projects, the Appalachian Trail, which traverses the headwaters of the streams that lead down into the Chesapeake, and the C & O Canal Park, paralleling the Potomac for nearly two hundred miles.

Perhaps the most valuable elements of the consulting project that Horne and Schwarz have been asked to undertake are the most tediously practical. The planners are to determine the best means, drawn from the arsenal of land protection techniques, to preserve the greenway corridors and then recommend development standards—trailway construction specifications, for example. All this information will be published in a technical manual that state and local officials, as well as citizen volunteers, can use to create a fully realized regional greenway network.

Such an ambitious-sounding program might seem suspiciously pie-in-the-sky had not earlier generations of land preservationists acquired a substantial fraction of the system, even though they had no sense that it *was* a system or that it would ever be called a *greenway network*. But, in this regard, Maryland may not be as unique as it seems. Indeed, Douglas Horne and Loring Schwarz believe that regional greenway systems throughout the United States can be created from seemingly unrelated greenway projects once a pattern is found and rationalized in the manner of Maryland's greenways-to-the-bay approach. They hope, along with Conservation Fund President Patrick Noonan—a member of the presidential Commission on Americans Outdoors, which had proposed greater use of greenways for outdoor recreation—that other states will look to Maryland as a model for regional systems based on natural landforms.

In fact, regional greenway networks—whether at the state, substate, or multistate level—would seem to be the next logical step for the greenway movement. Clearly, the authors of *Americans Outdoors* (the presidential commissions's 1987 report) intuited this next step with their proposal to "link together the rural and urban spaces in the American landscape." As might be expected in a report on outdoor recreation, the proposals for action were pretty much restatements or reaffirmations of ideas long on the agendas of recreationists. But the notion of linking urban and rural spaces stood out as something bold, new, and dramatic, especially for those unfamiliar with the larger implications of the greenway movement.

Today, great swaths of America's best rural resource lands, the vast majority in fact, lie within one or more urban fields—the extended magnetic circles of metropolitan influence which surround all major cities. So extended are they that some Chicago commuters on their way home from the Loop can almost catch a whiff of Iowa pig farms from across the Mississippi when they turn into their subdivision streets. In order to reach Washington, D.C., or Baltimore by starting time, cars back out of dark garages in West Virginia and drive through Maryland cornfields before the farmers have had their first cup of coffee. In California there are peo-

ple who buy tract houses in the Central Valley—where all the big vegeta-
ble producers operate—so they can afford a job in the San Francisco Bay
area, on the other side of the Coast Range. In effect, there has been an
interleaving of rural and urban land uses to a degree well beyond that
experienced in the leapfrog development of the 1960s and 1970s. This is
the phenomenon that the urban-rural greenway network concept—as
applied, for example, in the state of Maryland—implicitly acknowledges
and seeks to deal with.

From one point of view, the urban-rural linkage idea is downright
revolutionary, for in the United States of America it has been our policy
to try to *separate* the city from the country. New-town projects are meant
to soak up urban residential development before it leaks into rural landscapes. Agricultural land zoning is designed to stop urban encroachment
at some invisible border. Bond issues in wealthy communities are floated
to purchase land for parks and open space in an effort to retain an enclave
of pastoral ambience at any cost. Thus do the efforts to keep the city at
bay continue apace, but the interleaving goes on anyway.

In contrast, the impulse behind the greenway networks is to *integrate*
land uses rather than separate them—to *join* the urban and the rural into
a kind of normative American countryside—a land between the inner
city on one side and the unpopulated hinterlands on the other that is as
agreeable to farmers as it is to yuppies hanging out at the swimming pool
by the condo.

Doubtless, this vision relates to some sort of primal urge. The first
greenway network may have to be inaugurated a million and a half years
ago when a band of hominids hiked along a streamside—more or less
just for fun of it—which led them out of the Great Rift Valley of Africa
(whence the species arose a couple of million years before) and began the
colonization of the rest of the world. In such a manner may the concept
touch upon human instincts too deeply layered for us to understand.
Then again, the idea may not be as anthropological as all that but simply
a practical way to make the places where increasing numbers of us live—
an American countryside that is neither rural nor urban but a little of
both—legible, humane, and accessible.

The name of the enterprise we undertake to accomplish all these worthy goals is *regional planning*. And the most curious thing about regional planning in the United States of America is that we have so little of it compared with virtually every other civilized nation on the globe. I should not wish to argue that establishing greenway networks is equivalent to regional planning, but I would argue that they can be a forerunner to it, for as an infrastructure consciously created, greenways may have great power to help us envision effective regional-planning objectives. In the phrase of author Tony Hiss, what the urban-rural greenway infrastructure can create is "landscape connectedness." And connectedness has been the goal of regional planners for at least the past one hundred years.

According to Hiss, who wrote of these matters in the *New Yorker* magazine ("Encountering the Countryside," August 21 and August 28, 1988), the progenitor of the idea of linking city and country through regional planning was Benton MacKaye, who, taking his Appalachian Trail concept to the next logical step, proposed a greenway infrastructure (as I discussed in Chapter 1) of "dams" and "levees" that would contain the metropolitan flow created by highways. Writes Hiss, "MacKaye realized early in his life that landscape connections are often unwittingly severed by major technological innovations," especially motorways, but that "the countryside could rescue the cities" *if* urban and rural planning were integrated.

Oddly, this has never happened. America has developed educational systems, transportation systems, and we even seem to be on the verge of developing a health care system at long last. But comprehensive land-use planning on more than the most elementary level—mainly planning for zoning in towns and cities—seems to be beyond us. "It's my land," folks say, as if they were living alone on an island in the middle of the sea, "and no one is going to tell me what to do with it." As a result, the public values of a regional landscape become obliterated by the cumulative effect of self-interested private decisions. Whole ecosystems are rendered dysfunctional because development pollutes or silts up streams and rivers and decimates natural areas; ugliness prevails along the roadway; social disintegration is created by artificial separation of land uses. In a word, the lack of regional planning has produced a mess—"the mess that is manmade America," as one British planner puts it.

As I have said, regional greenway networks will not themselves clean up the mess. But the idea of establishing such an infrastructure might very well give us a new and less controversial approach to regional planning by providing a geophysical *framework* for it, which, unlike that of highways and high-tension lines, is the framework of the landscape itself. The aim, of course, is to produce a settlement pattern that Benton Mac-Kaye said would be adapted "to certain fundamental human desires." MacKaye assumed, as do we, that people desire ecosystems that work, beauty as opposed to ugliness, civic peace rather than civil strife. One day, perhaps, the networks of green can lead us there.

9

The World of Greenways:
Part II

MAD DOG MITCHELL AND DON HERNANDO'S
ARBOREAL ARCHWAYS

Canopy Roads Linear Parkway, Tallahassee, Florida

There is something about greenway-making which attracts un-conventional people—people whose imaginations are able to produce new approaches to making the places we live a lot more interesting and beautiful than they would otherwise be. Quite often, such people are outside the usual, Helen Hokinson run of preservers-of-place.

Take Chuck Mitchell, for example, ex-hippie (although not so *ex* as all that). A husky, athletic man, Mitchell and some counterculture friends from Florida State University decided fifteen years ago to build a group of houses cooperatively (i.e., do-it-yourself) after graduation and to stay in Tallahassee rather than return to hometowns or to graduate school (Mitchell was bound for Yale). Their approach was so unconventional that the city's building inspector started calling Mitchell and friends the "mad dog builders of Tallahassee." As it turned out, Mitchell got good at building houses and decided to go into it as a career. Hence, the Mad Dog Design and Construction Company—now a major contractor in north Florida.

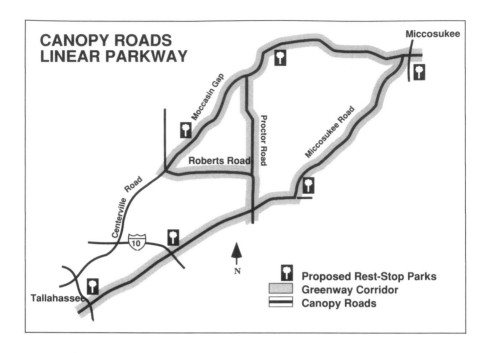

In 1988, Mitchell received an award from the National Park Service for discovering and preserving a major archeological site associated with Hernando de Soto (1499–1542) which had been spotted in the course of excavating for a development. Ordering the work stopped, Mitchell told the state archeologists to take all the time they needed to determine what might be down there. As it turned out, the time was well spent. What the archeologists discovered was nothing less than what appears to be the first European building site in the United States, dating to 1539. De Soto had stayed there for nearly five months, his first encampment on the brutal foray northward in search of gold.

As it happens, there is yet another connection between Mad Dog and Don Hernando. When not building or archeologizing, Mitchell works on a project of the Appalachee Land Conservancy to preserve Tallahassee's historic Canopy Roads, which de Soto doubtless used himself in exploring the region. The roads, which radiate outward from the city into the adjoining countryside, were the original routes used in pre-

Columbian times by various tribes of the Creek nation, including those whom de Soto had encountered. The roads were later taken over by the Spanish—who, following de Soto, settled permanently there—and after that, by the plantation owners. Some of the roads are still dirt surfaced and through centuries of use have sunk several yards below the grade of the surrounding fields. Huge live oaks line the roads and the spreading limbs, dripping with Spanish moss, create an arboreal archway—a green canopy over the ancient avenues. The roads are perfectly beautiful, yet, because they are narrow, without shoulders, and lined with a forbidding gauntlet of stout tree trunks, they are also unforgiving to motorists and deadly to bikers.

The transportation engineer's proposed solution to this problem—which was getting worse as Tallahassee's population increased—was to cut down the trees and widen the roads. But to Mad Dog Mitchell that idea was *truly* crazy. Reduce development on the roads, he and his colleagues urged, reduce the speed limit, establish alternate through-routes, and significantly acquire two hundred-foot right-of-way easements from the large landowners whose properties abut the Canopy Roads to provide for foot and bicycle trails. Such a tree-lined corridor would permanently protect the canopy as well as provide for recreation and non-polluting alternative transportation.

Working in concert with the Trust for Public Land, the Historic Tallahassee Preservation Board, the engineering firm of Post, Buckley, Schuh, and Jernigan, Inc., and sympathetic public agencies (the cast of characters is abundant), Mitchell and the conservancy got the Canopy Roads Preservation Plan adopted in principle by the Leon County Commission in February, 1988. The commission also established a Canopy Road coordinator, an executive position now held by Ed Deaton, a sociologist and refugee from California (although born in Florida), to implement an action program. Deaton has completed his own plan for preserving the Canopy Roads and is looking toward a referendum for a bond issue or special mil-rate tax assessment to acquire crucial rights-of-way and, in time, to develop them for recreational use.

One thing Mitchell, Deaton, and their colleagues have learned is that landowners may well be willing to provide a right-of-way to protect the canopy, but they are less inclined toward active recreational or community use of the corridors for off-road biking, hiking, and picnicking. Broward Davis, president of the Appalachee Land Conservancy, and a civil engineer, surveyor, and site planner with a large clientele, has been quite successful in seeing to it that the mandatory dedication of open space under the state's development-of-regional-impact regulations is devoted to the Canopy Road right-of-way. He has had no success so far, however, in inducing landowners to permit public access along the easemented strip voluntarily. Says Davis, "The canopy can be protected now. Development for recreational use we may well have to leave for another time."

Still, the canopy is going to be saved, with the descendants of de Soto's oaks looking much the same as their forebears did four and a half centuries ago. Whether active recreation becomes a part of it or not, Mad Dog Chuck Mitchell's Canopy Roads Linear Parkway program is a remarkable idea—building parks around a road rather than building highways through a park. Mad enough to be utterly sane.

MAKING THE CITY JUMP

Riverpark, Chattanooga, Tennessee

This story begins in 1815, when John Ross, otherwise known as Kooweskoowe, the blue-eyed, half-Scot chief of the Cherokees, built a landing on the Tennessee River to establish a center for trade for his people. Soon after, Ross's Landing was to become the city of Chattanooga. The trade increased, but like many cities built along rivers, Chattanooga turned its face away from its geographic and historic provenance, leaving the old buildings and storage yards and piers along the waterfront to dereliction and decay.

Doubtless Kooweskoowe would be pleased to know that his old landing, although never really forgotten, is today a focal point of a redevelopment project called Riverpark, whereby Chattanoogans hope to recapture their river heritage and give the city an economic shot in the arm in the process. Riverpark extends along a twenty-mile stretch of the

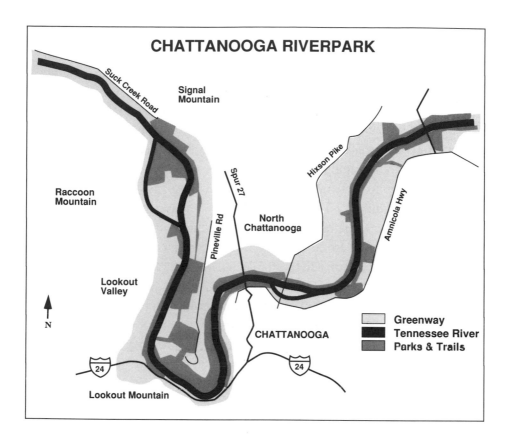

Tennessee River from the Tennessee Valley Authority's Chickamauga Dam to a place called *The Suck* in the Tennessee River gorge. At Ross's Landing, the epicenter of the project, the plan calls for a new hotel, office and apartment buildings, and, best of all, the $30 million Tennessee Aquarium. Seven stories high, it will be the only freshwater aquarium in the world, featuring what its publicists call "the unique freshwater system that flows out of the Appalachian mountain streams through the lakes and rivers of the Southeast."

Other features of the Riverpark plan include Riverwalk, a two-mile, $5 million linear park-and-trail system opened for use in mid-1989. River-walk is a part of a larger park-and-trail system called Riverway (there is a whole new language here) which, according to the master plan, would not only provide for recreation but also offer a means to "protect and improve the natural environment along the banks of the Tennessee River." Also planned is a new residential area called Heritage Landing, meant to complement the business development of the river. At Moccasin Bend, a huge "central park for the city" is planned with an archeological museum, amphitheater, Civil War museum, botanical garden, lake, tree-lined mall, marina, and golf course and with new housing and an office park adjoining. Elsewhere, there is to be a new industrial park called Riverport, intended to connect Chattanooga with every inland port on the Tennessee-Tombigbee, Ohio, and Mississippi River systems, generating $70 million in private investments and creating over one thousand new jobs. In the course of development of the port, the fifty-five-acre Amnicola Park will be established as a nature preserve and maintained by the Tennessee Wildlife Resources Agency. Beyond the city, the plan calls for a combination of new residential development and, where possible, the protection of the riverbanks in a natural state. Taken together, the redevelopment of the river is expected to generate the investment of an astonishing $750 million dollars in Chattanooga's future.

"Many cities develop daring dreams," says Jim Bowen, vice president of a corporation that serves as a kind of latter-day John Ross, "but few cities put in place an organization properly staffed and financed to help them accomplish the plans." The organization is the RiverCity Company. Once the master plan for Riverpark was completed, the RiverCity Company was, as proposed by the plan itself, created as a nonprofit corporation that would coordinate the redevelopment projects. It was given a $12 million nut to start with by eight local foundations and seven banks. The board of directors reflects, fifty-fifty, the public and private sectors. "Our purpose," says Bowen, "is to help city and county governments and the general citizenry accomplish high-quality development along the Tennessee River corridor and in downtown Chattanooga. We can hire professional assistance, buy land, make loans, and develop (as a last resource) to make this city jump.

"We've done things as varied [Bowen continues] as making a start-up loan for a local restaurant, guaranteeing private gifts toward the renovation of a local historic theater ($2.1 million), paying for design and pre-construction for a new park-and-trail system ($700,000), raising nearly $27 million in private gifts toward the construction of the Tennessee Aquarium, and loaning local governments $1.7 million toward the construction of the first phase of the Tennessee Riverpark."

Although many greenway projects on urban riverfronts attract new business, the mix of economic development and conservation is perhaps in a different proportion in Riverpark. As one Tennesseean has put it, "This greenway is supposed to make dollars, not cost them." Surely the thrifty Scottish chief of the Cherokees would have liked that idea plenty.

LA HISTOIRE DE LA PORTAGE DE CHECAGOU

The Illinois and Michigan Canal National Heritage Corridor, Chicago to La Salle, Illinois

That's what the French called it—at least part of it—*la portage de Checagou,* an overland carry from the Chicago River at the lower end of Lake Michigan to the Des Plaines River which, unlike the Chicago, did not run into the lake but westward, joining the Illinois River, which then flowed on to the Mississippi. *Sacrebleu!* Lugging those pelts and bateaux in the late-1600s, the early French trappers longed for a water route. But they were not the ones to build it, despite urgings to do so by Father Marquette and Louis Joliet in 1673.

Instead, the Illinois and Michigan Canal, one hundred miles long, would be dug, mainly by hand, by Irish laborers over a period of twelve years beginning in 1836. American industrialists of the Middle West financed the project; it was they, not the French *voyageurs,* who would make *Checagou* Chicago, hog butcher to the world, the city of broad shoulders. By 1848, the canal was complete, with fifteen deep locks of carefully fitted stone. The heavy barges could then move easily, hauled by mule and drover along a towpath that ran between the lake and a point beyond La Salle where the Illinois River became deep and broad on its own and turned south in a long gentle arc to meet the Mississippi north of St. Louis.

At last the boom was on. Warehouses and mansions sprouted in

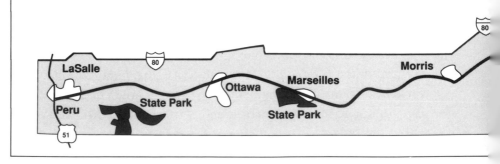

**THE I & M CANAL
NATIONAL HERITAGE CORRIDOR**

Lockport, which became the headquarters of the canal commission, whose members were recognized as the most powerful figures in Illinois in those days. On a hot August Saturday in 1858, in Ottawa, Illinois, another canal town, folks gathered from miles around to hear Senator

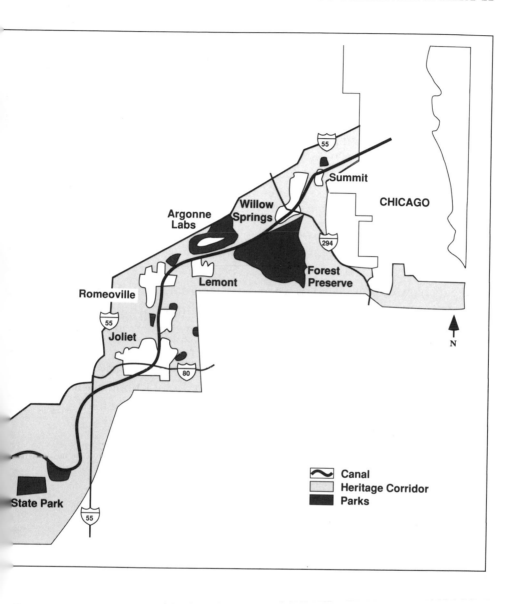

Douglas debate that funny-looking long drink of water from downstate. What was his name? Lincoln?

Yet the heyday of the Illinois and Michigan Canal was brief. After the Civil War, the new railroads mounted a serious challenge to the canal for freight business. Moreover, the waterway was decidedly preindustrial in design; with the cities booming in the latter half of the nineteenth century, a wider and deeper facility was needed. Accordingly, toward the end of the century, a new canal was dug, parallel to the I & M—the modern Chicago Sanitary and Ship Canal. Then in the 1930s, yet another canal was built—the Illinois Waterway. That did it. By 1933, the old I & M was closed for business, and the warehouses and mansions and old towns along it fell into a long period of decline. In the late 1930s, the CCC boys (Civilian Conservation Corps) adapted the towpath along the last sixty miles of the canal's length for limited recreational use, but the path was not maintained, and the locks fell into disrepair. There was no money for such frills in those Depression days. Then there was a war, and by the time it was over, the whole business was a pretty sorry mess. The most damaging blow came in the 1950s when the northernmost thirteen miles of the I & M were unceremoniously filled in to construct an expressway. Zoom zoom zoom went the traffic thoughtlessly over the wonderfully historic old canal.

Not a pretty story. But not the end of it. In 1963, an outfit called the Open Lands Project was organized in Chicago to do something about the accelerating rate of destruction of natural and historic sites in northern Illinois. After mounting several successful initiatives, the OLP remembered the old I & M Canal. After a lengthy and effective campaign, the project persuaded the state of Illinos to take over the rundown pathway the CCC had worked on—the sixty miles between Joliet and La Salle/Peru—and turn it into a state park. The new I & M Canal State Park was formally dedicated in 1974. It was a fine achievement but only a partial one. Actually, the OLP wanted the state to adopt the whole length of the canal, but park officials declared that the last twenty-five miles, from Joliet to Summit, at the edge of the city, were "too industrialized," just "too far gone" to do anything with.

One staff member of the OLP, however, did not buy that excuse—Gerald W. Adelmann. There were two reasons for his interest in the industrialized part of the canal. He was a trained historian (from Georgetown University) who, while working at the Smithsonian Institution in Washington, D.C., developed a keen appreciation of the fascinating artifacts of American industrial history. And he was a sixth-generation Lockporter, whose family memory encompassed the glory days of the old I & M. The canal was bred in the bone. After returning home from Washington, Adelmann joined the Open Lands Project and set about to restore the canal. "The problem," Adelmann told a reporter, "was how to make it all clear, and accessible, and linked together. . . . In all, it is a fascinating collection of historiana, spanning the whole of American technology—a huge open-air museum." Finally, in 1979, the OLP got the money together to undertake a detailed study of the industrialized stretch of the canal which had been ignored by the state. Adelmann's findings were striking, and together with the earlier information he developed while lobbying for the state park, they formed the basis of a series of articles about the canal in the *Chicago Tribune*. Score one for the Fourth Estate. The articles were instrumental in Senator Charles Percy's decision to introduce a bill in the U.S. Congress directing the National Park Service to study the entire length of the canal as a possible candidate for national park status.

The NPS study, completed in 1981, turned up some thirty-nine significant natural areas—glacial sloughs, virgin prairies, lakes, parks (including eleven state parks) and old woods—as well as over two hundred bona fide historic sites, ranging from Indian burial mounds to the Reddick Mansion in Ottawa where Lincoln and Douglas held their debate. Obviously, the canal corridor was a national treasure but hardly a typical national park. Much of the land was in private ownership and had great economic value to the region. Moreover, there were already state and local parks all along the length of the canal, albeit somewhat discontinuously. Clearly, a new approach had to be developed.

The new approach that Adelmann, the National Park Service, state and local officials, and business leaders came up with was to make the corridor a national park without having the Park Service own any of the land. It would be a national heritage corridor instead, locally administered, the first of its kind. Moreover, unlike most parks, this one had an economic as well as a preservation objective: to improve the climate, throughout the length of the corridor, for economic growth and development. For this reason, the project not only had the support of the usual conservation organizations but also of Chicago's heaviest hitters on the business and industry side. Stated Edmund Thornton, a former chairman of the Illinois Manufacturer's Association, "The I & M Canal settled the upper Midwest with industry and commerce. Industry and commerce should be proud of its heritage in the valley and should support efforts to preserve it."

The combination of environmental and business support proved irresistible to Congress. In 1984, a bill creating the Illinois and Michigan Canal National Heritage Corridor was enacted which encompassed a historic area 5 to 20 miles wide and 120 miles long. The legislation created a canal commission (although only a pale shadow of the original, of course) to coordinate conservation and development projects throughout the corridor. The commission was allocated an administrative budget of $250,000 annually but no capital budget.

Actually, the major player in advancing the natural and historic preservation of the canal is the same individual and the same organization that started it all—Gerald Adelmann and the Open Lands Project. Adelmann, who had resigned from the OLP to work exclusively on the I & M, rejoined Open Lands as executive director but remains as director of the Upper Illinois Valley Association, an offshoot of Open Lands set up in 1982 to promote the canal. Through research, publications, and fund-raising efforts, the association advances a long-range plan for the corridor: to create a continuous trailway, to preserve historic sites and natural areas, to figure out adaptive reuses for industrial properties, and to attract new commerce and industry to the corridor area.

It will take a while to restore the old I & M to its former glory—perhaps even longer than it took to dig it in the first place. But project by project, mile by mile, the dream is coming to pass for a renewed canal that pays off on the *voyageur* dream of a *portage de Checagou* in ways that even Father Marquette might think a miracle.

CIVIC PRIDE FROM GAP TO GAP

The Yakima Greenway, Yakima, Washington

Out where the hot basin and range country begins in central Washington State, there is Yakima, the "apple capital of the world," the boosters call it. It is a small, tidy, county seat town that is not without some serious economic and social problems. One of these is the community's dependence on agriculture with its associated boom-and-bust economic cycles. Another is more specific—endemic poverty and social anomie afflicting a large group of migrant agricultural laborers who, having followed the ripening crops northward, have simply stayed on in Yakima instead of returning south again. During the worst of times in the early 1980s, overall unemployment reached 22 percent because of these factors.

It is towns like Yakima (population, about 80,000 in the city and outlying areas) that professionals, young people, and the upwardly mobile usually want to leave. "Who needs this place?" they might ask—a small city beset with unemployment stemming from both agricultural and urban problems, a community isolated in the semidesert far from the bright lights and good jobs of Seattle-Tacoma 150 miles to the west. And yet, somehow, sanguinity prevails in this place, despite the isolation from the coastal metropolises. There are surely many reasons for this, but one of them, locally acknowledged, is the magnetic effect of the Yakima Greenway, no less, and of Yakima's remarkable Gap-to-Gap Relay, as joyous a civic enterprise as any in the state of Washington.

The Yakima River rises in the nearby Cascades, gathering a substantial flow from spring rains and snowmelt, and then descends southeastward into the arid landscapes of central Washington. Just north of Yakima, the river passes through a low, basaltic ridge called Selah Gap, south of which lies a broad agricultural valley where the abundant waters are used to irrigate orchards of apples and cherries, grape vineyards, and hop farms where the vines grow on tall *A*-shaped supports.

Below Selah Gap, the river skirts the city and then opens up, alternately braiding into separate channels, then rejoining, then braiding again in a lush natural corridor that has retained much of its pristine

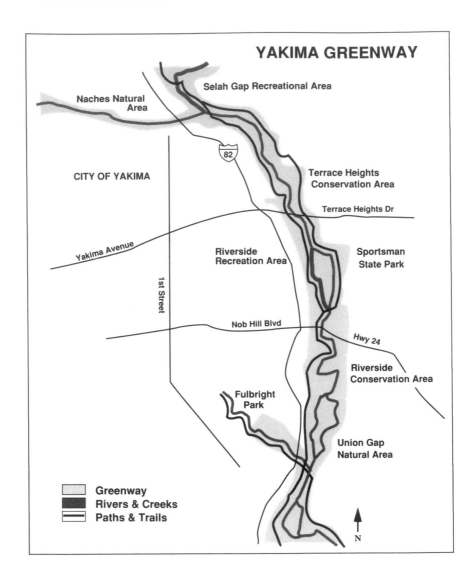

beauty despite the refuse dumps, gravel pits, materials storage yards, and cloverleaf interchanges for I-82, the interstate highway that parallels the river's course. South of the city the river makes an exit from the area in much the same way as it entered, at another cleft in another low basaltic ridge, this one called Union Gap. It is the stretch between the gaps, ten miles, which has become the Yakima Greenway.

Although now well known as a successful example of greenway-making, the project very nearly failed in its early years despite what appeared to be auspicious beginnings in the Washington state legislature. After piecemeal efforts to protect the riverway, beginning in 1949, state lawmakers, led by Yakima's Jim Whiteside, finally appropriated funds in 1975 for a study of the corridor between the two gaps with an eye to creating a greenway under state auspices. The Seattle design firm of Jones and Jones was retained, and by 1976 it had produced a greenway master plan featuring the preservation of wide strips of land along both sides of the river, a series of recreational and natural parks, and a continuous hiking and biking trail. A year later, Whiteside introduced a bill to create the Washington State Yakima River Conservation Area and assigned various state agencies to carry out the plan.

At last things were moving. Conservationists were heartened by the state's interest. But the idea of state-level control infuriated local developers and landowners for reasons all too familiar to river-savers. As it turned out, the developers prevailed, managing to convince the legislators to make the Yakima County commissioners responsible for implementing the conservation area plan. The developers were well aware that actions by locally elected commissioners could more easily be influenced than those of state bureaucrats far away over the mountains in Olympia. But the greenway opponents need not have worried. The county commissioners were facing other pressing priorities, and the plan was to be relegated to obscurity anyway. And so, after thirty years of effort, the last four of which had been intense, the Yakima Greenway had gotten exactly nowhere.

Then, in May, 1979, those who remained interested in the greenway plan called a what-shall-we-do meeting of city officials, county and state agencies, and conservation groups. The conferees quickly came to the conclusion that the Yakima County commissioners should appoint an official task force to investigate whether the Jones and Jones plan could *ever* be carried out. The commissioners were pleased to comply; a task force was appointed, drawn from the what-shall-we-do conferees. Meetings began in late 1979 and continued into 1980.

During this period, as options were being reviewed, a pivotal event

for the greenway came to pass: a visit from Joel Kuperberg, a highly re-
spected land conservationist and vice president of the Trust for Public
Land, headquartered in San Francisco. Kuperberg made a simple, and in
many ways, bold suggestion. Although many citizen-led conservation
groups yearn to "go public"—toward governmental auspices—
assuming that this is where official clout and cash money are to be had,
Kuperberg recommended just the opposite. Take the project "private,"
he said. The task force, conscious of past inaction, was quickly convinced
that Kuperberg was on the right track, and in March, 1980, the task force
recommended to the county commissioners that a private nonprofit
foundation be formed. The commissioners agreed, and within a month,
the Yakima River Regional Greenway Foundation was created to take on
the operational responsibility for carrying out the Jones and Jones greenway plan. It was this move, according to one of the foundation's incor-
porators and its current president, Dick Anderwald, that broke the log-
jam that had frustrated the implementation of the plan for so many years.

Anderwald, whose daytime job is as planning director for Yakima
County, is not one of those ideologically opposed to government sponsorship in land conservation. But a number of factors had become clear
to him and his associates. One was that government auspices had not
(and probably would not) result in a substantial amount of government
money for the project. Another was that popular local support was
needed to make the greenway a reality—the dimes and dollars from individuals, the contributions from businesses, and the grants from foundations. Clearly, it would seem contradictory to some for a government
agency, which used the taxing power to support its programs, to request
additional voluntary support for a special project.

Yet another factor in the decision to go private was that landowners
along the greenway—some of them philanthropically inclined—were
extremely chary of working with a government agency, whether state *or*
local. A citizen-led foundation, Anderwald and his colleagues decided,
could raise money, not suspicions.

Scarcely was the ink dry on the foundation's articles of incorporation
then the first gift of land, a twenty-acre parcel, was presented to the
greenway project. A few weeks later, a $5,000 donation was pledged by

the Kiwanis Club. A few months after that, a key thirty-one-acre parcel was offered on a bargain sale basis—at a price much reduced from appraised value. The following year, a landowner meeting was held at Bob Hall's Sunfair Chevrolet dealership (Hall is now the owner of the multiline Greenway Auto Plaza) where additional land gifts and bargain sales were sought. A few months later, the first major public fund-raising event was held, by the Greenway Tank Club, which suggested that citizens ride their bikes for a week and donate the cost of the tankful of gasoline they had saved. It was, observed the organizers, a way of saying *tanks* to the greenway.

What had happened? Suddenly, as one greenway leader put it, "the idea of a greenway had become something visible and joinable."

Although momentum to implement the Jones and Jones greenway plan was clearly well established in 1981, the first flush of success could not be sustained. Still, negotiations with landowners went forward. More fund-raising events were held—float trips, T-shirt sales—to raise money for land purchase and development. Then, in 1983, the local Pepsi Cola bottler donated funds for construction of the first pathway segment, an event that set off another flurry of activity. Within two months time, $450,000 had been raised from community sources ranging from $1 to $50,000 via a fund drive under the direction of the ever-faithful Jim Whiteside who had left the state legislature and become a county commissioner.

Following up on the idea suggested by the Pepsi donation, the foundation began working with various organizations and agencies to sponsor other segments of the greenway. The state government introduced plans to expand Sportsman's Park, a recreational facility in the central part of the greenway. The Kiwanis Club announced it would like to build Sherman Park at the southern end of the pathway, whereupon the Audubon Society kicked in $1,000 for a picnic shelter, and the Cub Scouts built picnic tables. At the end of 1983, the city gave the foundation permission to begin work on the Sarg Hubbard Riverside Park, a key recreation area to be built atop the former city dump. The state sent a check for $135,000 for development, and St. Elizabeth Health Foundation, along with the Wells Fargo Bank, gave $7,500 for a fitness trail to be constructed. The city donated masonry panels formerly used for bus kiosks which they reassembled to create handsome restrooms. Work-release prison inmates raked glass and tin cans out of regraded areas. And that is how the Yakima Greenway was made, foot by foot, acre by acre, park by park, dollar by dollar, and is still being made at this writing.

As a way to celebrate this remarkable civic achievement as well as to raise the wherewithal to continue the work, the foundation inaugurated what is now known throughout the West as the Yakima Greenway Gap-to-Gap Relay. The event was first held in 1985 with thirty-three teams. By 1989 there were 175 teams—the Gas Passers, for example, or Fudd's Crew, or Terrible Tim and the Turtles. The teams bike, paddle, and run over a killing forty-mile course up and down the greenway corridor. The winner gets first prize. The greenway gets land, money, and public support in greater measure than anyone thought possible in those dark days before Joel Kuperberg showed up with his suggestion they take the project private. Paradoxically, the result is a more *public* project than any government agency could conceivably have brought off. From a standing start, the foundation—which is to say the people of Yakima—has been instrumental in the preservation of 3,600 acres of land along the river and the construction of many miles of trails.

What does the presence of the greenway do for the self-esteem of the residents of Yakima? Perhaps no one can answer that question better than Dick Anderwald. A planner with a national reputation, Anderwald could have his pick of jobs almost anywhere, including his native Seattle—now so highly touted as the place to be on the Pacific rim. But when a visitor once asked him if Seattle didn't now beckon or if living in a small city didn't pall after a while, Anderwald was nonplussed. "Why, I couldn't get my wife and children to move away from here for anything," he said. "The greenway is not just something I work on; it's a terrific benefit for everyone who lives here, including us. We just love it. We're staying."

CONNECTIONS: REGIONAL PLANNING AND THE USES OF TRAILS

The Bay and Ridge Trails, San Francisco Bay Area, California

"The only time we really get to see the bay," says Susan Phillips, "is when we cross the bridges."

"The suburban office boom and sprawl in our rural areas," says Judith Kunofsky, "is robbing the bay area of its countryside."

No wonder. During the 1980s, the rate of population growth in the San Francisco metropolitan area increased as fast, or faster, than in any of the large urban regions of the United States (with the possible exception of Houston in its pre–oil glut period). New development seemed to be enfolding the bay, while at the same time spreading outward in a relentless march of shopping malls, suburban kitch office buildings, and *ticky-tacky,* a descriptive term that, as a matter of fact, originated in the San Francisco suburbs, courtesy of songwriter Malvina Reynolds.

Over the past quarter-century the bay area's leaders have tried any number of regional-planning approaches to control this runaway growth of what one local columnist calls "Baghdad on the Bay." The trouble is, there is more than one Baghdad. Indeed, there are scores of jurisdictions in the nine counties of the bay area, all jealous of their prerogatives and all eager for a larger slice of the economic pie. Historically, they have had some difficulty thinking as one political unit, and, as a result, uncoordinated growth appeared with a vengeance as early as the mid-1950s. Appalled at the loss of bay shoreline—sometimes through landfills of the bay itself—to industrial and residential development in the competing cities, bay area citizen leaders in the mid-1960s finally managed, through state legislation, to create the Bay Conservation and Development Commission (BCDC) to control the filling-in of the bay's wetlands for building sites. At the same time, the Association of Bay Area Governments (ABAG) was organized to promote cooperative planning among the cities of the region.

Meanwhile, People for Open Space, a civic organization founded in 1958 by the late Dorothy Erskine, a woman of indomitable public spirit

THE BAY AND RIDGE TRAILS

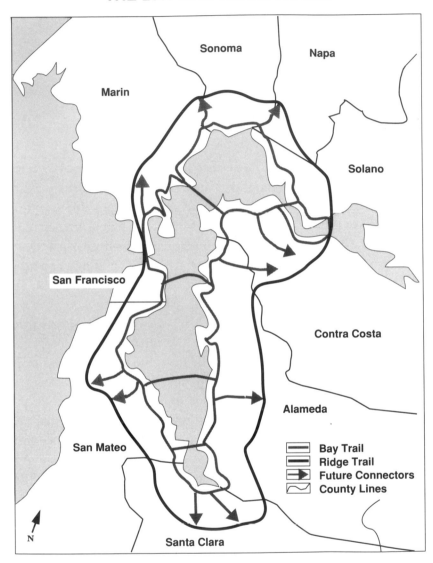

and drive, sought to protect the region's metropolitan countryside. The idea was to limit development within a de facto greenbelt surrounding the metropolitan area, a 3.8 million-acre girdle of parks, watershed lands, farms, rural estates, and ranches. The approach was modeled on the London Green Belt which had been established in 1938 and greatly expanded after the war. If such lands remained unexploited by the real estate boom in the bay area, the greenbelt could, at once, confine development to places already urbanized and provide authentic rural landscapes within striking distance of every bay area resident.

In yet another effort to mitigate the urbanization of the bay area, citizens urged the federal government to establish the Golden Gate National Recreation Area (GGNRA), a unit of the national park system which took over a number of large tracts of surplus military land around the bay, adapting them to recreational use rather than allowing them to be sold off and developed.

These were valiant and important efforts—the BCDC-ABAG planning, the POS greenbelt, the GGNRA's aggregation of parks—and not without effect. Less bayshore was filled, more rural open space was saved, increased recreational opportunities were provided. Yet these regional land-saving concepts did not, in themselves, provide as much public focus on the conservation of the region's natural resources and the impulse to cooperative action to protect them as their proponents might have hoped. During the 1980s, just as in the 1950s, 1960s, and 1970s, the steamroller of growth and development, fueled by a burgeoning population, lumbered on, from bayshore to highland.

Then, in 1987, two new ideas emerged with a potential to help change traditional popular and official attitudes about regional planning and land conservation. They were the Bay Trail, a program established by the state legislature to be carried out by the Association of Bay Area Governments, and the Ridge Trail, a cooperative effort spearheaded by the National Park Service and People for Open Space (since renamed the Greenbelt Alliance). Where once regionwide planning, so coolly rational and sensible, had a kind of lulling quality for the populace, the idea of a *trail,* of personal *access* to the bayside and to rural open space, seemed decidedly energizing. As it happened, the two trail ideas were floated within months of one another; in both cases, almost immediately after their announcements, local governments, civic organizations, and conservation groups signed on as cooperators and demanded action.

The Bay Trail program, established by a bill introduced by California state legislator Bill Lockyer (of Hayward, an East Bay city), directs the Association of Bay Area Governments to develop a plan and an implementation program for "a continuous recreational corridor that will extend around the perimeter of San Francisco and San Pablo Bays." A new idea? Well, yes and no. According to Susan Phillips, the ABAG executive in charge of getting the program started, the trail "has been a dream for a long time in the bay area" but never really thought to be possible. Heretofore, says Phillips, "the bay shoreline had been a place for landfills, factories, port facilities. But as communities have grown, they have begun to understand that the bayshore is an important focus in the lives of their residents, giving them a sense of place, and has high potential for recreational use."

Although the Bay Trail program was initiated by state legislation, the planning effort is really community based. Trail alignments have been designed by local residents at the ground level, not just by planners looking at a map. After many months of intensive effort, orchestrated by Phillips, the citizen inventory and alignment suggestions were recorded, and ABAG cartographers mapped the resultant trailway system. It turned out to be four hundred miles long—an assemblage of hardened bicycle trails, naturally surfaced footpaths, even boardwalks in marshy areas. Phillips estimates the eventual cost might run from $22 million to $33 million, to be funded by a variety of means—primarily local recreation budgets, augmented by proceeds from regional and state-level open-space bond issues, private donations, and some bicycle-path money from federal highway grants.

Although the estimate of cost may have caused some municipal officials around the bay to swallow hard, no one has really backed away from the concept. Officials know the Bay Trail is a good and vital idea and that with citizen support and enthusiasm it will eventually come into being. Lockyer says he will give the various governments some time to see how they do on their own. If it's too slow, he says he might introduce a bond-issue bill to finance part of the program. "We're hoping," Lockyer told the *San Francisco Chronicle* in 1989, "that a great deal of the trail system will be in place within the next ten years."

Meanwhile, out in the countryside, the Greenbelt Alliance saw the possibility of the beginnings of another circumferential route, this one along the ridge lines of the hills surrounding the bay. When William Penn Mott, then director of the National Park Service, was told about the idea, he exulted, saying that he too had been having such thoughts, indeed had considered the possibility of a ridge trail when he was director of the vast East Bay regional park system during the 1960s and 1970s. And so, the Ridge Trail was born. A good idea has many parents. And this was a good idea.

According to Kunofsky, scores of citizen groups, municipal agencies, and others attended an organizing meeting in November, 1987, formally constituting themselves as the Bay Area Ridge Trail Council. With the help of the Golden Gate National Recreation Area staff (of the National Park Service), the Ridge Trail organizers soon engaged volunteers to work out an alignment. Says Marti Leicester, an NPS staff member, "When the Greenbelt Alliance showed us how much of a necklace of green was already in place, we knew we had to go for it." Substantial parcels of ridgeline open space already existed in public ownership courtesy of the GGNRA, the Marin County Open Space District, the Greater Vallejo Recreation and Park District, the East Bay Regional Park District (Mott's old outfit), various California state parks, the Midpeninsula Regional Open Space District, and county parks in Santa Clara and San Mateo.

The principal trail-planning criteria developed by the Greenbelt Alliance, the park services, and others were that the trail route should (1) be located as close as possible to the highest ridgeline with a view of the bay and also be within an hour's drive from bay area cities; (2) traverse public open-space and watershed land to the fullest extent possible, minimizing the necessity to acquire easements across private property; and (3) provide links to existing and proposed trails systems. The general alignment—like the Bay Trail it amounted to roughly four hundred miles— took nine months to establish after extensive mapping, field research, and local debate. Then, the Ridge Trail Council began working with various municipalities to help them complete sections through their jurisdictions. Funding for the work would be borne by local governments along with grants from the various open-space bond issues and other sources. The trail council is hoping to establish an adopt-a-trail fund to encourage private subscription. Says Kunofsky: "Our goal is to complete all the segments of the trail across public lands in five years."

But there is more to this story than simply a trail. In fact, the very idea of this green*way* suddenly made the idea of the green*belt* much clearer to both officials and the civic leadership. The reason was that all the promotional activities aimed at getting people out into the landscape via walks, rides, trail days, and the like made vivid and urgent the need to protect the larger greenbelt. Says Greenbelt Alliance Executive Director Larry Orman, "Without actual or experiential access to land that is to be protected, it's hard to get people involved—which is why we expect the trail to sell the greenbelt to the people of the region." If he is right, the Ridge Trail project may be instrumental in producing the first London-style greenbelt in the United States.

To a lesser extent but no less valid, the Bay Trail is also expected to generate a greater public understanding of the bayshore's ecological and aesthetic function as a result of improved public access to it. What is more, the Bay Trail people and the Ridge Trail people agree that there should be interconnections—*spokes,* some call them, or *laterals,* located along stream valleys—between the two circumferential trails. Thus, taken together, the two trails and their spokes and laterals may well bring a sense of regional identity to the people of the San Francisco Bay area which no amount of abstract regional-planning theory could provide. Access and linkage are the keys. As Larry Orman puts it, "To the ordinary citizen, these linkages mean, 'I'm connnected.' " And when that happens, true regional planning has begun.

A historic church on Boston's Bay Circuit.

Canopy Roads Linear Parkway in Tallahassee (below) got its start even before Hernando de Soto moved his troops along these oak-lined routes 450 years ago. First built by Creek Indians, the roads are now historic greenway corridors that serve a growing population in this north Florida city. The Brooklyn-Queens Greenway—located in America's largest city, New York—connects 40 miles of parks and parkways that were designed by Frederick Law Olmsted in the nineteenth century and Robert Moses in the twentieth. The concept of planner Tom Fox (shown with his son on Olmsted's Ocean Parkway, bottom right), the B-QG links museums (such as the Brooklyn Museum, lower right) with public open spaces and historic areas from Fort Totten on Long Island Sound to Coney Island on the Atlantic shore. Chattanooga's new Riverpark is equally historic. Shown at right is a scene near Ross's Landing on the Tennessee River, the place where the city was founded by John Ross—otherwise known as Kooweskoowe—the half-Scot chief of the Cherokees.

32

33

34

35

36

Three photographs (top and right) show the range of benefits from Denver's pioneering Platte River Greenway. Even within the city limits, a jogger (top) passes by a beaver dam in a pristine stretch of riverway. Confluence Park (top right), where Cherry Creek enters the Platte, is the scene of city-wide concerts and cultural events. These days, the Platte River, once so polluted that citizens avoided it, can even provide "urban whitewater" for pro and tyro alike (below right). Another urban river, the Yakima, which passes through Yakima, Washington, is now the venue for the famous "Gap-to-Gap Relay" (above), in which contestants from all over the West race for 40 grueling miles up and down the course of the river afoot, by bike, and in kayaks. The event has sparked community pride beyond its sponsors' most optimistic projections.

37

38

39

40

In the San Francisco Bay area, two circumferential greenways will, when completed, provide a regional planning framework for one of America's most rapidly growing urban regions. Along the Bay Trail, Pinole Point (upper left) was acquired from a developer to provide a crucial trail link. Further along, Point Wilson (lower right) affords nearby residents dramatic views of the bay. The Ridge Trail (upper right and lower left) traverses the region's uplands. Each trail is approximately 400 miles long. In time lateral greenways located along stream valleys will connect the ridges with the bay.

41

43

Fishing along the Illinois and Michigan Canal, Illinois.

THE OUTER NECKLACE—
AN IDEA THAT REFUSES TO DIE

The Bay Circuit, Duxbury to Newbury, Massachusetts

Charles Eliot, Jr., son of Harvard's president and a young landscape architect in Frederick Law Olmsted's firm, headquartered in Brookline, Massachusetts, has just completed working on some details of Olmsted's plan for a linked series of parks around the city, but Boston's civic leaders have scoffed at it. Too visionary, they say. Too expensive, too. Why must we have parks so far into the country? Let's have parks where the people are, they say. The year is 1887. In time, Olmsted's linked parks will become known as Boston's famed Emerald Necklace, the proto-greenway that now encircles the inner city with most of the metropolitan area stretching out beyond it.

Young Eliot was struck with the concept of a necklace of parks, and it wasn't long before he had an even more ambitious idea than Olmsted's. Why not, urged Charles in 1890, create a board of trustees to acquire a garland of large park reserves much further out, so that people from the city could get into the *real* country. This idea led to the formation of the Trustees of Public Reservations and later, a metropolitan parks commission and the first metropolitan system of parks in the United States. Unfortunately, Eliot died (in 1897, at the age of 37) before his idea for a vast system of linked reserves encircling the entire Boston Bay region could be fully implemented. But as the new century unfolded, it was finally understood how visionary the plan for an outer ring of reserves really was.

At length, in mid-1929, the idea of an interconnected outer necklace had an opportunity to be proposed in a quite specific form, as a Massachusetts bay circuit, which was recommended by a special gubernatorial commission on the needs and uses of open spaces. (The commission included regional planner Benton MacKaye and young Charles Eliot II, nephew of Charles, Jr.) The circuit was to provide the connected string of parks (one version of the plan also proposed a motor route) that Charles, Jr., had envisioned. The plan could provide a means for people

THE BAY CIRCUIT

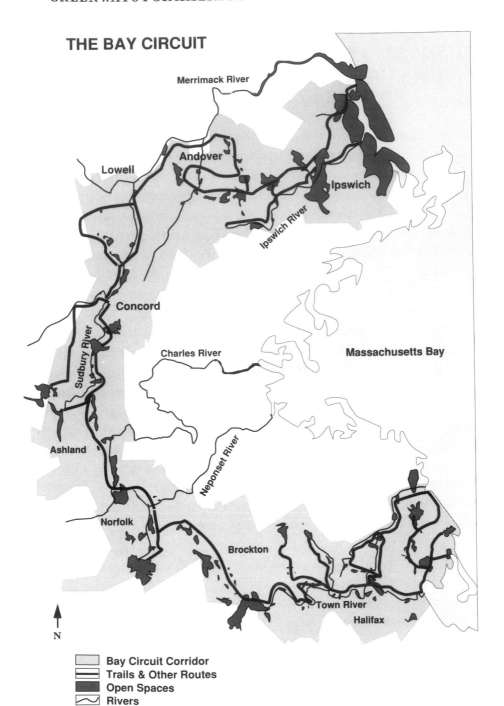

Merrimack River

Lowell
Andover
Ipswich
Ipswich River

Concord

Charles River

Massachusetts Bay

Sudbury River

Ashland

Neponset River

Norfolk
Brockton

Town River
Halifax

N

Bay Circuit Corridor
Trails & Other Routes
Open Spaces
Rivers

to explore and enjoy rural areas that were ten or twenty miles from the city, not two or three, as were most of Boston's existing natural parks, including those in Olmsted's Emerald Necklace. But the timing for this proposal was exquisitely unadventitious. In October of that same year, the New York stock market crashed, with devastating economic shock waves instantly felt in Boston, the nation's first (and a still-) dominant financial center. It was an event that not only pauperized investors but eclipsed civic projects as well. One of the victims was the Bay Circuit.

Then, in 1937, at a moment when the Great Depression was easing a bit, the Bay Circuit idea was revived again, this time directly by the Massachusetts Trustees of Public Reservations, the nongovernmental body created by the Massachusetts legislature in 1891, at the urging of Charles Eliot, Jr., to preserve regional landscape parks. Like one of the versions of the 1929 plan, the trustees' 1937 plan also called for a motor route through the circuit, although automotive transportation was not really its focus. The primary idea was to establish nonmotorized connecting lanes (for walking, horseback riding, or bicycling) and canoe routes that would link all major open-space areas and historic features around the circuit—the state forests, the trustees' own nature sanctuaries, and sites such as Walden Pond.

Like the 1929 plan, this new iteration of the Bay Circuit idea was to be a faithful replica, writ large, of the Emerald Necklace concept but not so costly, in relative terms, either to acquire or develop. Some new parks were proposed, but the connecting lanes would require minimal acreage, and the canoe routes were free. Since these were mainly natural areas, development would be unprepossessing, mainly a matter of pathways. It was, in fact, a splendid plan, building on the work of the 1929 open-space commission as well as doing full honors to Charles Eliot, Jr., and his mentor, *Mr. O.,* as Eliot called the great park-maker whose aesthetic theories the plan so well expressed.

Yet despite the trustees' valiant effort to make the idea interesting to the residents of Boston and its close-in suburbs, this plan, too, failed to be implemented. Soon enough, there was a war on, and no further thought to parks and recreation could be given. Then came the period of postwar readjustment and then a suburban housing boom that sent the edges of the metropolis rippling outward to and even beyond the old Bay Circuit corridor. Almost twenty years were to pass before the idea was taken up again. But it had remained very much alive in the mind of Charles Eliot II.

With the arrival of postwar affluence, it seemed to Eliot II that it was time yet again to dust off the old plan. According to Paige Mercer, who has written a detailed, unpublished paper on the history of the Bay Circuit project, the 55-year-old Eliot had been appointed a professor of landscape architecture at Harvard in 1954, and a year later he got his class to map the old Bay Circuit. A year after that he agitated for a Bay Circuit greenbelt act that would expand on the 1937 plan.

In 1956, Governor Christian Herter did in fact sign into law a program that was intended to connect all the public and quasi-public open spaces of the circuit but only by means of a tourist route along existing roads rather than through the purposeful acquisition of open-space linkages. Indeed, the statute was so vague and unspecific that from today's vantage point it seems less of an honest program than a sop to conservationists' demands. No money was appropriated, no new powers conferred. Under the law, some signs saying *Bay Circuit* were erected (a few still survive), and that was it. The only circuits around the city, it would appear, would be strictly automotive—Route 128 (which would become I-95) and later another circumferential interstate, I-495, built farther out. The two superhighways bracketed the unrealized Bay Circuit corridor between them in a slumgullion of suburban development.

Still, the idea would not stay dead. In 1983, a planner in the state's Department of Environmental Management saw a way to correct the shabby treatment the Bay Circuit idea had suffered for so long. Using the old Christian Herter program as a legal basis—for the act had never been repealed—the planner, Bob Yaro, cannily slipped a Bay Circuit title into a 1984 state bond authorization for environmental projects. And so it was that the Bay Circuit concept finally got funded, and Yaro has since become quite well known (he is now at the Regional Plan Association in New York City) for creative solutions (as was this one) to difficult regional-planning problems. The Bay Circuit appropriation wasn't much—$3.25 million—but it brought the concept, that old Lazarus of an idea, back to life once again.

According to Susan Ziegler, the present administrator of the Bay Circuit project, there was, at the outset, confusion as to whether the Bay Circuit was to be simply a broad band of open, rural land, ten to twenty miles in width, given planning recognition but no specific program for creating, or something more concrete such as the 1937 Trustees of Reservations trail-and-canoe route linkage concept. After discussion, the latter approach was chosen at the urging of Charles Eliot II. Comprehensive goals and objectives were developed, which Ziegler boils down to this formula: "a network of parks and open spaces that are connected by various roads, trails, and waterways and with various points of interest featured along the way."

The trouble was, $3.25 million was not much of a budget, given 1980s land prices, to acquire the connectors. Accordingly, Ziegler and a staff of three put a great deal of emphasis on cooperative projects. They started working with the fifty towns on the circuit, contacting their boards and councils and civic groups, and parceled out its budget in small grants in an effort to get localities to give open-space preservation priority to the all-important linkages. Such grants were made to twenty-eight communities to implement the Bay Circuit plan locally. Additionally, a major new state park was acquired, plus four regional linkage areas. Despite these efforts to make the money go as far as possible, in less than two years the initial program funding was substantially committed. Ziegler and her staff were counting on a 1987 environmental bond issue to provide additional support to continue the work. As it turned out, the bond issue passed, but the Bay Circuit program did not share in it. A powerful legislator, representing an urban district, said he didn't see how the circuit could benefit city people. Parks ought to be where the people are. Echoes of the objections to the original Emerald Necklace were heard.

There was more bad news. In the following year, severe financial problems beset the state of Massachusetts, leading to a Bay Circuit staff cut, leaving only Ziegler and planner Leslie Luchonok to carry on the program. The two of them retained their enthusiasm, however, and began working on a series of guides—pamphlets financed under the Department of Environmental Management's administrative budget which could provide maps of the local byways, trails, and canoe routes in various sectors of the circuit. This, plus some signage, will, they believe, maintain and maybe even build regional interest in the project until new funding appears.

End of story? Maybe not. As Leslie Luchonok points out, the basic elements of the circuit are largely in place—the astonishing quantity of preserved open-space land within the corridor, thanks to the Eliots and others. Local conservation commissions and land trusts located on the circuit have been assiduously acquiring natural areas off their own bat all along. Putting it all together, as the Trustees of Reservations proposed in 1937, is even more sensible now than it was then. And there is a historic imperative operating here, too, as Bob Yaro understood so well—an innovative park-planning tradition that stretches back one hundred years.

Despite more adversity than would seem believable, the Bay Circuit concept hangs on, insisting on implementation. Clearly, the strength and logic of it could not have been more thoroughly tested. If the politicians of Massachusetts fail to understand that, some conservationists believe it may be time for nongovernmental auspices to take over—to do finally what Charles Eliot, Jr., Charles Eliot II, Bob Yaro, Susan Ziegler, and Leslie Luchonok have devoted a substantial part of their careers to doing—connecting up the gems of the outer necklace so that the Boston area will have its two garlands of green at last.

FROM OLMSTED TO MOSES TO FOX

The Brooklyn–Queens Greenway, Coney Island to Fort Totten, New York

New York City. The Big Apple. Times Square. Broadway. If you can make it here, you can make it anywhere. But *that* New York isn't the half of it. In fact, it is a good deal less than half of it. The biggest chunk of the Big Apple, in both area and population, is in just two of the city's five boroughs, Brooklyn and Queens.

BROOKLYN - QUEENS GREENWAY

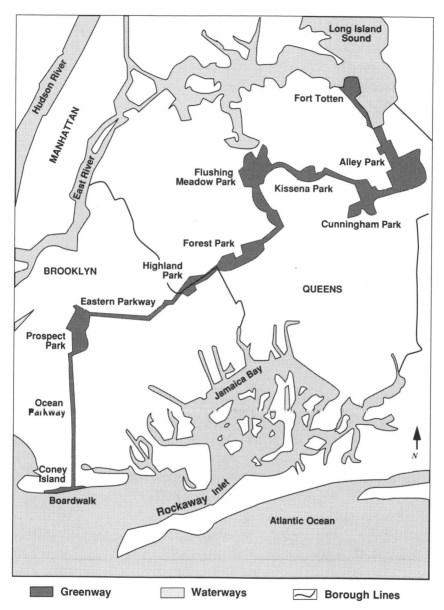

Although they share highways, power grids, sewer systems, and subway lines, the connection between these two boroughs has always been a tenuous one, both geographically and culturally. Queens people rarely venture into Brooklyn, fearing they will get lost in the maze-streets of the old city that was once independent of New York and is peopled by all manner of strange folk, Hasidic Jews in Borough Park, yuppies on Park Slope, boom-box kids in Bedford-Stuyvesant. To the Brooklynites, Queens is equivalently terra incognita. Anyone who lives in Queens, they will tell you, has somehow got to be kidding. It is a *parvenu* borough, with noisy airports surrounded by brick tract houses, as opposed to their tradition-steeped Brooklyn Bridge and old neighborhoods.

But now, thanks to a Brooklyn native, Tom Fox, a linkage between the geography and culture of the two boroughs is finally being created— actually as well as symbolically. The linkage may be described, at once, as a historic imperative and as just about the niftiest idea for a long time in a city that needs such ideas desperately. Can *anything* link Brooklyn and Queens other than the ordinary kinds of urban infrastructure? Yes it can, and it is called a *greenway*—the Brooklyn-Queens Greenway, to be exact.

The seed for this idea was planted in Flatbush, where Fox grew up during the 1950s and would ride his balloon-tired bike down Ocean Parkway. He could go all the way to Coney Island if he wanted. Buy a red hot at Nathan's Famous if he wanted. Or he could ride the other way along this wide boulevard, with the auto-free pathway alongside it, all the way to Olmsted's Prospect Park and the zoo, if he wanted. This is what is known as kids' heaven: to lace up your magic Keds and pedal your Columbia bike as fast as you can, the handlebar tassels fluttering in the wind, and get to a place you have never seen before. The idea of it made a profound impression on young Tom Fox.

But he grew up, and there was Brooklyn College with its beautiful Ivy League-looking campus. And then there was Vietnam, not so Ivy League. And then a job with the National Park Service, working for the Gateway National Recreation Area, an aggregation of various waterfront sites around New York's lower bay.

The great problem, then and now, with the Gateway National Recreation Area was that its constituent units—Sandy Hook in New Jersey, Breezy Point and Floyd Bennett Field on Long Island, the Great Kills Park and South Beach on Staten Island—were widely separated. To get people from one park of the GNRA to another remains the great unsolved problem for this 1970s addition to the national park system. Connections were much on the mind of those who, like Tom Fox, were charged with the responsibility of making our nation's gateway park comprehensively meaningful to its users. Even after he left the National Park Service to work for a nonprofit community-organizing group in Washington, D.C., linking people and places seemed to Fox what any city needs. So, in the early 1980s, he went back in New York to organize the Neighborhood Open Space Coalition on the basis of just such sentiments. He would pull the groups together, link them, and therefore give them a larger impact than any simple addition of their good works could provide.

One day in 1985, Fox was, as he says, "just looking at a map of New York City," thinking open-space thoughts, when he noticed how many parks there were in Queens and how they sort of ran together. His mind drifted back to the days of the Keds and the Columbia bike and exploring the wonders of Ocean Parkway, and he let his finger trace a route from Coney Island northward along the parkway to Prospect Park and. . . . Hey, wait a minute! You can also ride *out* of Prospect Park, along Eastern Parkway toward Queens. Like Ocean Parkway, this thoroughfare comes equipped with a pathway separated from the automobile traffic. What's more, with a couple of jogs and a stretch along residential streets, you can actually get to Highland Park in the borough of Queens. *Queens?* Look here, another little jog to Forest Park, then another six blocks to Flushing Meadow Park, where the two world's fairs had been located. Then, after a string of parks through the center of the borough, you take a hard right into Kissena Park, to Cunningham Park, to Alley Pond Park, and finally to Fort Totten *on the Long Island shore!* There you are: forty bike-miles (fourteen crow-miles) from deepest Brooklyn to farthest Queens! Talk about your linkage!

As Tom Fox and his associate Anne McClellan have since written in an infectious feasibility study of the route, the greenway could "link thirteen parks, two botanic gardens, the New York Aquarium, the Brooklyn Museum, the New York Hall of Science, the Queens Museum, Shea Stadium, the National Tennis Center, the site for 1939 and 1964 world's fairs, two environmental education centers, three lakes and a reservoir—with a bicycle/pedestrian path running from the Atlantic Ocean to the Long Island Sound." And here is the beauty part: by virtue of these parks, parkways, and cultural sites, the greenway's landbase is 90 percent in place already, thanks to Frederick Law Olmsted and Robert Moses, the great park-makers of the middle of the nineteenth century and the middle of the twentieth, respectively.

On the Brooklyn side, Olmsted had conceived of great avenues leading into and out of Prospect Park in 1866. They would not be simple roads but instead broad carriageway boulevards with wide, planted margins. He called them *park ways,* the first use of that term. And they still are parkways, functioning as Olmsted wished them to. His original idea was to have Ocean Parkway approach Prospect Park from the South Shore, pass through it, and head north toward Manhattan, eventually to connect with the great parks of that city. The plan was too visionary for the politicians and bureaucrats to approve, even then. Instead, the boulevard out of the park was later rerouted and became Eastern Parkway, extending into the countryside toward Queens. But the general objective remained the same: to provide approaches to the park which were as grand as the park itself—to prepare the mind and spirit properly for the park experience. And the park was worth it. The 526-acre Prospect Park was, Olmsted believed, his finest achievement.

On the other side of the Kings County line, where Eastern Parkway was headed, lay Queens. In those days, Queens was mainly farmland and marsh, not really part of the metropolis. But that was to change. By the 1920s it had become solidly suburban but not so built up that a new generation of park- and parkway-makers could not plan their projects boldly. And no one was bolder than Robert Moses. Although one of Moses's parkways broke a link in Tom Fox's greenway that must now be reconnected, his hunks of parkland, including those associated with the world's fairs and the skein of parkways he built to deliver the visitors to them, provide the crucial lands than can now deliver a walker or cyclist through much of Queens away from vehicular traffic.

Although all of the land is already in the public domain, this does not mean that creating the Brooklyn-Queens Greenway is easy. The cost of development and of reforging the missing links needed to make a continuous trailway is steep. To determine how steep, Fox and his Neighborhood Open Space Coalition colleagues developed a fine-grained greenway development plan—right down to the signage, reflectors, and the cost of paint. Their estimate for development of the greenway (not including some $160 million worth of park, road, and public works improvements to be applied along the route that were otherwise scheduled by the city) ranges from $3 million for a bare-bones trailway to $18 million for a deluxe model greenway.

Despite items included in the budget such as a veloway bridge to get bikers across Northern Boulevard ($2.2 million) and the construction of a new trail through the Coney Island section ($3 million) and widening and rebuilding the bikeway strip along Eastern Parkway ($4.6 million), New York City, broke as it is, has taken this project to its heart.

Actually, such a price tag is not much for a city whose total budget is greater than that of most nations. Indeed, many see the greenway as an investment that multiplies the utility of the parks and cultural facilities that are linked along the route's forty-mile length. Because the importance of Coney Island, Prospect Park, and Flushing Meadow to the city is so great, an increase in accessibility could justify the cost of the greenway many times over. And such a humane calculus is not at all beyond the reach of New York's politicians. The NOSC plan was accepted by the Parks Department and the Department of Transportation almost as quickly as it was completed. Within a year, the first section of the new greenway, from Coney Island to Prospect Park, had been opened for use, and work on other sections begun. At the reopening of the bikepath on Ocean Parkway, Henry Stern, New York's parks commissioner, observed, "I can't think of any project that has produced so much enthusiasm." Transportation Department head Ross Sandler, mindful of the Olmsted heritage, called the completion of the greenway a historic imperative. Former Mayor Koch mounted a ten-speed, grinned for the photographers, and for once did not put his foot in his mouth. Given such a send-off, Tom Fox figures the greenway will be completed, although perhaps not fully developed, by 1995.

And so it is that at last some long-divided parts of the city are being brought together—courtesy of Frederick Law Olmsted's Brooklyn parks and parkways, Robert Moses's manifold projects in Queens, and the concept of linking them together provided by Tom Fox and the Neighborhood Open Space Coalition. In the neighborhoods of both boroughs, the parks are called *pawks*. Lord knows how the local youngsters are going to pronounce the word *greenway*. But you had better believe they're soon going be using it, as in "Hey, ma, I goin' out on the greenway."

And before she can yell something about not being late, a kid on a bike will be riding away, tassels streaming from the handlebars, pedaling off to somewhere he's never been before.

LESSONS IN RIVER-MAKING AT SHOEMAKER U.

The Platte River Greenway, Denver, Colorado

Joe Shoemaker, a tough-talking, abrasive state legislator, now retired, literally founded a river. Unless you are God, that is a tricky piece of business. But that's what Shoemaker did. He started with a miserable, pestiferous, flood-ridden sewerway fouled by 250 drainage pipes carrying the unspeakable fluids of a city into it; a channelized dump, filled with piles of broken concrete, rubber tires, waste oil, stoves, refrigerators, and, in one particularly nasty section, rejected chicken feathers from a bedding factory. And he made of it the most important park and recreation facility in the city of Denver. From a river that had from the earliest days divided rich from poor, Shoemaker found a way to connect a city that had once been wedged apart. The vehicle for this miracle was the Platte River Greenway, a project that has been the model for a dozen or more urban river greenways in cities throughout the United States.

The story begins in 1965, when the Platte escaped its banks and flooded the city of Denver. This had happened many times before, but

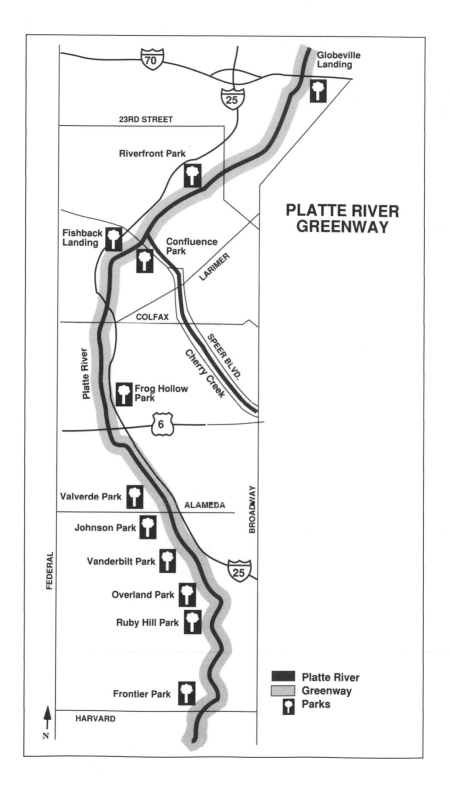

PLATTE RIVER GREENWAY

Platte River
Greenway
Parks

173

1965 was different. The normal flow of the river is three hundred cubic feet of water per second. Seriously high water is three thousand cubic feet per second. But after fourteen inches of rain fell in an upstream watershed area, the flow on June 16, 1965, was recorded at 150,000 cubic feet per second. This was more than a hundred-year flood—that is, a flood with a one in a hundred chance of happening in any given year. This was a five hundred-year flood! As Shoemaker has written of the event, the Platte, "this forgotten nothing of a river, remembered itself to everyone . . . with an unforgettable $350 million bill for damages. A century of disrespect and disregard had been revenged in a few unforgettable hours."

The response of the city government after the 1965 flood was to commission a Platte River redevelopment plan at a price tag that Shoemaker can scarcely believe even now. The study, eighty-four slick pages in length, cost $680,000. But that wasn't the worst of it. The redevelopment plan, featuring massive new apartment buildings and a huge park flanking a completely reorganized riverway, was Babylonian. The money the planners estimated was needed to carry out the redevelopment staggered everyone: a cool $630 million.

It was a loopy idea, even for the 1960s, and the plan fell from grace almost from the time it was conceived, even though a committee called SPARC (the South Platte Area Redevelopment Committee) was formed to promote its implementation. But the committee, unlike the planners, was unfunded and soon fell apart. Meanwhile, upstream dams were built, and other abatement measures were undertaken, virtually eliminating the possibility that another 1965-style flood could happen again. And that appeared to be that. The city cleaned itself up and once again forgot about the Platte. Except the future of the river started nagging at Joe Shoemaker, who had been a public works commissioner for Denver before being elected to the state legislature in 1962.

By the time the 1965 flood hit, Shoemaker had ascended to the chair of the Joint Economic Committee of the Colorado legislature, acknowledged to be the most powerful position of all, in an operational sense, in the state's political arena. He was a rough, tough deal-maker in the public's interest. A favor-giver and a favor-getter. Captains of Denver's industry came hat in hand to curry favor. Powerful bureaucrats tugged at their forelocks in his presence. When a new mayor was elected, Democrat William McNichols, he, too, sought out Chairman Shoemaker, for state-level budgetary approval was needed to carry out many city programs. Shoemaker was helpful, even though the mayor was of a different political party. Republican Shoemaker had no reason not to work with McNichols. He did not covet that job. Instead, he wanted to take a shot at being governor and in 1974 began to test the waters for his party's nomination.

Mainly, Shoemaker was itchy, an affliction that comes to many, if not most, accomplished people in midcareer. As the chairman of the Joint Economic Committee, he was beginning to tire of the endless infighting. Needing a real issue to sink his teeth into, for personal as well as political reasons, Shoemaker, on a whim, decided to pay a visit to Mayor Bill McNichols. Striding into McNichols's office with no appointment, the story has it, he said without preamble, "Well, what are we going to do about the Platte River?".

"Funny you should ask that," McNichols replied. "I was thinking about what *you* might do about the Platte." So saying, the mayor slid a list of names across the desk, explaining that they were some of the people who might want to serve on the newly formed, nine-member Platte River Development Committee. The mayor said he would like to pick two citizen-members but that Joe could pick all the rest, whether they were on the list or not. "You're not bound to select any of these," said McNichols, "You're the chairman."

"I am?"

"You are, if you want to be. All I can give you is a capital budget of $1.9 million. The rest is up to you. You're probably the only person in Denver who can save that river."

Flattery will get you everywhere in politics. Shoemaker gladly agreed. Anyway, maybe the redevelopment issue would help him with the nomination.

On the other hand, compared with the $630 million the earlier redevelopment plan had called for, $1.9 million was impossibly paltry. The newspapers thought the idea was silly—just another committee that would bite the dust even faster than SPARC. But characteristically, the scorn served to sharpen Shoemaker's resolve rather than weaken it. He chose his members with care. Avoiding officials and bureaucrats altogether, he tapped only those civic leaders who represented major interest groups and ethnic populations—blacks and Chicanos, Jewish business executives, WASP conservationists and preservationists. Two young planners, Rick Lamoreaux and Bob Searns, were detached from the city planning department to serve as staff. For Searns, who had recently earned a master of architecture degree at the State University of New York at Buffalo and had come to Denver meaning only to get a job to "support my skiing habit," the assignment to the committee was a crucial factor in his career. "My real education as a planner," says Searns, now the head of his own firm, "was at Shoemaker U."

At the beginning of the project there were no plans, at least not published ones. Shoemaker forbade them. Instead, he divided his citizen-members into four teams and told each team it had a half-million dollars. Each was to make a park node somewhere along the 10.5-mile riverway as it passed through the city of Denver. After the sites had been agreed on and design and construction bids sought, Rick Lamoreaux prepared a map of their locations. But he had also done one other thing—and this was a kind of plan perhaps, albeit for internal use only: he connected the sites along the riverway with the thick line of a green marking pen. "Why not," he suggested, "link the parks into a 'greenway' all along the river?" No one had ever heard the term *greenway* before, but the idea made sense. Shoemaker liked it immediately.

As it turned out, there was only money enough for two nodal parks: one called Confluence Park, located where Cherry Creek enters the Platte, the place where the city of Denver had originated; and the other, Globeville Landing, at "the armpit of Denver," so-called by its residents, the minority poor who lived in the old stockyards area. Shoemaker got the city to agree that the land required—in both cases, municipally owned sand and gravel pits that had been converted to solid waste dump sites—could be developed as greenway pocket parks. But he told the committee that he wanted a mile of trailway built along the river in each location. He had learned that trick from reading about famed New York highway builder, Robert Moses. "The psychology of highway building," says Shoemaker, "is you put a ten-mile section of interstate out there in the middle of nowhere, and everyone says, 'When the hell are you going to finish this highway?' So you go to the politicians who control the money and tell them that the people are screaming that the highway ought to be completed."

The fact is, the technique worked for Shoemaker as well as it did for Moses. There is now a paved trail all the way down the Platte, if not on one side, then on the other, and in some places both. In securing trail easements from the city, industrial owners, and the railroad, Shoemaker also relied on a bit of Moseslike cunning, including a veiled threat to bring a legal complaint against a recalcitrant landowner whose property, Shoemaker guessed, might be significantly undervalued on the tax rolls. The trail easement Shoemaker sought was forthcoming the next day.

At one point during all the maneuvering, a member of the committee asked Shoemaker what legal authority empowered him to cut deals on behalf of the city and county of Denver. The committee had no real charter except as a citizens' advisory group. Shoemaker replied that he had told the mayor he wanted no specific powers vested in the committee. None. Zip. "Why in the world not?" asked the member. "Because," said Shoemaker, giving utterance to what is now called *Shoemaker's Law,* "to have no power in a situation like this is to have *all* power." For those who might not understand the paradox, he pointed out that any real power conferred upon the committee by the city would have to be specific and therefore limiting. Since there were no specifics, there were no limits. QED. And so the favors were called in, the arms got twisted, foundations were cajoled, industries threatened, bureaucracies bullied, and the greenway began to come together.

It was Shoemaker's Law, in fact, that led the committee, after several years of operating as a mayoral advisory group, to reconstitute itself as a nonprofit foundation. No municipal "powers" would be lost, since they were only an illusion anyway. But a foundation could receive grants and individual contributions directly rather than having to work through city agencies—an awkward situation that often discouraged giving in certain instances. So in 1977, the Platte River Greenway Foundation was formed, planners Lamoreaux and Searns quit their city jobs and came to work full-time for Shoemaker, and the committee members became the foundation's trustees. As it turned out, the idea was inspired. Of the total of $14 million raised to create the greenway, half of it was obtained from private sources, including a significant fraction from small donations. By 1980, the trails had been linked, seventeen pocket parks built, and four boat chutes in the riverway were constructed so that kayakers could use the river as urban whitewater. There were new footbridges and amphitheaters and nature education areas, and much else. Today, 150,000 people a year use this greenway.

The Platte River Greenway Foundation still thrives, seeing to it that the greenway is well maintained; and they are expanding the work along the Platte and its tributaries, moving both north and south into the suburbs and even creating linkages to trails in other parts of the state. But it is toward Denver's part of the Platte that Shoemaker feels his greatest obligation. "I will stay as chairman of the foundation until the day I die," he says.

Rick Lamoreaux and Bob Searns have gone their separate ways now. But they will never forget the lessons learned at Shoemaker U: The best plan is not to have one, at least not too soon; to build a trail to nowhere is the way to get trails built everywhere; and Shoemaker's Law—to have no power is to have all power. There is one other: To love your city, and its people, and to honor them with total devotion to true public service. As it turned out, Joe Shoemaker never did become governor. He gave his city a river instead.

10

The Practical Matters

The most important question is, What are you going to do on Monday morning?

—*AMERICAN BUSINESS ADAGE*

This is a chapter for those who want to get down to the actual business of making greenways. It summarizes the lessons from the several dozen projects discussed in the essay chapters and in the two World of Greenways sections. And it draws on the abundance of practitioner-written reports and pamphlets published by government agencies and nonprofit conservation organizations wishing to provide detailed guidance, mainly to citizen groups, on just exactly how to do it.

I hope the reader will forgive me for being direct about some of the practical matters. After you have analyzed a wide range of projects, you begin to form opinions about what works and what does not. Here is what I think works.

GETTING STARTED: THE RECONNAISSANCE

Nothing beats taking a look. It is remarkable how often, especially in government-sponsored greenway projects, a thorough reconnaissance is made later rather than sooner—or worse, is left to technical planners late in the project, or, even worse than that, is never done at all. The failure to understand the resource from a ground-eye view at the outset can be a terrible disadvantage, causing a slow start, a nonstart, even ultimate failure.

Many projects—winners all, such as Denver's Platte River Greenway, for example, or the Brooklyn-Queens Greenway—undertook a reconnaissance at the very beginning. In Denver, Joe Shoemaker force-marched his advisory committee, some of them skeptical about the whole idea, on an arduous day-long inspection of the Platte. They found 250 sewer pipes, and it made such a profound impression that what started out as a project to create a few parks wound up creating a whole greenway. For the Brooklyn-Queens Greenway, the first thing Tom Fox did was to take a forty-mile bike ride. The published account of the trip along the route Fox dreamed up for his greenway was so effective that it garnered him a National Endowment of the Arts grant to develop a detailed plan.

You may be a high-powered government official or a corporate CEO used to having people submit reports and bring your coffee. Forget all that. Walk as much of the greenway corridor as you can, or paddle it, or bike it, or at least cruise slowly with the windows down in the family station wagon. Take notes, take pictures, talk to people along the way. Now you are ready to begin.

GETTING ORGANIZED

There are three basic organizational approaches. The first is for a government agency to do all the planning, handle all corridor acquisition and development, serve as the exchequer, and own and operate the greenway forever. A good many successful projects are handled this way. The Boulder (Colorado) Greenway, for example, one of the finest in the land, is and always has been the work of municipal government. With regard to municipal or regional *systems* of greenways, such as the successful Capital Area Greenway program in Raleigh, North Carolina, governmental auspices are a requirement, although nongovernmental groups may do local planning and implementation. One key finding is the need for the government agency to be independent of typical functional departments such as transportation, parks and recreation, public works, or the like.

Ideally, the work should be assigned to a greenway commission that has no other duties and therefore no potential conflicts of interest.

The second approach is to eschew government sponsorship in favor of a private, nonprofit association. There are fewer projects of this sort, but it is possible, even necessary in many cases, not to involve government in any substantial way. Bob Myhr's Ferryboat Corridor Greenway in Puget Sound's San Juan Islands is one of these.

The third organizational approach is to add one and two together, a public-private amalgam that can create an entirely different compound with wonderful properties. In fact, I have seen enough greenway projects to conclude that in nearly every case of a single (nonsystem) greenway endeavor, a governmental cum private group partnership should be the organizational mode of choice: ideally in the form of a single-purpose, publicly authorized greenway foundation, with a board of directors representing citizen organizations, business corporations, professional and academic associations, and government departments. The foundation can be legislatively chartered or the outgrowth of a governmental committee or can simply arise on its own. The Chattanooga Riverpark project is an example of the former, the Yakima Greenway took the middle approach, and Casper's Platte River Parkway is an example of the last type.

The greenway foundation has the benefits of a private nonprofit organization in that it can cut deals with landowners, moving quickly and decisively. At the same time, it can avoid the chief disadvantage of the private group, which is a lack of authority, either actual or implied by official status. A strictly private greenway organization has no more clout than any group of citizens, but a public-private foundation can often borrow the governmental powers it needs by working closely with public agencies—for the regulation of land, for example, or the use of public funds and authorities for acquisition, construction, and maintenance.

A greenway foundation can also avoid the drawbacks of public-only greenway auspices, which may have governmental authority but only a limited geographic jurisdiction. In addition, a greenway foundation avoids the problem of greenway policy decisions being subject to political pressures and sudden structural change, as when the other party throws the rascals out: sometimes they are the very rascals supporting a greenway project. Moreover, when sources of public funding are limited (as they usually are), the government-only greenway agency will have little capacity to raise money through private subscription. How often do most of us make a voluntary contribution to a government agency? By contrast, a greenway foundation can be a most attractive recipient of donations and grants and can derive continuing income from membership dues.

THE RESEARCH BASE

It is likely that a great deal of basic research data is available for any given greenway project area: ecological, geological, and hydrological studies; geographic and topographic studies; historic and ethnographic studies. The one study that probably has not been done is a corridor landownership inventory—a matter of going to the assessor's office; taking a look at the plats; and determining, tract by tract, who owns what, with special emphasis on the existing public and quasi-public open space that will constitute the starting point for creating the greenway corridor. This information can be plotted by hand on a working map, using pasted-together United States Geological Survey quandrangles as the base map. (Some find it useful to take the taped-together topo maps to a graphic arts shop that has a giant photocopying machine that can produce a clear copy on a single sheet with the colors dropped out—much easier to work with.) In addition to ownership, the working map can also show different zoning classifications (residential, industrial, special districts), environmental constraints on land use (floodplain, steep slope, and similar regulations), and subdivision requirements (cluster development, open-space set-asides). The zoning and regulatory information is available from municipal or state planning offices.

It is important to emphasize that the map in this case is a kind of topographic notebook for use by those working closely on the project; it is not artwork for public presentation or precise measurement for the archives. No cartographer is needed.

I am certainly not suggesting some superscientific computerized resource analysis either, especially at an early stage. At some point this kind of work may be appropriate but not at the outset. The GIS approach (stands for Geographical Information System) has been well developed by government planning agencies. It has its place, which is later if you can afford it and if your greenway program is an especially elaborate one. The Hudson River Valley Greenway, for example, will computer-map owner- ship, resource, infrastructure, regulatory and related data for a wide swath of the valley, parcel by parcel. The trouble with a GIS for most projects, however, is that it can be a substitute for action. It tends to sup- press a sense of creative possibility, overloading the project at the idea- generating stage with such an excess of data-manipulation possibilities that options may be constrained rather than opened up.

There are a good many other research needs that will present them- selves: public attitude surveys, for example, or economic studies, both of which can be extremely valuable. The trick, however, is to resist the temptation to keep on conducting research to the point of procrastina- tion in the matter of presenting the greenway concept for serious public discussion and of developing a civic consensus on the general validity of the project—a step that, under ordinary circumstances, should be taken sooner rather than later for any proposed greenway.

COMMUNICATING THE CONCEPT

In the main, greenway-making is by its nature an extremely visible con- servation activity. The very linearity of a greenway means that its exis- tence, or lack of it, will affect many lives. Quite often, in fact, greenways must deal with a full-blown socioeconomic cross-section—rich neigh- borhoods and poor ones, estate owners and factory workers—along a greenway corridor that might encompass every level of development density and every type of land use. A greenway, therefore, whether along a river, a ridge, a stream, a road, a canal, or a rail line, tends to be a small-*d* democratic endeavor, best carried out in full sunshine and with a sense of participation by all the parties—which are multitudinous.

It is for this reason that the most successful greenway projects make a serious effort early on to communicate their greenway concept to a broad audience. This process, I hasten to add, is not the same as physical green-way planning, which comes later (and is discussed below). Unfortu-nately, many greenway projects move from an idea that is known and understood by only a small group of advocates directly to a detailed plan before a public consensus has had a chance to develop.

Actually, what is needed at the early stages of a project is an interim document that is descriptive and suggestive rather than anything pre-scriptive and authoritative. Tony Hiss, a writer on regional-planning is-sues, calls such publications *vision documents*. Although other communi-cations efforts should take place, of course—magazine and newspaper articles, slide shows, and special publicity-generating events such as pro-motional walks—the basic consensus-seeking source of information about the greenway idea should be the words and pictures and drawings of the vision document, presenting the proposed greenway in a context that is inherently interesting and compelling to the general reader.

ECONOMIC EFFECTS

According to conventional wisdom, the only way to sell a greenway is to show its economic value: how many jobs it provides, how much it in-creases business income and therefore sales tax revenues, how it improves real estate values. If well presented, the primary social benefits of green-ways—urban amenity, recreation, ecological diversity, historic and sce-nic preservation—ought to be sufficient in themselves to rationalize the public cost. In the real world, however, greenway-makers will sooner or later have to demonstrate how well their greenway will pay.

For some urban area redevelopment greenways such as the Riverpark project in Chattanooga, the primary social benefit *is* economic, produc-ing new investment and resulting in new jobs, rather than an issue aside. But for a good many greenways, the economic effects are thought to be entirely negative—specifically that the greenways will remove land from the tax rolls and decrease the value of adjacent taxable properties. This, some believe, adds insult to injury in that not only does a greenway re-quire an initial public investment and continuing expenditures for main-tenance, but it reduces municipal tax revenues as well. Occasionally the insult-and-injury analysis may be true but not as invariably as greenway adversaries claim. More often it is not true at all. In fact, noneconomically oriented greenways can produce a quite positive economic effect as an ancillary benefit.

Let us begin with the "they're taking land off the tax rolls" complaint—oft heard with regard to any open-space preservation effort. In the case of greenways, the land used may have only a slight value to begin with, and so it produces only a minimal lowering of tax income. Riparian corridors, for example, are usually zoned against development for reasons of public safety in the event of floods. Such zoning has already eliminated most of the taxable value of this land. Similarly, in the case of railway corridors proposed to be converted to greenways, the prior abandonment, not the idea of a greenway, is what has reduced the tax revenues. Even in those cases in which an abandoned right-of-way permits property to revert to adjacent owners, the potential for such a thin strip of land to produce significant new tax revenues is—although certainly possible—unlikely.

What about greenways not associated with public or quasi-public rights-of-way such as streams and railway corridors? Here, too, the tax effect of land acquisition (or a right in land such as a trail or conservation easement) along a narrow strip would hardly seem to be significant. In fact, the existence of a greenway in any of these situations is far more likely to have a positive effect on tax revenues and to produce some substantial public cost *savings* as well.

The cost savings with regard to land acquired for a greenway are most obvious in the case of riparian projects that reduce the cost of future flood damage. As I reported in the profile on Tucson's linear park system, local government studies showed a substantial savings by establishing a greenway, even if it required relocating some residences away from a floodway, in contrast to the projected cost of later mitigation.

Positive economic effects of a greenway corridor arise because of an increase in the value of taxable properties adjacent to the greenway. In an urban setting, this is almost beyond argument since the value of land for office buildings and apartment houses or condominiums will be enhanced to some degree by adjacency to any public amenity of this sort.

The property-value problem arises in suburban and countryside areas where the presence of a greenway is often thought by some landowners as having a negative effect on value because of a loss of privacy and the possibility of inviting vandalism or even worse crimes. The fear is that the greenway will provide a new access route for nonlocal people into heretofore isolated residential and farm areas.

In some cases, unfortunately, the expresson of this concern is a surrogate for racism, economic prejudice, or a generalized xenophobia, and therefore rational discourse has little effect. For those landowners actually interested in the facts of the case, however, the indications are that greenways increase property values, not the reverse. There are several ways to predict the property-value effects in advance. One is to identify an existing greenway running through an area similar to a proposed corridor—in a nearby town, if not locally—and take a look at assessments (available at the assessor's office) before and after the greenway was established to see if there are any differences. A better approach is to identify a control area similar in essential respects to the corridor neighborhood but without a greenway and compare the changes in assessments between the two areas.

Yet another approach was taken by the city of Seattle's engineering department concerning the city's heavily used Burke-Gilman Trail (discussed in Chapter 4) that passes through residential neighborhoods. In this case, researchers simply interviewed the three groups of people that could shed some light on economic impacts—real estate agents active in the areas, the police officers who patrolled it (to determine the actual as opposed to the presumed level of vandalism), and the homeowners themselves.

The real estate people regarded the trail as, at best, a sales plus that helped them to attract buyers and, at worst, neutral in effect. Indeed, today agents routinely advertise properties as being on or near the trail. According to the report (see citation under "Seattle" in the Published Reports section of the List of Principal Sources), "property near but not immediately adjacent to the Burke-Gilman Trail is significantly easier to sell and, according to real estate agents, sells for an average of 6 percent more as a result of its proximity to the trail. Property immediately adjacent to the trail, however, is only slightly easier to sell. The trail has no significant effect on the selling price of homes immediately adjacent to the trail."

According to the police, says the report, "officers interviewed stated that there is not a greater incidence of burglaries and vandalism of homes along the trail. They attribute that fact to the absence of motor vehicles. They noted that problems in park areas are generally confined to areas of easy motor vehicle access."

As for the residents, nearly two-thirds of those interviewed believed that the trail "increased the quality of life in the neighborhood." The researchers uncovered not a single resident who thought the trail should be closed. The report concludes that "concerns about decreased property values, increased crime, and a lower quality of life due to the construction of multiuse trails are unfounded. In fact the opposite is true. The study indicated that [such] trails are an amenity that helps sell homes, increase property values, and improve the quality of life."

THE ISSUES OF RECREATIONAL ACCESS

As the foregoing indicates, concerns about public access to greenways are often tied up with economic impacts. Economics aside, however, access issues create their own kinds of problems and opportunities. The rule to keep in mind is that greenways do not necessarily require public recreational use, but without it (with some exceptions), the projects are harder to sell to both the public and the policy-makers. The history of modern greenway-making over the past twenty-five years—from the Staten Island Greenbelt to the San Francisco Ridge Trail—has shown that if people have recreational access to a proposed greenway, they more readily grasp its utility and importance. In many cases, they grasp the importance of preserving the surrounding landscape as well. The obvious corollary to the rule of access is that the route must be continuous—even if unfortunate public-road detours or connectors are necessary—to catch the imagination of the public. An interrupted trailway is not a trailway at all but simply an aggregation of separate pedestrian or bicycle paths that are not perceived as being unitary in any practical way.

The access rule must have exceptions, of course. Chief among these are some scenic-drive greenways wherein the access is essentially visual—through a windshield. In addition, there are some river-based greenways such as the Willamette in Oregon and the Oconee in Georgia for which the access route is by water rather than along the banks. In a great many projects in rural and some suburban settings, conservationists are often concerned about recreational trails intruding on areas that are extremely sensitive ecologically—where rare plants or animals may be found, for example. Usually these concerns can be met by making sure the trail routes simply avoid fragile areas, which is preferable to having a discontinuous trail. Moreover, recreational impact can be lessened by limiting greenway use to walkers rather than developing trailways (by grading and surfacing) intended to attract throngs of joggers and bikers more concerned with how they look in their Reeboks and sweatbands than with the natural corridor they are speeding through.

Indeed, in greenway-trail design, the degree of development relates more or less precisely to the intensity of use. Greenways established for commuting and recreation such as the Burke-Gilman Trail in Seattle obviously get more traffic than the woods paths through the sylvan precincts of exurban Redding, Connecticut. Sometimes, in fact, the bikers and joggers, who tend to demand trails paved in concrete or asphalt, become so numerous that they drive out other users. On the typical all-purpose paved trail (usually built eight feet wide, although many designers now think they ought to be ten, with a center stripe), the joggers usually do not have altercations with bikers, since their actions on the trailway are predictable: they run more or less straight ahead. A saunterer, however, might suddenly swerve over from one side of a trailway to another to check out a wildflower, only to suffer a serious accident with a speeding cyclist (or even a runner). The main problem is the low-handlebar speedster, who is to the pedestrian users of a greenway what an eighteen-wheeler is to a Chevette on the interstate.

Some greenway planners believe that this incompatibility between users (I have not even mentioned bridle paths, which present an additional problem) can erode public support of greenways, and in recent years the planners have proposed separate trails for the different uses. Sometimes the trails are constructed side by side, sometimes with different alignments, often on either side of a river or stream.

Greenway projects that agonize over a need for multiple trails should count themselves lucky. A great many greenways have foundered on a more elementary problem—what might be called the catch-22 of greenway-making. The catch is this: the surest way to get public support for most greenways is to promote public access; yet the surest way to acquire a greenway corridor across private land is to promise that public access will be prohibited. The Canopy Roads project in Tallahassee ran afoul of this exact problem. The solution was to avoid confrontation with landowners, which could be done because the scenic benefits of the greenway could be achieved without trailways being part of the formula. However, in many cases in which a greenway without a trail could be expected to garner little public support, the catch can delay, if not doom, a project.

In 1980, the Minnesota Department of Natural Resources conducted a study addressing this very problem. The study method was to compare landowner attitudes about privacy and related impacts on a pair of proposed trails with landowner attitudes along a pair of similar trails already established. On the question of local versus "urban" users, it turned out that although 65 percent of landowners along the proposed trail assumed the trail was intended primarily for nonlocal use by people "from the big cities," nearly 100 percent of landowners along the developed trails believed they were primarily for local use and enjoyment. On the proposed trails, nearly 75 percent of landowners thought that if a trail were constructed, it would mean more vandalism and other crimes. By contrast, virtually no landowners along the two constructed trails (0 and 6 percent, respectively) agreed with the statement, "trail-users steal."

Although there may be little evidence to suggest that greenway trails produce disturbance to private landowners adjoining them to anywhere near the degree that landowners expect, the fears are likely to persist. Accordingly, greenway-makers must do what they can to help eliminate the threat of privacy loss and crime. In the state of New Jersey, to offer one example of how this might be done, a program has been established to provide grants for projects that seek to reduce the impacts of trails on landowners. According to the official brochure of the Open Lands Management Program, if a property owner will "open up his or her land to the public for one of several types of outdoor activities," the state in turn will provide funds to "eliminate the problems and hazards to the property owner."

The problems and hazards that the Open Lands Management Program has in mind include such matters as the accumulation of trash; people wandering off the trail into areas that would intrude on the landowner's privacy; the occasional act of senseless vandalism; and, perhaps most serious of all, the possibility of a liability suit being brought by a venturous hiker who has fallen down an old cellar hole off the trail in the woods. To meet these concerns, the program will provide funding, on a project basis, to pay for trash collection, parking areas, signage prohibiting this and that, and fencing to keep trail-users away from areas the landowner would like to remain private. It will also pay the costs of repair due to vandalism and pay the premiums on any special liability insurance the landowner wishes to take out—although in general, an owner's liability is limited in most states in the case of public recreational use of private land.

Another way greenway planners can reduce landowner objections (while still hanging on to the concept of a continuous trailway) is through trail design and management. As I stated earlier, the degree of development of a trail seems to determine the intensity of its use. Where thousands might use a dual bikeway with picnic and other recreation areas provided along its length, hundreds would use a paved trail with limited facilities, and only scores (or less) a woodland path. That a trail should be continuous does not imply that it need be continuously paved, especially through private-land areas. There, trails can dwindle to simple footpaths, which tend to be unattractive to people the landowners are concerned about—unruly youths, nonlocals, or those with larceny (or worse) on their mind.

ON PLANNING

The big question on planning—by which I mean getting a professional (usually a landscape architect) to prepare a physical plan for a greenway—is not *whether,* but *when.* At some point, you have to draw lines on a map and color the space between them green, then put a dotted line along where the trail is supposed to go, and then add other features as you choose. You have to get specific about such matters as how wide, how steep, what paving (if any), what plants, what benches, what bridges, what signs, and whatnot. And then you have to work out the hardest detail of all: How much?

After the plan is made, you then have to show it to somebody— usually the public or the public's elected or appointed representatives. The responses can range from "Let's go for it!" to "Are you out of your mind?" In between is the proverbial shelf on which so many well-intentioned plans gather dust.

More often than not, the dust problem, if not outright rejection, is inevitable if the plan is prepared too early in the life of a project; its previousness makes it seem gratuitous, like a form of special pleading. The reason is McLuhanesque: a physical plan is a medium with a not-so-subtle message, especially so when the plan is presented before any significant policy consensus has been reached. The exactitude of the God's-eye view maps and the trailway cross-section drawings, the expert jargon, and the highly rationalized prescriptive approach implies (whether meant or not) "this way or no way." If forced to choose, the public's answer is often the latter. In short, a premature plan tends to suppress creative civic energy rather than engender it.

For the most part, the leadership of successful greenway projects either knows the secret of plan timing through experience or has intuited it. I am mindful of Joe Shoemaker's unwillingness to publish any kind of plan at all until the construction work had actually started on Denver's Platte River Greenway. By contrast, Al Edelman in Portland, Oregon, understood that the 40-Mile Loop concept—which had been around since 1903 and in its 140-mile version had been ripening for about ten years—was ready for action. Given the number of jurisdictions involved, the Alphonse and Gaston problem seemed insurmountable. Yet Edelman knew that a true public consensus had been reached, so he commissioned a quite technical, detailed, and authoritative plan right down to the size of pea gravel and design of the signage. The plan was anything but gratuitous. The timing was exquisite, the effect galvanic.

NAILING DOWN THE CORRIDOR

Get the free land first. The starting point is land already dedicated to park and recreation use. For land in other kinds of public ownership, the effort must be to convince its managers—the local waste-management authority, for example, in the case of a riverside landfill—to dedicate a strip for greenway use, if not now, then eventually. Land in quasi-public ownership—a cemetery, a golf course—presents a different kind of problem but usually a nonmonetary one. The object here is to have the owners convey a right-of-way easement for a trail, assuming the land is in a more or less permanent open-space use. (Note: Planners tell me that you must locate a trail across a golf course on the hook side of a fairway rather than the slice side, lest trail-users get beaned.) Land in private industrial use may present a special problem in that its owners or managers may not wish to donate a permanent easement but rather an access agreement over a limited term of years. As for railroad land, the conditions are variable and legally complicated, as I discussed in Chapter 4. In a good many circumstances, however, thanks to the railbanking law, this land too may not require purchase.

Land in private residential ownership should be left for last—even if it is the best and most crucial land for the project. Public enthusiasm for the greenway should be given time to make itself felt. A good deal of private land can be acquired at no cost or at low cost if the landowner believes in the importance of the greenway. In working with landowners, the old salesman's rule should be followed for corridor acquisition: make the easy calls first.

Here is a summary of salient tips from the experts experienced in private land acquisition:

—Land for the corridor need not be conveyed in fee—that is, in full title, free and clear. A negative, conservation easement may be all that is necessary for corridor areas not actually open to the public— adjoining a trail for example, or the view involved in a scenic route. A *purchase in fee* means to purchase all rights in land. An easement acquisition concerns only certain rights, including the negative right to prohibit development or otherwise change the use of land. A positive easement (access agreement) is required for a trailway itself or other public access to an area, however.

—The land along rivers and streams in most cases is already protected to some degree by floodplain zoning. It therefore has little if any new-development value and may be acquired in fee or easement for a corridor relatively cheaply, assuming a willing seller and assuming the land is vacant.

—In special cases, already developed land in a floodplain can be acquired from owners under grants from the Federal Emergency Management Agency under its flood insurance program, assuming local law prohibits development or redevelopment in the floodplain. To qualify, existing properties within the floodplain which have been damaged must have lost greater than 50 percent of their value through a flood disaster.

—Land along ridgelines, another favored route for greenways, is often in private ownership and may have significant development value. With ridgeline trails, however, there is more flexibility in routing than with riparian greenways, so a corridor can be routed through land whose owners are sympathetic to a project or through land too steep to be developed economically.

—Trail easements can be piggybacked on public utility rights-of-way such as sewer easements or power lines.

—In most jurisdictions, residential developers are required to donate part of their site for park or recreational use. If privately owned land ready for development is located along a potential greenway corridor, arrangements should be made with municipal authorities and with the developer for this land (and not some other part of the site) to be dedicated as part of the corridor.

—Residential development plans can also be modified to produce corridor land (over and above mandatory dedications) by means of cluster development (keeping overall housing density the same but reduc-
ing individual lot sizes to produce an open-space surplus). This may
also be achieved by allowing the transfer of development rights
(TDR) from a greenway corridor to another site not in the corridor,
permitting the builder to construct the same number of housing units
overall.

—Greenway authorities (whether governmental or a public-private
foundation) can also produce corridor land by various purchase-and-
resale approaches. For example, a large parcel may be purchased outright from a private owner, the land needed for the greenway corridor
divided from it, and the remainder resold either as a single parcel or
further subdivided into multiple parcels. In the latter case, it is altogether conceivable that the authority might come out of the transac-
tion with no financial loss or even with a surplus that can be used to
acquire corridor land elsewhere. If the division of the property is im-
practical, then a conservation easement with a trail right-of-way can be
placed in the deed and the parcel resold in its entirety with covenants
protecting the corridor and providing public access along a trail established in perpetuity.

—Some public authorities favor purchase and leaseback (to adjoining
farmers, for example) rather than purchase and resale. In cases other
than state or federal scenic highways, however, for which this approach is sometimes used, purchase and resale with restrictions is
probably a better means to establish a greenway corridor since it elimi-
nates the need to administer leases.

—Philanthropic land donation (fee or easement) or a bargain sale of land
to a greenway authority should always be sought but rarely expected—especially now that lowered income tax rates make land donation less desirable from an estate-planning standpoint. The best approach is to involve the landowners along the corridor in the project at
the outset. Then the opportunity for a donation of land will arise naturally. When it does, ask—and it may be given.

DEVELOPMENT AND MAINTENANCE

Here is another rule: In developing a greenway (after the corridor has been secured), do it segment by segment, completing each entirely before moving on to the next. A completed segment becomes, in effect, an advertisement for what the whole greenway will look like when the job is finished, thereby engendering public enthusiasm and support.

For recreation-oriented projects, the preferred development model appears to be the beads-on-a-string type greenway—a paved trail connecting nodes that provide for picnic benches, restrooms, and so on. For nature-oriented greenways, the nodes disappear, and often the paving does too. There is, in both cases, a strong sense on the part of planners that greenways ought not to be overdeveloped, for reasons of cost as well as basic concept. They are not linear parks. If somehow they become linear parks, the maintenance problem increases.

And maintenance *is* a problem. In the enthusiasm of creation, many greenway-makers have told me, maintenance seems unimportant, but over the years the failure to provide for it in the initial planning can undo a greenway. The trail has to be kept in repair, the signs replaced when necessary, the trash picked up—all manner of mundanities. The questions to ask are: "Who is going to do it?" and "Where is the money going to come from?" There is no right answer: the task can be carried out publicly or privately, by volunteers or under a municipal budget, but the penalties for not addressing the questions can be severe, leading to the erosion of public interest in a greenway and conceivably to its abandonment.

GETTING HELP

There is no point in reinventing the wheel. Those who wish to create a greenway or a greenway system really should contact people of various kinds to get help. Most useful of all will be (1) those who have worked on similar greenway projects elsewhere; (2) national or regional organizations and government agencies that can provide specialized expertise; and (3) professional greenway-planner/consultants who may sometimes

be associated with a nearby university department or are in private practice. Here are the specifics:

1. To get in touch with similar greenway projects, one place to start is
    American Greenways, a program of the Conservation Fund. As a na-
    tional nonprofit group, American Greenways wishes to encourage
    individual projects as well as regional systems. (See the Afterword by
    Keith Hay for a more complete description of this program.) Of spe-
    cial interest is its greenway project data base, which began life as a set
    of notecards prepared in the course of researching this book and has
    since been expanded and is kept up to date. A request made to the
    data base can fetch the names, addresses, and phone numbers, plus
    background information on over one hundred greenway projects,
    some of which might provide crucial guidance at a crucial time. Con-
    tact American Greenways, The Conservation Fund, 1800 North Kent
    Street, Suite 1120, Arlington, Virginia 22209; telephone 703-523-6300.

2. There are scores of organizations that can provide specialized techni-
    cal assistance; but at the risk of angering some good friends, let me
    list those that the prospective greenway-maker should contact first.
    Just a few calls will put you into the network of greenwayites.

    —On matters of organization (especially of greenway foundations,
      as discussed earlier), general operations, and legal matters con-
      cerning land preservation, a helpful informational contact is the
      Land Trust Alliance, 900 17th St., N.W., Suite 410, Washington,
      D.C. 20006; telephone, 202-785-1410. Also, you should contact the
      Trust for Public Land, 82 Second Street, San Francisco, California
      94105; telephone, 415-495-5660. The latter organization has a field
      staff in regional offices throughout the country and may be able to
      provide some direct consultation.

    —For greenways concerned with rail corridor conversions, in whole
      or part, get in touch with the Rails-to-Trails Conservancy, 1400
      16th Street, N.W., Washington, D.C. 20036; telephone, 202-797-
      5400. The conservancy has a large number of local chapters and
      can provide expert legal, organizational, and operational advice on
      conversion and trailmaking.

    —For riparian greenways, contact American Rivers, 801 Pennsyl-
      vania Avenue, S.E., Suite 303, Washington, D.C. 20003; telephone

202-547-6900. This is an organization with a great deal of expertise in its membership as well as in its professional staff. In addition, you should contact the Rivers and Trails Conservation Assistance Program, National Park Service, Recreation Resources Assistance Division, P.O. Box 37127, Washington, D.C. 20013-7127; telephone, 202-343-3780. This new program provides technical assistance in trail and river corridor planning via nine regional National Park Service offices.

—For upland trail-based greenways, contact American Trails, a coalition of trailway organizations located at 1516 P Street, N.W., Washington, D.C. 20036; telephone, 202-797-5418. Also, contact the NPS Rivers and Trails program, address above.

—Greenway projects involving scenic-highway corridors should contact the Coalition for Scenic Beauty, 216 Seventh Street, S.E., Washington, D.C. 20003; telephone, 202-546-1100. For historic corridors, it is the National Trust for Historic Preservation, 1785 Massachusetts Avenue, N.W., Washington, D.C. 20036; telephone, 202-673-4165. The headquarters office will put you onto one of the trust's six regional offices.

3. When the time comes to develop a full-scale plan for a greenway or greenway system, a landscape architect will be needed. You can contact the landscape architecture department at a nearby university or the Information Resource Manager, American Society of Landscape Architects (ASLA), 4401 Connecticut Avenue, N.W., Fifth Floor, Washington, D.C. 20008; telephone, 202-686-2752. The ASLA will provide a list of landscape architects in your area, plus the address and phone of the local ASLA chapter.

A WORD ON MONEY

Greenway-making is as much a matter of scrounging as it is of making genteel applications to government and foundation funding sources. The fact is, scroungers make by far the best greenway leaders simply because, by rooting around, they somehow find the grants, the in-kind services, donated materials, and, significantly, the gifts of land. There is no way to provide tips for the art of scrounging; scroungers are born, not made.

For the rest of it, fund raising consists of a combination of T-shirt sales (and their ilk, including maps, books, buy-a-foot-of-greenway campaigns, and other means of producing citizen support for a greenway project) and more formal requests for aid. It would appear that the T-shirt approach should not be dismissed, because local citizen support is the best recommendation a project can have in terms of interesting outside funders in the project.

The contacts described above will doubtless be the best sources for information on government grants-in-aid at the national or (more likely) the state level where funds from open-space bond issues may be available. At present, there is no specific federal source for the funding of greenway projects. Federal assistance is available, but it is often in odd, roundabout ways best discovered through contact with American Greenways or another organization or with the Rivers and Trails Conservation Assistance Program of the National Park Service (listed above).

Philanthropic foundations should not be overlooked. Research undertaken by Darlene Thomas, research assistant for this book, uncovered forty-three national, twenty regional, and ninety-three state-level philanthropic foundations that have a special interest in greenways and similar projects. It is true that such foundations are inundated with requests. At the same time, they *are* obliged to give their money to *somebody,* so it might as well be to your greenway. The trick of it is simple: ask the foundation to which you wish to apply for their guidelines for application and then *follow them exactly.* Detailed information is available from the Foundation Center, 1001 Connecticut Avenue, N.W., Washington, D.C. 20036; telephone, 202-331-1400. The center will put you in touch with a branch office or with one of its one hundred cooperating libraries around the country, where you can personally search out the foundations most likely to be interested in your project.

11

The Greenway Imperative

In the beginner's mind there are many
possibilities, but in the expert's there are few.
—SHUNRYU SUZUKI, *Zen master*

After Bill Flournoy created the plan for the Capital Area Greenway in Raleigh, North Carolina, he took a job with state government, leaving to others the long-term execution of the concept he crafted. As it worked out, the greenway program got off to a slow start. It was based primarily on securing the corridors in the course of (mainly) residential development, with builders providing dedicated streamsides as part of their site plans. (Under the law, those refusing to do so would have to allow the city a year either to come up with funds to purchase the land or to decide to forego it.) At the time that Flournoy conceived of this, the 1965–75 development boom was on in Raleigh, but by the time the greenway program was finally put in place in the mid-1970s, the rate of development was beginning to slow down. Few miles of greenway were created. Then, in the 1980s, development heated up again in and around Raleigh. It was then that a landscape architect named Charles Flink applied for and got the job of greenway-planner, a position invented by Raleigh and now well established in many North Carolina cities. Over the next few years, Flink did so well with the city greenway system that many now associate its success with him as much as with Flournoy, and deservedly so, even though he did not stay long. Flink left the city planning department in 1986, preferring to set up in business as a full-time, independent greenway-planner.

As it happens, Chuck Flink (to use the nickname he favors) was one of the first people I interviewed about greenways. We took a walk along one of the many trails in the Raleigh system and then talked for several hours in his office, a bustling but somewhat underfurnished suite of rooms in a commercial building on the edge of town. As one of a small (but growing) number of independent landscape architects with a specialty in greenway consulting, he is by nature a promoter, so the entrepreneurial life suits him. And his reputation has grown rapidly. Before my visit, someone who did not know Flink personally gave me the impression that he was the grand old man of greenways. At the time that I visited Chuck Flink, in the spring of 1988, he was just twenty-eight years old.

It occurred to me then, and it seems true now, that in interviewing Flink, I was interviewing the future of greenways in America. And so, I asked him why he was devoting all his energies to this one—still rather obscure—specialty.

He took a moment to answer. "My personal point of view," he said slowly, "is that we're at a critical stage in the world. We have reached the point where we need to think about what kind of environmental future we're going to have. I believe we can live in harmony with our environment; we don't have to go out there and pave every square inch. But we need a new ethic for living in our world. That's why I do what I do.

"By preserving the land in its natural state," he explained, "you allow the natural system as God designed it to function. If you think of greenways as a means to provide a place for biological communities in their natural state to be maintained, and if at the same time you provide human access to the greenway corridor, you have given people a means to look at our world in a different way."

Those were lofty thoughts, and well put, but the relation of greenways to the larger issues of the environment was not immediately clear to me. Greenways, as an artifact, would seem to have little to do with planetary survival. They are nice but so what? As I was considering these matters, Flink's discussion veered suddenly into the personal.

"We were living in a brand new subdivision near St. Louis, in Creve

Coeur, just northwest of the city," Flink said, apropos of something I missed because of my interior argument about whether greenways had anything to do with, say, global deforestation. "There was a very large tract of land behind us with a stream called Sunny Brook. The backyard sloped down to the stream, and on the other side the land sloped up again steeply in a big woods. We used to play down by the stream and in the adjoining woods all the time. We would dam up the little creek; it was only about three or four feet wide. We would tramp up and down the streamway; it seemed to my sister and me and to the little kids we played with that we had gone miles and miles, but probably it was only a few hundred yards. We'd look at the frogs and turtles and salamanders, the typical intimate stream life you find in a place like that. One time we built a fort up in the woods overlooking the stream, our domain. I was six years old. It was a secret place for all of us kids." Chuck Flink paused to look at me, to see if I was listening.

"Then a tragic thing happened," he continued. "One day the bulldozers came and cleared everything. All the mothers came out and lay down in front of the bulldozers. One neighbor beat on one of them with a broom and screamed. She just screamed and screamed. But it didn't do any good. The woods were cleared, the brook was put in a pipe and covered with asphalt. A road was put over Sunny Brook and the woods became apartment houses.

"It was traumatic," Chuck Flink concluded. "I often think about that; sometimes I still experience that feeling of loss."

What Flink described evidently became a controlling metaphor for his life. The loss of a creek mattered to him. And it should matter to us. The poet Robert Frost understood this point, as he makes plain in a twenty-four-line poem entitled "A Brook in the City," concerning a similar event. It was written in the early part of the twentieth century, but the lines are wholly apposite to what Flink was telling me, to the underlying impulse to preserve so small a thing as a child's playbrook in a St. Louis suburb.

Frost begins by telling how his brook once ran by a farmhouse, embracing the house, in fact, in a course shaped like an "elbow crook," as if to provide safety and comfort. The brook was a familiar place, so familiar the poet could recall how when he would dip his hand in the steady current, the water would "leap his knuckle," and how he would test the crossing currents of the brook by casting a flower into it. But here, in this New Hampshire town, just as in Creve Coeur, a new city street had to be built. The poet observes that the meadow grass could easily be paved over, and the woods would offer no resistance for the trees could be cut into fireplace lengths and consumed. But what of the brook? How would the street-builders cope with what was, in fact, unstaunchable? The bleak solution, the poem relates, was to send the brook to "live and run" underground, in a "sewer dungeon," a banishment of an "immortal force," represented in this one small brook, which perhaps would have dire consequences we could barely understand. Frost concludes with these lines of warning:

> No one would know except for ancient maps
> That such a brook ran water. But I wonder
> If from its being kept forever under
> The thoughts may not have risen that so keep
> This new-built city from both work and sleep.

That so keep the new-built city from work and sleep. Thus we are reminded that "The Environment," with which we are much preoccupied these days in terms of ozone layer and rainforest and carbon monoxide, begins at the edges of our shoes as we explore along a streamside path, at the tips of our fingers as the racing waters curl around them, and in the bordering woodlands in which we, hugging our knees, sit still as a stone, watching a deer glide softly by.

Greenways, therefore, should be seen as a beginning in a journey toward an environmental consciousness—a way for people to practice as well to promote the protection of the ecosphere, starting at the edges of their shoes; a way for people to express "a necessary land ethic," in the phrase of Aldo Leopold for whom the *land* meant all the soils and waters and creatures and plants of the world and the ways in which these elements interact with one another.

In the city of High Point, North Carolina, Chuck Flink told me, the sponsors of a local greenway program raise money for it by asking people to buy a foot of the greenway for $25—which is actually pretty close to the cost of constructing twelve linear inches of an eight-foot-wide path along the streamsides of the city. In return, you get a deed-like certificate that indicates which foot, or feet, you have bought and a T-shirt reading "One foot at a time" on the front and "Ask me where my feet are" on the back.

I realize there must be detailed and quite technical municipal planning maps and engineering specifications for such greenways. And comprehensive programs and policies must be drafted up by government lawyers. But plans and policies, necessary and helpful though they may be, do not themselves create the greenways along our Sunny Brooks, offering protection to them as representatives of the immortal force. The greenways come into being one footstep at a time through individual choice and collective action. And who is to say that such modest steps as these will not begin a historic journey with ethical possibilities unimaginable?

AFTERWORD

This remarkable book marks a milestone in achieving a goal I have had for decades—a goal that is shared by thousands of Americans who have experienced a similar and all-too-common tragedy. Returning as adults to the world of nature we enjoyed in our youth—to a local creek, woods, park, lake, or some other special place—we found it to be not only much smaller than it once was but often altered beyond recognition or totally destroyed by the forces of urbanization and the deeds of short-sighted planners and developers. It is sad that future generations of boys and girls will rarely have the same opportunity to experience, as we did, the peace, the ever-changing sights and sounds of the seasons, and the endless fascination of nature that was available to us so close to home.

For most of my working life, I have attempted to discover ways to preserve such unique places in this increasingly congested and highly developed living environment of ours. For this reason, I was among those who proposed to the 1987 President's Commission on Americans Outdoors that an important way to achieve a more equitable balance between thoughtless development and the wise use of our remaining natural systems would be to establish and protect green corridors across America. Connecting open spaces to form a living landscape of such corridors was indeed the answer to our ardent quest to link local creeks, rivers, and wetlands with parks, wildlife reserves, and other recreational and historical amenities. The Commission's recommendation to "establish a network of greenways across America" was aggressively pursued by Patrick

F. Noonan, a member of the President's Commission and the president of the Conservation Fund, who had lost a special place of his own in his native Maryland. He is responsible for my personal involvement with the greenway movement and for helping to secure the funding that made it possible for the Conservation Fund to sponsor the publication of this book and to undertake the "American Greenways" program.

We set out to understand the contemporary greenway movement, to define the "greenway" concept, and to develop a program that would assist states and local communities in achieving their respective greenway-building initiatives. The only way to accomplish this task, we discovered, was to begin a personal reconnaissance of successful greenway projects across the nation and to learn who and what made them successful. To undertake such a survey, to interview the hundreds of people who are involved in creating greenways, and to reduce the voluminous notes and materials into an interesting and compelling book for the "common reader" would require the combined talents of a scholar, a gifted writer, and an experienced land conservationist. By good fortune, I was able to persuade a long-time friend and colleague who embodied such talents, Charles E. Little, to take on the task. With this book, he has provided the nation with a contemporary analysis and definition of the physical and conceptual nature of greenways and the proven methodologies for creating them.

Once the book was underway, I compiled information on how best to design a program to meet the informational and service needs of greenway-makers at the local, county, and state levels. Thus, the American Greenways program was established in 1987 by the Conservation Fund to provide such tools. The Fund is a national, not-for-profit, scientific and educational organization that is committed to advancing land conservation in the United States. Its programs are financed by individual gifts and foundation and government grants.

The Conservation Fund's American Greenways program, as funding becomes available, plans not only to encourage the wide distribution of *Greenways for America* but also to provide a number of important services. Among them are: a national "greenways data base" that will ensure a means for greenway-makers to get in touch with one another; a "greenways referral service" for those who wish to consult with individuals, organizations, and public and private agencies that provide greenway-related services; the provision of grants for demonstration projects that can serve as model greenways and that offer new approaches to financing, ecological and economic analysis, and other areas of greenway-making; the publication, in cooperation with others, of a series of technical monographs on all aspects of greenways; the arrangement of greenway conferences and, when necessary, the publication of their proceedings; and the creation of a national greenways awards program and other communication projects to help advance the greenway idea.

It is my hope that everyone who reads this timely book will be inspired to help us achieve the goal of protecting those remaining special places in the city and countryside where nature still reigns, where the opportunity to find tranquility still abounds, and where our quality of everyday life can be enriched.

KEITH G. HAY, *Director*
American Greenways Program
The Conservation Fund
Arlington, Virginia

PRINCIPAL SOURCES

INTERVIEWS

Gerald W. Adelmann, Upper Illinois Valley Association, Chicago, Illinois.
Charles E. Aguar, University of Georgia, Athens, Georgia.
Kristi Akers, Platte River Parkway Trust, Casper, Wyoming.
Dale Allen, Trust for Public Land, Tallahassee, Florida.
Richard Anderwald, Yakima River Greenway Foundation, Yakima, Washington.
Maude M. Backes, Delaware and Raritan Greenway Alliance, Pennington, New Jersey.
Charles E. Beveridge, American University, Washington, D.C.
Charles Birnbaum, Walmsley and Company, New York, New York.
Jim Bowen, RiverCity Company, Chattanooga, Tennessee.
Hooper Brooks, Regional Plan Association, New York, New York.
Christopher N. Brown, Rivers and Trails Conservation Program, National Park Service, Washington, D.C.
Timothy D. Brown, Town of Cary, North Carolina.

Interview entries show affiliations at the time of the interview. Most interviews were conducted in person, some were by means of telephone calls, and many included both. By and large, only those individuals interviewed at some length are included here, although many others provided key pieces of information. Virtually all contacts (about two hundred for the eighty projects analyzed) supplied the author with an abundance of published material. Nevertheless only those items of more than purely local interest are listed. Here and there I have supplied a comment and, when appropriate, a publisher's address, so that the list may be used as a kind of technical appendix. The complete research files for the book have been given to North Carolina State University, Raleigh, to form the basis for a national greenway archive. For more information, contact: University Archives, The Libraries, Box 7111, North Carolina State University, Raleigh, NC 27695; telephone (919) 737-2843.

David Burwell, Rails-to-Trails Conservancy, Washington, D.C.

Douglas Cheever, Heritage Trail, Inc., Dubuque, Iowa.

Karen Cragnolin, French Broad Riverfront Planning Committee, Asheville, North Carolina.

Broward Davis, Broward Davis and Associates, Inc., Tallahassee, Florida.

Meg Downey, *Poughkeepsie Journal,* Poughkeepsie, New York.

Albert Edelman, 40-Mile Loop Land Trust, Portland, Oregon.

J. Glenn Eugster, National Park Service, Philadelphia, Pennsylvania.

Craig Evans, Walkways Center, Washington, D.C.

Charles A. Flink, Greenways, Inc., Raleigh, North Carolina.

William L. Flournoy, Jr. North Carolina Department of Environment, Health, and Natural Resources, Raleigh, North Carolina.

Richard T. T. Forman, Harvard School of Design, Cambridge, Massachusetts.

Al Foster, Meramec River Recreation Association, Frontenac, Missouri.

Leigh Fowler, Platte River Parkway Trust, Casper, Wyoming.

Tom Fox, Neighborhood Open Space Coalition, New York, New York.

William E. Fraser, Collin County Open Space Program, McKinney, Texas.

Stella Furjanic, Appalachee Land Conservancy, Tallahassee, Florida.

Merle D. Grimes, Platte River Greenway Foundation, Denver, Colorado.

Mary Anne Guitar, First Selectman, Town of Redding, Connecticut.

Robert P. Hagenhofer, Sourland Regional Citizens Planning Council, Flemington, New Jersey.

James R. Hinkley, planning consultant, Pittsboro, North Carolina.

Tony Hiss, *New Yorker* Magazine, New York, New York.

Linda Hixon, attorney, Chattanooga, Tennessee.

Jean Hocker, Land Trust Alliance, Alexandria, Virginia.

Robert Kendrick, Chamber of Commerce, Asheville, North Carolina.

Caroline King, Hudson River Valley Greenway Council, Albany, New York.

Kenny King, boat guide, Eugene, Oregon.

James Knight, Oregon Land Conservation and Development Commission, Salem, Oregon.

William A. Krebs, Maryland Department of Natural Resources, Annapolis, Maryland.

Judith Kunofsky, Greenbelt Alliance, San Francisco, California.

Douglass Lea, author and editor, Waterford, Virginia.

Marti Leicester, Golden Gate National Recreation Area, National Park Service, San Francisco, California.

Philip H. Lewis, Jr., Environmental Awareness Center, University of Wisconsin, Madison, Wisconsin.

Nina Lovinger, Oregon Natural Resources Council, Eugene, Oregon.

Leslie Luchonok, Bay Circuit Program, Massachusetts Department of Environmental Management, Boston, Massachusetts.

Anne Lusk, Stowe Recreation Path, Stowe, Vermont.

Anne McClellan, Neighborhood Open Space Coalition, New York, New York.

Stuart H. Macdonald, Trails Program, Colorado Division of Parks and Outdoor Recreation, Denver, Colorado.

Edward T. McMahon, Coalition for Scenic Beauty, Washington, D.C.

Chuck Mitchell, Mad Dog Design and Construction Company, Tallahassee, Florida.

John G. Mitchell, Redding Conservation Commission, Redding, Connecticut.

Allan H. Morgan, Sudbury Valley Trustees, Wayland, Massachusetts.

Robert O. Myhr, San Juan Preservation Trust, Lopez, Washington.

Larry Offerdahl, Department of Parks and Recreation, McKinney, Texas.

Keith Oliver, Pima County Transportation and Flood Control District, Tucson, Arizona.

W. Kent Olson, American Rivers, Washington, D.C.

Larry Orman, Greenbelt Alliance, San Francisco, California.

Anne Peery, Trust for Public Land, Tallahassee, Florida.

Susan P. Phillips, Association of Bay Area Governments, Oakland, California.

Robert Rindy, Oregon Land Conservation and Development Commission, Salem, Oregon.

Hal Salwasser, U.S. Forest Service, Washington, D.C.

David S. Sampson, Hudson River Valley Greenway Council, Albany, New York.

Ann Satterthwaite, planning consultant, Washington, D.C.

Klara B. Sauer, Scenic Hudson, Inc., Poughkeepsie, New York.

Loring LaBarbera Schwarz, environmental planner, Arlington, Virginia.

Robert M. Searns, Urban Edges, Denver, Colorado.

Susan E. Sedgwick, St. Louis County Department of Parks and Recreation, Clayton, Missouri.

Jeff Shoemaker, Platte River Greenway Foundation, Denver, Colorado.

Joe Shoemaker, Platte River Greenway Foundation, Denver, Colorado.

Nancy Smith, Clarke County Parks Department, Athens, Georgia

Valerie Spale, Save the Prairie Society, Westchester, Illinois.

William T. Spitzer, Recreation Resources Assistance Division, National Park Service, Washington, D.C.

Brian L. Steen, Big Sur Land Trust, Carmel, California.

Mark Thornton, City of Allen Department of Parks and Recreation, Allen, Texas.

William Thornton, park planner, Plano, Texas.

Jean Webb, French Broad River Foundation, Asheville, North Carolina.

Susan Ziegler, Bay Circuit Program, Massachusetts Department of Environmental Management, Boston, Massachusetts.

BOOKS

Blake, Peter. *God's Own Junkyard*. New York: Holt, Rinehart, and Winston, 1964.

Boyle, Robert H. *The Hudson River: A Natural and Unnatural History*. New York: Norton, 1969.

Caro, Robert A. *The Power Broker: Robert Moses and the Fall of New York*. New York: Knopf, 1974.

Diamant, Rolf, et al. *A Citizen's Guide to River Conservation*. Washington, D.C.: Conservation Foundation, 1984.

Dykeman, Wilma. *The French Broad*. Knoxville: University of Tennessee Press, 1955.

Eliot, Charles W. *Charles Eliot, Landscape Architect*. Boston: Houghton Mifflin, 1902.

Goodman, Paul, and Percival Goodman. *Communitas*. New York: Random House, 1947.

Houle, Marcy Cottrell. *One City's Wilderness: Portland's Forest Park*. Portland: Oregon Historical Society Press, 1988.

Howard, Ebenezer. *Garden Cities of To-Morrow*. 1898. Reprint. Cambridge, Mass.: MIT Press, 1965.

Leopold, Aldo. *A Sand County Almanac*. New York: Oxford University Press, 1949.

Longgood, William. *The Darkening Land*. New York: Simon and Schuster, 1972.

McHarg, Ian L. *Design with Nature*. Garden City, N.Y.: Natural History Press, 1969.

MacKaye, Benton. *The New Exploration*. New York: Harcourt Brace, 1928.

McLaughlin, Charles Capen, Charles E. Beveridge, and David Schuyler, eds. *The Papers of Frederick Law Olmsted*, vols. 1–5. Baltimore: Johns Hopkins University Press, 1977–. This important ongoing project will total twelve volumes. The general reader will find the introductory essays of each volume to be most useful.

Mueller, Marge, and Ted Mueller. *The San Juan Islands*. Seattle: The Mountaineers, 1988.

Mumford, Lewis. *The City in History*. New York: Harcourt, Brace, and World, 1961.

President's Commission on Americans Outdoors. *Americans Outdoors: The Legacy, the Challenge*. Covelo, Calif.: Island Press, 1987. Contains a major recommendation on greenways.

Rae, John B. *The Road and Car in American Life*. Cambridge, Mass.: MIT Press, 1971.

Roper, Laura Wood. *FLO: A Biography of Frederick Law Olmsted*. Baltimore: Johns Hopkins University Press, 1973.

Schuyler, David. *The New Urban Landscape: The Redefinition of City Form in Nineteenth-Century America*. Baltimore: Johns Hopkins University Press, 1986. A first-rate study of parks and urban amenities.

Shoemaker, Joe, with Leonard A. Stevens. *Returning the Platte to the People*. Denver: The Platte River Greenway Foundation, 1981. A fascinating case history of a premier urban river greenway. Full of tips for pro and tyro alike. Available from the foundation at 1666 S. University Blvd., Denver, CO 80210.

Stein, Clarence. *Toward New Towns for America*. New York: Reinhold, 1951.

Stevenson, Elizabeth. *Park Maker: A Life of Frederick Law Olmsted.* New York: Macmillan, 1977.

Stokes, Samuel N., et al. *Saving America's Countryside: A Guide to Rural Conservation.* Baltimore: Johns Hopkins University Press, 1989. An up-to-date and extremely useful citizen's how-to manual with policy-oriented case studies.

Tishler, William H., ed. *American Landscape Architecture: Designers and Places.* Washington, D.C.: Preservation Press, 1989.

Whyte, William H. *The Last Landscape.* New York: Doubleday, 1968. The definitive book on metropolitan open space. See especially Chapter 10, "Linkage," for an early essay on greenways.

PUBLISHED REPORTS, REGIONAL STUDIES, AND PLANS

Albert H. Halff Associates, Inc. *A Linear Greenbelt Park Study.* Allen, Tex.: City of Allen, 1986.

Association of Bay Area Governments. *Project Description: San Francisco Bay Area Trail, Initial Environmental Study, and Possible Bay Trail Segments.* Oakland, Calif.: n.d. (1988). Write: ABAG, P.O. Box 2050, Oakland, CA 94604-2050.

Bay Area Trails Council. *The San Francisco Bay Area Ridge Trail Technical Coordinating Guidebook.* San Francisco, Calif.: n.d. (1988). Description of the Ridge Trail project and procedures for establishing the trail corridor. Write: Judith Kunofsky, Greenbelt Alliance, 116 New Montgomery St., Suite 640, San Francisco, CA 94105.

Beveridge, Charles E., and Carolyn F. Hoffman. *The Master List of Design Projects of the Olmsted Firm, 1857–1950.* Boston: Massachusetts Association for Olmsted Parks, 1987.

Canopy Road Advisory Committee. *Canopy Roads Preservation Plan.* Tallahassee, Fla.: 1988. Write: Appalachee Land Conservancy, P.O. Box 14266, Tallahassee, FL 32317.

Carr, Lynch Associates, Inc. *Tennessee Riverpark: Chattanooga.* Chattanooga, Tenn.: RiverCity Company, 1985. How to think big—master plan for a multimillion-dollar riverfront redevelopment program cum greenway. Address: The RiverCity Company, 701 Broad St., Chattanooga, TN 37402.

City of Boulder, Colorado. *Boulder Creek: A Plan for Preservation and Development.* Boulder, Colo.: n.d. (1984?). Write: Gary Lacy, Boulder Creek Project, City of Boulder, P.O. Box 791, Boulder, CO 80306.

City of Casper, Wyoming. *Master Plan: Platte River Parkway.* Casper, Wyo.: 1982. Photocopies may be available from the Platte River Parkway Trust, P.O. Box 1228, Casper, WY 82602. See also citation under Platte River Parkway Trust.

City of Raleigh, North Carolina. *Administration's Response to the Capital Area Greenway Master Plan.* Raleigh, N.C.: 1986. The most recent comprehensive document on the expansion of the greenway system. Address: City of Raleigh, 222 W. Hargett St., Raleigh, NC 27602.

Colorado Division of Parks and Outdoor Recreation. *State Recreational Trails Master Plan/Nonmotorized.* Denver: 1985.

David Evans and Associates, Inc. *40-Mile Loop Master Plan.* Portland, Ore.: 40-Mile Loop Land Trust, 1983. An excellent model for a detailed greenway plan. Not generally available, but the 40-Mile Loop Land Trust may send you a photocopy if you cover the cost. Address: 519 S.W. Third Ave., Portland, OR 97204.

Defenders of Wildlife. *Preserving Communities and Corridors.* Washington, D.C.: 1989. A collection of useful papers on wildlife corridors. Available from Defenders of Wildlife, 1244 Nineteenth St., N.W., Washington, DC 20036.

Diamond, Henry L., et al. with Douglass Lea. *Greenways in the Hudson River Valley: A New Strategy for Preserving an American Treasure.* Tarrytown, N.Y.: Sleepy Hollow Press, 1988.

Ensor, Joan, and John G. Mitchell. *The Book of Trails,* 2d. ed. Redding, Conn.: Redding Conservation Commission and Redding Land Trust, 1985. A classic. Write: Town Office Building, Redding, CT 06875.

Eubanks, David. *Old Plank Road Trail-Community Impact Study. Chicago: Open Lands Project, 1985.* Approach to cost and privacy issues of trails. Write: Open Lands Project, 220 S. State St., Suite 1880, Chicago, IL 60604-2103.

Federal Highway Administration. *Scenic Byways.* Washington, D.C.: 1988. An important policy document on scenic road designation and protection. Available from the Federal Highway Administration, Department of Transportation, 400 7th St. S.W., Room 4210, Washington, DC 20590. Ask for publication FHWA-DF-88-004.

Flournoy, William L., Jr. *Capital City Greenway: A Report to the City Council on the Benefits, Potential, and Methodology of Establishing a Greenway System in Raleigh.* Raleigh, N.C.: 1972. This is the plan (a thesis for a master's degree) that started the greenway movement in North Carolina and many other states. Out of print, but contact the author for a possible photocopy at North Carolina Department of Natural Resources, P.O. Box 27687, Raleigh, NC 27611-7687.

Fox, Tom, and Anne McClellan. *The Brooklyn-Queens Greenway: A Design Study.* New York: Neighborhood Open Space Coalition, 1988. Specifications and cost estimates for the BQG. Write: Neighborhood Open Space Coalition, 72 Reade St., New York, NY 10007.

Fox, Tom, Anne McClellan, and Maria Stanco. *The Brooklyn-Queens Greenway: A Feasibility Study.* New York: Neighborhood Open Space Coalition, n.d. (1987?). First rate. Available from the coalition, address above.

Friends of Parks, Recreation, and Conservation in Westchester, Inc. *The Bronx River Parkway Reservation.* White Plains, N.Y.: n.d. (1985?). Available from Westchester County Department of Parks, 618 Michaelian Office Bldg., White Plains, NY 10601.

Greenbelt Alliance. *Reviving the Sustainable Metropolis.* San Francisco, Calif.: n.d. (1989?). On metropolitan growth in the San Francisco urban region, with emphasis on a bay area greenbelt. Address: 116 New Montgomery St., Suite 640, San Francisco, CA 94105.

Harris, Larry D. *Conservation Corridors: A Highway System for Wildlife*. An ENFO Report. Winter Park, Fla.: Florida Conservation Foundation, 1985. Available from Environmental Information Center, 1203 Orange Ave., Winter Park, FL 32789.

Hixson Chamber of Commerce. *North Chickamauga Creek Greenway: Preliminary Master Plan*. Hixson, Tenn.: 1989. Excellent example of a suburban greenway project plan. Address: Hixson Chamber of Commerce, P.O. Box 727, Hixson, TN 37343.

Jones, Stanton. *The Davis Greenway*. Davis, Calif.: 1988. A first-rate plan integrating the Davis bikeways with a greenway system. Write: Department of Environmental Design, University of California, Davis, CA 95616.

Kunofsky, Judith, and M. Thomas Jacobson. *Tools of the Greenbelt*. San Francisco, Calif.: People for Open Space (Greenbelt Alliance), 1985 (see address under Greenbelt Alliance).

Land Trust Exchange. *1989 National Directory of Conservation Land Trusts*. Arlington, Va.: 1989. Lists 748 local groups, many of which are undertaking greenway projects. Available from the LTE at 900 17th St., N.W., Suite 410, Washington, D.C. 20006.

Marist Institute for Public Opinion. *A Survey of Public Attitudes on the Hudson River Valley*. Poughkeepsie, N.Y.: Marist College, n.d. (1987?). "By greater than 2:1, residents in the Hudson River Valley believe that [a greenway] is a good idea even if it limits development in their county." Available from Scenic Hudson, Inc., 9 Vassar St., Poughkeepsie, NY 12601.

Maryland Department of Natural Resources. *Patapsco Greenway: A Redevelopment Concept for the Lower Patapsco River Valley*. Annapolis, Md.: 1987.

Mid-Atlantic Regional Office, National Park Service. *Riverwork Book*. Philadelphia, Pa.: 1988. Write NPS at 260 Customs House, 200 Chestnut St., Philadelphia, PA 19106.

Mitchell, John G. *High Rock*. New York: Friends of High Rock, 1976.

Montagne, Charles H. *Preserving Abandoned Rights-of-Way for Public Use: A Legal Manual*. Washington, D.C.: Rails-to-Trails Conservancy, 1989 (see address under Rails-to-Trails Conservancy).

National Park Service. *Rivers and Trails Conservation Assistance Program Annual Report*. Washington, D.C.: 1988. Describes NPS technical services and provides addresses of regional greenway specialists. Contact Christopher N. Brown, Manager, NPS Rivers and Trails Conservation Program, P.O. Box 37127, Washington, DC 20013.

North Central Texas Council of Governments. *Rowlett Creek Interjurisdictional Watershed Management Program*. Arlington, Tex.: North Central Texas Council of Governments, 1987. Address: P.O. Drawer COG, Arlington, TX 76005-5888.

Olson, W. Kent. *Natural Rivers and the Public Trust*. Washington, D.C.: American Rivers, Inc., 1988.

Pima County Department of Transportation and Flood Control District. *Preliminary Discussion Document for a Regional Permit Application under Section 404, Clean Water Act, Submitted to U.S. Army Corps of Engineers, Los Angeles District.* Tucson, Ariz.: 1987.

_____. *General Mitigation Approach for 404 Permits.* Tucson, Ariz.: 1988. Features natural greenways as opposed to engineering structures for flood mitigation. Write: Pima County DOT & FCD, 1313 S. Mission Rd., Tucson, AZ 85713.

_____. *River Park Design Guidelines.* Tucson, Ariz.: 1988. Description of Tucson greenway system. Address above.

Pima County Open Space Committee. *The Findings of the Pima County Open Space Committee,* with a supplemental report, *Open Space in Pima County.* Tucson, Ariz.: 1988. Discusses Tucson greenway system. Write: Pima County DOT & FCD, 1313 S. Mission Rd., Tucson, AZ 85713.

Platte River Parkway Trust. *1987 Annual Report to Board and Membership.* Casper, Wyo.: 1987. Especially good report showing an urban river greenway program in action. Address: P.O. Box 1228, Casper, WY 82602.

Rails-to-Trails Conservancy. *Converting Rails-to-Trails: A Citizen's Manual for Transforming Abandoned Rail Corridors into Multipurpose Public Paths.* Washington, D.C.: 1987. This indispensable manual is updated from time to time. Available from the RTC, 1400 16th St., N.W., Washington, DC 20036.

_____. *Sampler of America's Rail Trails.* Washington, D.C.: 1988.

Redding, Connecticut Conservation Commission. *Redding Open Space Plan.* Redding, Conn.: 1984. Features the Redding Greenbelts proposal. Address: Town Office Building, Redding, CT 06875.

St. Louis County Department of Parks and Recreation. *Lower Meramec River Management Study.* St. Louis: Meramec River Recreation Area Coordinating Committee, 1980.

Satterthwaite, Ann, with John G. Mitchell. *Appalachian Greenway.* Harpers Ferry, W. Va.: 1975. A proposal to expand the Appalachian Trail into a greenway.

Scenic Hudson, Inc. and National Park Service. *Building Greenways in the Hudson River Valley: A Guide for Action.* Poughkeepsie, N.Y.: 1989. Write: Scenic Hudson, 9 Vassar St., Poughkeepsie, NY 12601.

Seattle Engineering Department. *Evaluation of the Burke-Gilman Trail's Effect on Property Values and Crime.* Seattle: 1987. Available from City of Seattle, Engineering Department, Bicycle Program, 600 4th Ave., 9th Floor, Seattle, WA 98104.

Shaw, William W., et al. *Wildlife Habitats in Tucson: A Strategy for Conservation.* Tucson, Ariz.: School of Renewable Natural Resources, University of Arizona, 1986.

Sourland Regional Citizens Planning Council. *The Sourland Legacy.* Neshanic Station, N.J.: 1989. Available from the council at Box 538, Neshanic Station, NJ 08853.

Tucker, Dean F., and Hugh A. Devine. *Town of Cary Parks, Recreation, and Greenways Survey: Final Report.* Cary, N.C.: 1989. An exhaustive citizen survey on all kinds of greenway issues such as the preference of asphalt over dirt for paths (a draw). Address: Cary Planning Department, 316 N. Academy St., Cary, NC 27511.

U.S. Army Corps of Engineers. *Survey Report and Environmental Assessment of Rillito River and Associated Streams.* Los Angeles, Calif.: 1988. On Tucson's floods.

U.S. Environmental Protection Agency. *National Water Quality Inventory: 1986 Report to Congress.* Washington, D.C.: U.S. Government Printing Office, 1988.

U.S. Office of Coastal Zone Management, National Oceanic and Atmospheric Administration. *Improving Your Waterfront: A Practical Guide.* Washington, D.C.: U.S. Government Printing Office, 1980.

Urban Design Assistance Team (AIA) and Community Assistance Team (ASLA). *The Riverfront Plan.* Asheville, N.C.: French Broad Riverfront Planning Committee, Inc., 1989. The assistance teams are from the state chapters of the American Institute of Architects and the American Society of Landscape Architects. Both organizations provide pro bono "charettes" to help localities develop new planning concepts. This project represents the first time the two groups teamed up. The plan is available from the French Broad Riverfront Planning Committee, P.O. Box 15488, Asheville, NC 28813-0488.

Urban Drainage and Flood Control District. *The South Platte River: A Plan for the Future—Chatfield to Brighton.* Denver, Colo.: 1985. Shows relation of flood control to greenway planning for forty miles of the South Platte, through Denver and four counties north and south of the city. Write: UDFCD, 2480 W. 26th Ave., Suite 156-B, Denver, CO 80211.

Whyte, William H. *Cluster Development.* New York: American Conservation Association, 1961.

————. *Securing Open Space for Urban America: Conservation Easements.* Washington, D.C.: Urban Land Institute, 1959. Contains the earliest reference to *greenways* as such which I have been able to find.

Wilburn, Gary. *Routes of History: Recreational Use and Preservation of Historic Transportation Corridors.* Information Series 38. Washington, D.C.: National Trust for Historic Preservation, 1985. A useful how-to paper, with case histories, by a former National Trust lawyer. Address: National Trust, 1785 Massachusetts Ave., N.W., Washington, DC 20036.

Wilkins, Suzanne, and Roger Koontz. *Connecticut Land Trust Handbook.* Middletown, Conn.: The Nature Conservancy and the Conservation Law Foundation of New England, 1982. Despite its focus on New England, this is a generally useful how-to handbook for setting up and operating land trusts to conduct greenway projects. Available from the Nature Conservancy at 55 High St., Middletown, CT 06457.

UNPUBLISHED PAPERS

Backes, Maude. "The Delaware and Raritan Greenway: A Regional Vision Realized through Local Action." Photocopied conference paper, December 1988.

Burwell, David. "Trail Blazing for Tomorrow: A National Greenway Network." Conference Paper, 27 July 1989.

Cheever, Douglas. "Primer for Rail-Trail Proponents." Photocopied paper, n.d. This two-page how-to for rail-trail conversion is a masterpiece. Write: Heritage Trail, Inc., 900 Kelly La., Dubuque, IA 52001.

Coalition for Scenic Beauty. "Environmental Coalition Backs Scenic Byways Legislation." Press release, 22 February 1989. Contains summary of scenic highway bill (q.v., Miscellaneous Documents, below).

Conservation Fund. "Greenways to the Bay." Photocopied paper, n.d. (1989). Concept description for a statewide greenway system for Maryland.

Coyle, Kevin J. "Strategies and Tools for Protecting Greenways." Photocopied paper, 30 November 1987. Good summary, by a lawyer, of greenway acquisition techniques. Available from American Rivers, 801 Pennsylvania Ave., S.E., Suite 303, Washington, DC 20003.

Dawson, Kerry J., and Mark Francis. "Open Space and Livability in Davis." Photocopied paper, 28 October 1987. Proposes a wildlife and natural area system based on greenways. Write: Department of Environmental Design, University of California, Davis, CA 95616.

Eugster, J. Glenn. "Steps in State and Local Greenway Conservation Planning." Photocopied paper, 19 February 1988.

Forbes, Christina C. "Greenway Development Statutes and Programs." Photocopied paper, 22 August 1988. Deals with federal and New York state statutes and programs.

Hay, Keith. "Wildlife Corridors for Metropolitan America." Photocopied paper, 1986. Submitted to the President's Commission on Americans Outdoors.

Houck, Michael C. "Urban Wildlife Habitat Inventory: The Willamette River Greenway, Portland, Oregon." Galley proofs for an article, n.d. (1986?).

Huckelberry, C. H. "Flood Damage Reduction through Flood-Prone Land Acquisition." Photocopied report to Pima County (Tucson) Board of Supervisors, with an accompanying memorandum of recommendations, 31 October 1985. Write: Pima County Department of Transportation and Flood Control District, 1313 S. Mission Rd., Tucson, AZ 85713.

Lewis, Philip H., Jr. "The Environmental Awareness Center." Draft manuscript for a publication, n.d.

Lusk, Anne. "How to Build a Path in Your Community." Photocopied paper, 1986. Lessons from the Stowe Recreation Path. Address: Anne Lusk, R.D. 2, Box 3780, Stowe, VT 05672.

Macdonald, Stuart H. "Building Trails with Community and Political Support." Photocopied paper, n.d.

Maryland Department of Natural Resources. "Program Open Space: A Brief History." Photocopied paper, n.d. (1988?).

Mercer, Paige. "Charles Eliot's Bay Circuit Greenbelt Project." Manuscript paper for a graduate course, 25 May 1989. Address: 300 Topsfield Road, Ipswich, MA 01938.

Minnesota Department of Natural Resources. "Living Along Trails: What People Expect and Find." Mimeographed paper, 1987 (revised). Results from a 1979–80 survey of landowners. Available from: Trails Program Section, Minn. DNR, Box 52, 500 Lafayette Rd., St. Paul, MN 55155-4052.

Myhr, Robert O. "Private Coastline Conservation Management: The Land Trust in the San Juan Islands, Washington." Photocopied paper, n.d. On the activities and procedures of the trust. Address: San Juan Preservation Trust, Route 1, Box 2114, Lopez Island, WA 98261.

Rails-to-Trails Conservancy. "The Number of U.S. Rails-to-Trails Conversions Passes 200-Mark: 27 Million Used them in '88." Press release, 9 February 1989. Contains state-by-state breakdown of rail-trail miles in the United States.

Reichenbach, Kristina. "Illinois Greenways: Opportunities and Opposition." Master's degree thesis, 15 May 1989. A fine paper on the politics of greenway-making, with cases in point covering the Fox River, I & M Canal, Middle Fork of the Vermilion River, Rock Island Trail, Heartland Pathway, and the Shawnee Trail, all in Illinois. Address: R.R. 1, Box 371, Petersburg, IL 62675.

Schwarz, Loring LaBarbera. "Maryland Greenways." Photocopied report on 1989 workshop discussions concerning a state-level program, n.d.

Steen, Brian L. "The Big Sur Coast: An Area of Natural Grandeur." Manuscript chapter for a report, n.d. (1987?). Write: Big Sur Land Trust, Box 221846, Carmel, CA 93922.

Trustees of Public Reservations of Massachusetts. *The Bay Circuit: A Practical Plan for the Extension of the Metropolitan Park System and the Development of a State Parkway through a Number of Reservations in the Circuit of Massachusetts Bay.* Boston: 1937. A significant document in greenway history. Available at the library of the Harvard School of Design, Cambridge, Mass.

Yakima River Greenway Foundation. "A Brief Historical Synopsis of the Yakima River Regional Greenway." Photocopied paper, n.d. (1985?).

Ziegler, Susan. "The Bay Circuit Program." Draft manuscript for a government report, n.d. (1988).

ARTICLES

"American River Parkway: A Plan for All Seasons." *Open Space Action* (August 1969): 32–33. On an early greenway subject to a recent court suit to protect water flow. See entry under Hodge in "Miscellaneous Documents," below.

Beauchamp, Tanya Edwards. "Renewed Acclaim for the Father of American Landscape Architecture." *Smithsonian* (December 1972): 69–74. On Olmsted.

Brunnemer, Nancy M., and Owen J. Furuseth. "Mecklenburg County [N.C.]

Greenways: A Planned Open Space Network of Floodplains." In *Proceedings of the Tenth Annual Conference of the Association of State Floodplain Managers,* 35–40. Madison, Wisc.: Association of State Floodplain Managers, 1986.

Budd, William W., et al. "Stream Corridor Management in the Pacific Northwest. I. Determination of Stream-Corridor Widths." *Environmental Management* 11 (1987): 587–97.

Burwell, David. "Viewpoint: Rails-to-Trails." *Wilderness* (Winter 1986): 60.

California State Senate. *Senate Bill 100.* Sacramento, Calif.: 1986. Bill by William Lockyer which provides for a recreational corridor for San Francisco and San Pablo Bays—the so-called *Bay Trail.* Amends Division 5, Chapter 11, California Public Resources Code.

Carlson, Christine, et al. "A Path for the Palouse: An Example of Conservation and Recreation Planning." *Landscape and Urban Planning* 17 (1989): 1–19.

Cohen, Paul L., et al. "Stream Corridor Management in the Pacific Northwest. II. Management Strategies." *Environmental Management* 11 (1987): 599–605. (Cf. article citation under Budd, above.)

Coyle, Kevin J. "The Role of the Developer in Greenway Acquisition." *National Wetlands Newsletter* (September-October 1988): 10–12.

Cragnolin, Karen. "Who Created the Plan for Asheville's Riverfront?" *Asheville* [N.C.] *Citizen* (8 September 1989): 6D–7D.

Dalsemer, Richard. "Land Trust Sponsors Proposition 70." *Big Sur Land Trust News* (Spring 1988). Write: the Big Sur Land Trust, Box 221864, Carmel, CA 93922.

Didato, Barry. "How Green Is My Valley?" *Hudson Valley* (March 1989): 33–34.

Diringer, Elliot. "Tentative Ruling on American River Water Flow." *San Francisco Chronicle* (15 June 1989): A9. An important judicial decision. See entry under Hodge, in "Miscellaneous Documents," below.

Donaldson, Scott. "City and Country: Marriage Proposals." In *American Habitat: A Historical Perspective,* edited by Barbara Rosenkrantz and William Koelsch, 279–98. New York: Free Press, 1973.

Egan, Timothy. "Seattle Bid to Make Old Rails New Trails." *New York Times* (12 March 1988): 6.

Evans, Craig. "Bringing Walkways to Your Doorstep." *Parks and Recreation* (October 1987): 30–35.

Flournoy, William L., Jr. "A Nonlinear Approach to Open Space." *Carolina Planning* 15 (1989): 50–54. *Nonlinear* refers to greenway planning and implementation procedures, not to geomorphology.

Forman, Richard T. T. "An Ecology of the Landscape." *BioScience* 33 (1983): 535.
———. "Emerging Directions in Landscape Ecology and Applications in Natural Resource Management." In *Conference on Science in the National Parks,* 59–88. Washington, D.C.: National Park Service, The George Wright Society, 1986.
———. "The Ethics of Isolation, the Spread of Disturbance, and Landscape Ecology." In *Landscape Heterogeneity and Disturbance,* ed. Monica Goigel

Turner, 213–29. New York: Springer-Verlag, 1987.

Forman, Richard T. T., and Michael Godron. "Patches and Structural Components for a Landscape Ecology." *BioScience* 31 (1981): 733–40.

Frenkel, Robert E., et al. "Vegetation and Land Cover Change in the Willamette River Greenway in Benton and Linn Counties, Oregon: 1972–1981." In *Yearbook of the Association of Pacific Coast Geographers,* ed. James W. Scott, 46, (1984): 63–77. Corvallis, Ore.: Oregon State University Press, 1985.

"Gap to Gap." Yakima (Wash.) *Herald-Republic* (3 June 1988): 1F–12F. Special section published annually describing the Gap-to-Gap relay and listing the teams.

Gayle, Lisha. "Greenbelt: Group Is Fighting to Expand Meramec's Parks, Open Space." *St. Louis Post Dispatch* (15 May 1989): 1W–2W. On the Meramec River Greenway.

"Greenspaces and Greenways Are Growing Across the Region." *The Region's Agenda* (a Regional Plan Association [New York] publication) (February 1989): 1–4.

"Greenway Council: Think Big." Editorial, *Poughkeepsie Journal* (21 May 1989): 6C.

Hall, Alice J. "The Hudson: 'That River's Alive'." *National Geographic* (January 1978): 62–88.

Hiss, Tony. "Reflections: Encountering the Countryside." A two-part article. *New Yorker* (21 August 1988): 40–69 and (28 August 1988): 37–63. A thoughtful essay. Part 2 bears on regional-planning issues as they may affect greenway-making.

Hocker, Jean. "Greenways and Land Trusts: A Natural Partnership." *Land Trusts' Exchange* (Summer 1987): 6–7.

Hofford, William H. "The French Broad: A River Reborn." *Journal of Freshwater* 8 (1984): 24–26.

Huber, Joan. "Patriot's Path." *New Jersey Outdoors* (October 1984): 10–11.

Jackson, Donald Dale. "The Long Way 'Round: The National Scenic Trails System and How It Grew. And How it Didn't." *Wilderness* (Summer 1988): 17–24.

Kihn, Cecily Corcoran, et al. "Conservation Options for the Blackstone River Valley [R.I.-Mass.]." *Landscape and Urban Planning* 13 (1986): 81–99.

King, Caroline. "Is a Greenway Feasible Here?" *Land Trusts' Exchange* (Summer 1987): 14–15. On a proposed greenway along New York's Delaware and Hudson Canal.

Klose, Kevin. "Chicago's Canal Connection: A New National Park Brings a Historic Water System Back to Life." *Washington Post* (12 August 1984): E1, E6.

Kusler, Jon, and Anne Southworth. "Greenways: An Introduction." *National Wetlands Newsletter* (September-October 1988): 2–3.

Lea, Douglass. "Partial Pathways: An Abbreviated Guide to the [National Scenic Trails] System As It Is." *Wilderness* (Summer 1988): 25–35.

Lewallen, John. "Anne Taylor and the Raleigh Greenway." *Sierra Club Bulletin* (March 1976): 41–44.

Little, Charles E. "Linking Countryside and City: The Uses of 'Greenways.'"

Journal of Soil and Water Conservation (May-June 1987): 167–69.

Lusk, Anne. "Greenway in Vermont." *Parks and Recreation* (January 1989): 70–75. On the Stowe Recreation Path.

Macdonald, Stuart H. "Building Support for Urban Trails." *Parks and Recreation* (November 1987): 26–33.

McIlwain, Joy. "Saving Land for the Future." *Tallahassee Magazine* (Summer 1987): 31–33. About the Canopy Roads.

Martin, Julia Ibbotson. "Greenbelt Still Belongs to the People." *Staten Island Advance* (24 January 1988): A1, A6. First in a series of a retrospective articles on the Staten Island Greenbelt. Others: (25 January 1988): A1–A2; (26 January 1988): A3; and (27 January 1988): A3.

Meagher, John. "EPA's Contribution to the Greenway Effort." *National Wetlands Newsletter* (September-October 1988): 7–9.

Merriman, Kristin. "Greenways: A New Face for America." *Outdoor America* (Summer 1988): 22–23.

Miller, James Nathan. *The Great Billboard Double-Cross. Reader's Digest* (June 1985): reprint ed., 1–8.

Morris, Philip. "Streamside Open Space: It's a Natural." *Southern Living* (March 1974): 61–67.

Nelson, Arthur C. "An Empirical Note on How Regional Urban Containment Policy Influences an Interaction between Greenbelt and Exurban Land Markets." *APA Journal* (Spring 1988): 178–84.

Nunnally, Pat. "Iowa's Heritage Trail." *American Land Forum* (March-April 1987): 23–27.

Pritchard, Paul. "Americans Outdoors." *National Parks* (May-June 1987): 12–13. On the President's Commission for Americans Outdoors, which recommended citizen action on greenways.

"Public Shocked by Trail Damage in Iowa, Seattle." *Trailblazer* [newsletter of the Rails-to-Trails Conservancy] (April-June 1988): 1, 4.

Rogers, Ray. "In Land We Trust." *San Francisco Magazine* (July-August 1988): 35–36.

Rohling, Jane. "Corridors of Green." *Wildlife in North Carolina* (May 1988): 22–27.

Ross, Rosanne K. "Park with a City in It." *American Forests* (November 1978): 13–15, 48–49. On the Raleigh greenway system.

Sampson, David S. "The Hudson River Valley Greenway: A Case for Market Environmentalism." *Environmental Law Section Journal* 8 (September 1988): 14–16.

"The San Antonio River Walk: An Urban Masterwork Appreciated, Not Always Understood." *Water & Our World* (March-April 1988): 5–7.

"Saving Hudson Valley's Heritage." Editorial, *Poughkeepsie Journal* (27 December 1987): 8C.

Schurr, Karl, et al. "How a Natural River Can Increase the Community's Tax Base." *American Rivers* (December 1985): 6–7.

Searns, Robert M. "Denver Tames the Unruly Platte: A Ten-Mile River Greenway." *Landscape Architecture* (July 1980): reprint. A good description of the Platte River Greenway by a planner in on its creation. Write: Urban Edges, Inc., 1624 Humboldt St., Denver, CO 80218.

Seidensticker, John. "From the Ridge of the Fan." *Zoogoer* (November-December 1988): 27–30. Discusses a network of greenways around Washington, D.C., which connect with the National Zoo in Rock Creek Park and other open-space areas.

Spale, Valerie. "Greenway Connects the Past and Future." *Chicago Sun-Times* (17 July 1987): 38. About the 31st Street Greenway.

Spanbauer, Mary Kay. "Ribbons of Green." *Wildlife and Parks* (June 1988): 12–14.

Stallings, Constance. "Rights of Way." *Open Space Action* (May-June 1969): 15–21. An early article on rails-to-trails conversions which accurately predicted the importance of this movement.

Sullivan, John. "The Greening of New York." *New York Daily News Magazine* (25 September 1988): 11–12, 70. Roundup of greenway projects in the New York City boroughs.

Sutton, Edward D. "Ancient New England Highways: The Hanover 'Greenways' Controversy." *Vermont Law Review* 9 (1988): 373–413. About a failed effort (based on a 1761 ordinance) to convert an abandoned town highway right-of-way into a greenway.

Trudeau, Richard. "A Vision for a Living Network of Greenways." *California Parks & Recreation* (Fall 1988): 11, 13–18.

MISCELLANEOUS DOCUMENTS

Burwell, David, and Robert Brager. *Preseault and Preseault v. Interstate Commerce Commission, et al.* Washington, D.C.: Supreme Court of the United States, October term, 1989. Amicus Curiae brief by Rail-to-Trails and others in support of ICC in a case originally brought in Vermont by landowners adjacent to a railroad right-of-way who claimed that its conversion to a recreational trail was an unconstitutional taking of their property without just compensation. An excellent roundup of laws pertaining to rail-trail conversions. Availble from RTC, 1400 16th St., N.W., Washington, DC 20036.

Hodge, Richard A. "Preliminary Tentative Decision," *Environmental Defense Fund v. East Bay Municipal Utility District.* Superior Court of California, County of Alameda, 12 June 1989. Restrains the water district from lowering the flow of water on the American River which would have degraded the American River Greenway in Sacramento.

"The Hudson Valley Greenway Study." New York State Environmental Conservation Law, §49-0104, 16 August 1988 (McKinney 1989.) Copies of the statute are available from the Hudson River Valley Greenway Council, 2 City Square, Albany, NY 12207.

Lindberg, Mike. *Draft Resolution.* Portland, Ore.: 1985. Provides for intergovern-

mental cooperation in implementing the 40-Mile Loop Master Plan commissioned by the 40-Mile Loop Land Trust. Address: 40-Mile Loop Land Trust,
519 S.W. Third Ave., Portland,OR 97204.

Massachusetts Department of Environmental Management, the Bay Circuit Program. "Land Acquisition Criteria." Boston: 1987. Internal document describing a point system to establish land acquisition priorities for the Bay Circuit
greenway corridor. May be available from Massachusetts DEM, Bay Circuit
Program, 225 Friend St., Boston, MA 02114.

McDade, Joseph M., and Morris K. Udall. *Multi-Objective River Corridor Planning Workshops*. Washington, D.C.: 1989. Compendium of witnesses responses
from six field hearings held during 1988 by Congressmen McDade and Udall
dealing with riparian greenways.

New Jersey Department of Environmental Protection, Delaware & Raritan Canal Commission. "D & R Canal State Park." Brochure on the history of the
park. Available from the Delaware and Raritan Canal Commission, 25 Cal-
houn St., CN 402, Trenton, NJ 08625.

Oregon Land Conservation and Development Commission. *Willamette River
Greenway Program*. Salem, Ore.: n.d. Document contains the state law
providing for the Willamette River Greenway, legislative history, commission
orders, and rules and regulations regarding implementation. Available from:
LCDC, 1175 Court St., Salem, OR 97310.

Peters, Schmaltz, Fowler & Inslee, P.S. *By-Laws of Yakima River Regional Greenway Foundation*. Yakima, Wash.: 1985. A good model for a public-private greenway foundation. Write: Yakima River Greenway Foundation, 103 S. Third St.,
Yakima, WA 98901.

U.S. Congress, House of Representatives. "Scenic Byways Study Act of 1989
(H.R. 1087)," 22 February 1989. Introduced by Congressman James Oberstar
(D-Minn.). A companion bill was introduced into the Senate by Senator Jay
Rockefeller (D-W. Va.).

U.S. Court of Appeals, Eighth Circuit. *Glosemeyer, et al. v. Missouri-Kansas-Texas
Railroad, et al.* 5 July 1988. Key decision upholding the constitutionality of the
federal railbanking law.

U.S. Department of the Interior, National Park Service. *Chesapeake and Ohio
Canal*. Map of the (Maryland/D.C.) National Recreation Area, a national park
greenway, with a text description and history, n.d.

————. *Cuyahoga Valley*. Map of the (Ohio) National Recreation Area, a national park greenway, with a text description and history, n.d.

————. *Ice Age Trail*. Map of the (Wisconsin) scenic trail with a text description and history, n.d.

U.S. Forest Service, Pacific Northwest Region. *Columbia River Gorge National
Scenic Area: Final Interim Guidelines*. Hood River, Ore.: 1987. Background and
land-use policies pertaining to this intergovernmental greenway. Address:
U.S. Forest Service, Columbia River Gorge National Scenic Area, 902 Wasco
Ave., Hood River, OR 97031.

ACKNOWLEDGMENTS

This book is only partly my doing. The basic information came from all those I interviewed, many of whom graciously provided conducted tours and all of whom equipped me with a wealth of written material about their work. These kindly folks are named in the list of Principal Sources.

The original idea of the study, much of the funding work, and the patience of Job, are the selfless contributions of Keith G. Hay, colleague, friend, and director of the American Greenways program of the Conservation Fund, Inc., which has sponsored this book. He also helped assemble the photographs for the three galleries—including some of his own. Withal, Keith Hay's leadership, not only for this project but for the national greenway movement, has been as remarkable as it has been crucial. The shape of the book, intellectually as well as structurally, is in significant part the reflection of the sound editorial judgment of George F. Thompson, a publishing consultant to the Johns Hopkins University Press. Thompson is as fine an editor as I have ever worked with. Darlene Thomas, a cultural anthropologist, served as research assistant, contacting those who responded to my author's query as well as interviewing nonprofit organizations, government agencies, and charitable foundations with an interest in greenways. Her contribution was invaluable to me in the writing of this work and can also serve as the basis for later technical and scholarly analysis by others.

I would also like to acknowledge the support of Jack Goellner, the director of the Johns Hopkins University Press, for his keen interest in and commitment to the project, and Patrick Noonan, president of the sponsoring Conservation Fund, for writing the foreword to the book and for administering the grants—principally from the National Endowment for the Arts and the American Conservation Association—that made it possible for me to take on the work.

Marge Nelson handled the copyediting and indexing with grace, dispatch, and consummate skill. I should also like to thank Noel Grove of the National Geographic Society for many courtesies, not to mention some memorable bottles of claret; and Phil Schermeister, a contract photographer for the society, who so generously supplied many of the color photographs. Harriet Wright, a long-time collaborator, drew the maps; Ann Walston handled the design of the book; and Kim Johnson managed the production. I am grateful to them all.

During the research phase of the work, Jean Hocker and the Land Trust Alliance helped speed me on my way by putting me in touch with the many local land trusts working on greenways. Those who helped out in various logistical ways during my field trips were Charles Vernon, Andrew Traldi, Beth and Bob Fixsen, Paul A. Clement, Patricia Maida, Charles T. Little, Diana and David Dawson, Sue Sheats and Isaac Taylor, Alison and John Mitchell, Catharine Vernon, Dorothy and Tom Pariot, Arlene and David Sampson, Nancy Vernon, and a good many more.

There were many reviewers of pieces of the manuscript, among them: Charles E. Beveridge, Tony Hiss, Richard Anderwald, Klara Sauer, John G. Mitchell, Robert Hagenhofer, Tom Fox, Susan Ziegler, David Burwell, Gerald Adelmann, Chuck Mitchell, Douglas Cheever, William Flournoy, Brian Steen, Susan Sedgwick, Judith Kunofsky, Keith Oliver, and Charles T. Little. The manuscript as a whole was reviewed by David Schuyler, Frank J. Popper, George F. Thompson, and Keith Hay. They all did their level best to help me get it right. That I didn't manage to here and there is, of course, my fault, not theirs.

Lastly, I would have been unable to undertake the project at all without the help of my wife, Ila Dawson Little, a professor of English literature, terrific traveling companion, and alternate driver for most of the many weeks spent afield on research.

PICTURE CREDITS

GALLERY I

1. Phil Schermeister, courtesy National Geographic Society
2. Charles Aguar
3. J. Weiland (© J. Weiland)
4. Oregon State Parks
5. Phil Schermeister, courtesy National Geographic Society
6. Phil Schermeister, courtesy National Geographic Society
7. Tim Burke
8. Matthew McVay/ALLSTOCK
9. Anne Lusk
10. Phil Schermeister, courtesy National Geographic Society
11. R. Harrison Wiegand
12. Phil Schermeister, courtesy National Geographic Society
13. Keith G. Hay
14. Phil Schermeister, courtesy National Geographic Society

GALLERY II

15. Kathleen Thormod Carr (© Kathleen Thormod Carr)
16. Clois Ensor
17. Chuck Flink
18. Bill Flournoy
19. Chuck Flink
20. James Bleecker (© James Bleecker)
21. Chip Porter
22. James Bleecker (© James Bleecker)
23. Doug Cheever
24. Phil Schermeister, courtesy National Geographic Society
25. Herb Liu
26. Gretta Kraft
27. Keith G. Hay
28. Phil Schermeister, courtesy National Geographic Society
29. Phil Schermeister, courtesy National Geographic Society

PICTURE CREDITS

GALLERY III

30. Massachusetts Department of Environmental Management
31. James Valentine
32. John Rawlston/The RiverCity Company
33. Tom Fox (© Tom Fox)
34. Misha Erwitt, *New York Daily News*
35. Keith G. Hay
36. Yakima Greenway Foundation
37. Keith G. Hay
38. Phil Schermeister, courtesy National Geographic Society
39. Bob Walker (© Bob Walker)
40. Phil Schermeister, courtesy National Geographic Society
41. Phil Schermeister, courtesy National Geographic Society
42. Bob Walker (© Bob Walker)
43. Upper Illinois Valley Association, (© Holland)

CHAPTERS 3 AND 9

The sixteen maps were created by Harriet Wright.

INDEX

Adelmann, Gerald, 146–48
Aguar, Charles, 111–12
American Greenways program, of
  Conservation Fund, 196, 198
American Rhine. *See* Hudson River Valley
  Greenway
American River Parkway (Sacramento), 82
American Rivers (organization), 196–97
American Society of Landscape Architects,
  197
Americans Outdoors (President's Commission
  on Americans Outdoors), 37, 93, 133
American Trails (organization), 197
Amoco, donation from, to Platte River
  Parkway, 83
Anderwald, Dick, involvement of, with
  Yakima Greenway Foundation, 90, 152–54
Apalachee Land Conservancy, 138–40
Appalachian Trail, 102n; origins of, 18–20
Architectural planning, for greenway, 191–92
Arizona greenways, in Tucson: along Rillito
  River, 81; Pima County River Parks, 30,
  48–54
Army Corps of Engineers, U.S., 50, 97
Asheville, N.C., French Broad Greenway in,
  84–90
Association of Bay Area Governments, 155,
  157–58
Athens, Ga., Oconee River Greenway in,
  111–12, 188
Automobile, first appearance of, in America,
  12
Automobile route, as greenway, 117–28. *See*

also Historic route, as greenway; Scenic
  route, as greenway

Backes, Maude, as director of Stony Brook
  Greenway, 116
Bacon, Edmund, as possible coiner of term
  "greenway," 23–24
Baltimore, Md., 84, 87
Bay Circuit (Mass.), 19, 121, 161–66
Bay Conservation and Development
  Commission, 155–57
Bay Trail (San Francisco), 155–60
Benbow, Terry, involvement of, with Staten
  Island Citizens Planning Association, 95
Bennett, Edward H., involvement of, with
  40-Mile Loop, 77–78
Berkeley, Calif., origins of Piedmont Way
  in, 9
Beveridge, Charles E., 9–10
Bicycle, first appearance of, in America, 12
Big Sur Foundation, 73
Big Sur Land Trust, 73
Big Sur Viewshed, San Luis Obispo to
  Monterey, Calif., 70–76, 122
Billboards, prohibition of, 70, 75–76, 124–28
Birnbaum, Charles, 11
Blackstone Canal (R.I.), as greenway, 99, 121
Blake, Peter, *God's Own Junkyard*, 124
Boland, Walter, involvement of, with French
  Broad Greenway, 88
Book of Trails, The (Ensor and Mitchell), 56
Boston. *See* Bay Circuit; Olmstead Parkway,
  Emerald Necklace as

229

Charles E. Little is a former advertising executive who, in his mid-thirties, resigned from a Madison Avenue ad agency to devote his creative energies to land conservation and community planning. Since then, his books, published papers, and magazine articles have led to many innovations in conservation policy, including national legislation for farmland protection and new approaches to cooperative planning for outstanding landscape areas. He has served as executive director of the Open Space Action Institute (New York City), senior associate at the Conservation Foundation (Washington, D.C.), head of natural resources policy research at the Congressional Research Service of the Library of Congress, and founder and president of the American Land Forum. Since 1986 he has been a full-time writer. Born and brought up in southern California, he now lives in Kensington, Maryland, with his wife, Ila Dawson Little, a professor of English literature.

Greenways for America
by Charles E. Little
George F. Thompson, *Project Editor*

Designed by Ann Walston

Composed by Brushwood Graphics Inc.
in Galliard text and display

Printed by The Maple Press Company
on 60-lb. Glatfelter Eggshell offset
and bound in Rainbow Linque
with Lindenmeyr Elephant Hide endsheets

Picture galleries were printed
by The John D. Lucas Printing Company
on 80-lb. S. D. Warren's L.O.E. Dull